Blood, Sweat & Tyres

By The Hairy Bikers

The Hairy Bikers' Meat Feasts
The Hairy Dieters: Good Eating
The Hairy Dieters: Eat for Life
The Hairy Dieters: How to Love Food and Lose Weight
The Hairy Bikers' Asian Adventure
The Hairy Bikers' Great Curries
The Hairy Bikers' Perfect Pies
The Hairy Bikers' Big Book of Baking
The Hairy Bikers' 12 Days of Christmas
The Hairy Bikers' Mums Still Know Best
The Hairy Bikers' Mums Know Best
The Hairy Bikers' Food Tour of Britain

THE HAIRY BIKERS

Blood, Sweat & Tyres

THE AUTOBIOGRAPHY

Si King & Dave Myers

W&N
WEIDENFELD & NICOLSON

Copyright © Byte Brook Limited and Sharp Letter Limited 2015

The right of Si King and Dave Myers to be identified as the authors
of this work has been asserted in accordance with
the Copyright, Designs and Patents Act 1988.

This edition first published in Great Britain in 2015
by W&N
an imprint of the Orion Publishing Group Ltd
Carmelite House, 50 Victoria Embankment,
London EC4Y 0DZ
An Hachette UK Company

1 3 5 7 9 10 8 6 4 2

A CIP catalogue record for this book
is available from the British Library.

Hardback ISBN: 978 1 4746 0050 7
Trade Paperback ISBN: 978 1 4746 0306 5

Typeset by Input Data Services Ltd, Bridgwater, Somerset

Printed and bound by CPI Group (UK) Ltd, Croydon CR0 4YY

The Orion Publishing Group's policy is to use papers
that are natural, renewable and recyclable and made
from wood grown in sustainable forests. The logging and
manufacturing processes are expected to conform to the
environmental regulations of the country of origin.

Every effort has been made to fulfil requirements with regard to
reproducing copyright material. The author and publisher will
be glad to rectify any omissions at the earliest opportunity.

www.orionbooks.co.uk

Si
For my mam, Stella, and my dad, Graham.
I hope I'm making you proud.

Dave
For my wife, Liliana, who I love dearly and who
understands me – for which I am eternally grateful.

The Hairy Bikers
For the late John Stroud. Without him,
none of this would have happened.

Contents

Contents

1

Dave's

Cheese-and-Potato Pie, Killer Fishcakes and Toffee Apples

'Mam can't cook, she's not well. I've made your tea.'

My dad looked worried when I took a home-made cheese-and-potato pie out of the gas stove and hauled it onto the kitchen table.

'What's wrong with your mam, David?' he asked, eyeing the steaming pie.

'Not sure,' I shrugged. 'She went to bed because she didn't feel well. I was playing with me wagon train game, on the floor. Then I heard a thump.'

'A thump?'

'Aye, a thump. I went upstairs and Mam was on the bedroom floor. She'd fallen out of bed, so I helped her get back in, and then I made your tea, 'cos I knew you'd be hungry when you got in from work.'

Dad looked very concerned now. I was only seven years old and I thought he was bothered about my cooking. 'It's alright,' I assured him. 'I used the *Radiation* cookbook. I think I've done the pastry right. I rubbed the butter into the flour and all that . . .'

Dad wasn't listening. He had turned on his heel and was bolting up the stairs two at a time, so I shrugged my shoulders and went back to playing with my wagon train game on the floor.

When my dad eventually came back down he was crying, and it is no exaggeration to say that from that day on, my life was never the same again.

My father was the foreman of the local paper mill in Barrow-in-Furness and my mother had been a crane driver at the shipyard until she gave up work to have me, on 8 September 1957.

For the first seven years of my life my mam and dad had an absolute ball bringing me up. They didn't have much money but they spoilt me with time, and in all my early memories we are having fun and just being a very happy, close-knit family of three.

We lived in a tiny two-up-two-down terraced house on Devon Street in Barrow. My mam, Margaret, stayed at home and looked after me while my dad, Jim, worked shifts from either 6 a.m. to 2 p.m., 2 p.m. to 10 p.m. or 10 p.m. to 6 a.m. He'd started working at the paper mill at the age of twelve, and by the time I was seven he'd clocked up five decades of service.

Both my parents were widowed when they fell in love and married in the Fifties, and they didn't plan or expect to have a child together. My mother was forty-one when her belly started to swell. She feared she had an ovarian cyst and was absolutely over the moon when she discovered her 'cyst' was actually me, starting my journey into the world.

'When I came out the doctor's I danced down the street as though I were walking on air,' Mam told everybody who would listen. 'Honestly, I couldn't feel the pavement beneath my feet. Me! Pregnant! At my age! Can you credit it?' She found a four-leaf clover that day, and for years afterwards she carried it in her purse, along with a black-and-white picture of me.

My dad was fifty-five years old when I was born, but their age definitely proved a benefit rather than a barrier to bringing me up, at least at the start of my childhood. Nothing was too much trouble, and they were the best and most patient parents ever.

Both Mam and Dad had suffered their fair share of heartache in their previous marriages, which I think made them appreciate their second chance at happiness all the more. Dad had been very young when he married his first wife, Ida. They had a son together, Kenneth, who was more than thirty years older than me, but Ida developed heart disease early on in the marriage and my poor dad ended up nursing her for many years.

'Son, never steam open a letter that isn't addressed to you,' he said to me once. 'That's how I found out about Ida's heart. I steamed open a letter from the hospital, and it said she had three years to live. I nursed her for twenty-five years after that, thinking each year was her last.'

My mam grew up on Walney Island, just off the coast of Barrow, with three sisters who were all very close. She became a crane driver during the war, before working as a waitress in the Lake District and returning to the shipyard after the war ended.

'They used to say women had a more delicate touch,' she would laugh, as she regaled me with tales of climbing up the huge ladders to the cranes and manoeuvring them about the busy shipyard. She was very vivacious, my mam, and when I think of her talking to me when I was a young boy I always picture her smiling, full of life and energy.

Mam's first husband died of tuberculosis, and she met my dad on a coach trip to Belgium. They had a wonderful romance; I've got one of Dad's love letters to my mam from that time, which was truly written from the heart. After they married, Mam gave up the prefab she lived in and moved into the Devon Street house my dad owned.

They were both comparatively well-off in those days, and it was after another coach tour, this time to Lucerne in Switzerland, that Mam found out she was expecting me. There's a lovely photo of my parents, posing with a comically large glass of beer and looking very content. I like to think I was conceived as a result of the invigorating Swiss air rather than the beer, mind you!

Mam's friends and sisters had had their babies much earlier than her, and so when I was born I was a bit of a novelty and they doted on me. All the women set about knitting me baby clothes, and I had two jumpers with cranes from the shipyard on the front, called 'Little Alf' and 'Big Alf': the locals had names for all the cranes. I also had another jumper that was yellow and white and cuddly, which apparently I called my 'scrambled egg' jumper; even then I was interested in grub!

I can't really remember the jumper to be honest, but I do have a very clear, early memory of when I was just two years old, playing on the floor of the back kitchen with a clockwork monkey toy, while Mam cooked the tea. She was a fabulous cook and was often baking and preparing food while I played at her feet. I can still picture her now. Mam had two cookery 'bibles' that were often propped up on the Formica kitchen top while she worked – the famous Be-Ro flour cookbook and the *Radiation* cookery book, which was embossed with the proud words: 'For use with the "New World" regulo-controlled gas cookers'.

The smell of fresh cakes and pies always filled the room when I was a small boy; it was magic. Sometimes Mam would leave bread to rise in front of the fire, which made the whole house smell delicious, and in the summer she'd make fabulous bramble jelly from blackberries me and Dad picked from the hedgerows.

Sunday roast was my favourite. She'd make a roast chicken dinner with sage-and-onion stuffing, mash and cauliflower cheese, and I always felt happy and loved when the three of us sat around the table together and tucked in.

Whenever she was in the kitchen, Mam always had her beige ceramic mixing bowl in her hands because she used it for everything, whether she was baking bread or scones, cooking a hot pot or pickling onions. The same bowl got washed and re-used time and time again. It was the same with the pressure cooker, which was her other kitchen staple. One time the seal blew and the whole kitchen was decorated with mushy peas. Mam was covered too; I remember thinking she looked like the Jolly Green Giant. However, there was no question of chucking the pressure cooker out. No, the seal was replaced and the heavy old pan went on to cook hundreds and hundreds more broths, soups and spuds.

Anyhow, on this particular day, when I was two years old and playing with my toy monkey, Mam was using the beige ceramic bowl to make fishcakes. They were one of her specialties and she always used fresh hake from Hartley's fishmonger, which she poached in milk with a dried bay leaf. Once the fish was cooked she'd mix it with potato and parsley, shape it and then dip it in beaten egg before coating the patties in those luminous orange breadcrumbs that you could probably see from Mars. Next she'd make a delicious cheese sauce with the milk she had used to poach the fish in.

While she was doing all this, I was playing happily on the tiled floor, chewing on my clockwork monkey and wondering when my tea was going to be ready.

'Mam!' I suddenly spluttered. 'Urghhh!' I started coughing and making a huge fuss, because I'd swallowed the key used to wind up the monkey.

'Mam! Urghhh, urghhh, urghhh!'

'What is it, David? What's the matter?'

'De kreey,' I managed to croak, pointing at my throat. 'De kreeey!'

'Crayon? Oh, you daft 'apeth! You've swallowed a crayon. Oh, never mind, it's only a crayon, it'll melt.'

It wasn't until a little while later, when Mam was clearing away my clockwork monkey and the fishcakes were frying in the pan, that she twigged what had happened.

'David! Where's the key?' she asked in alarm. 'Did you swallow the monkey's *key*? Oh no, you didn't, did you? Not the *key*!'

We didn't have a car and I can remember Mam running down the road to our neighbour, old Mr Gibson, who owned the local chemist, and shouting: 'He's swallowed a key! He's swallowed a key!'

Despite having a nasty lump in my throat, it was an exciting adventure to be driven to the local hospital in Mr Gibson's car, and I can still remember the wonderful smell of old leather and vinyl filling the air. Mam, of course, wasn't quite so enraptured by the turn of events, and she was flapping and fretting like mad. An X-ray eventually showed I'd need a general anaesthetic to have the key removed, because it was lodged horizontally across my oesophagus and looked like something out of a *Tom and Jerry* cartoon on the black-and-white image. The next thing I remember is sleeping in a cot with bars and eating ice cream; it was absolutely delicious.

Incidentally, I cooked Mam's recipe on TV many years later, during our series *Mums Know Best*. I called it 'Killer Fishcakes', explaining that my mam's fishcakes were always massive, but really it was a bit of a joke between me and Si, because he knew all about how I nearly killed myself as a small boy while Mam was engrossed in her fishcakes.

Anyhow, my mam's home cooking was a fabulous part of my early childhood, and I have lots of happy memories linked to food. For my fifth birthday Mam presented me with a wonderful iced sponge cake in the shape of a number five, invited all my mates round for a party and gave them each party bags filled with short-bread and home-made sweets. Mam was great like that, always making an effort to keep up with the younger mums and making sure I didn't miss out on anything.

I also remember her treating me to bags of Salt 'n' Shake crisps whenever she could afford them, because I couldn't get enough of them.

'Mam, what have we got a belly button for?' I asked her one night, lifting my jumper and peering down at my tummy as I sat at the kitchen table.

Quick as a flash she responded: 'Belly button? Oh, that's for when you eat crisps in bed. It's where you put the salt that comes in the little blue bag.'

She had a twinkle in her eye, as usual, but I was too little to see she was only teasing. I took her at her word and, three weeks later, guess what? I had a terrible rash all around my belly button.

Dad was very proactive and good-humoured too. On his way home from work he'd go mushrooming, and would turn up with big field mushrooms that Mam would fry with bacon. They tasted fabulous, but the best bit of all was making a sandwich and soaking it in the wonderful black gravy that came from the mushrooms. Dad would often be covered in cuts because he'd clambered over a barbed-wire fence to get to the best mushrooms. Looking back, he must have been in his sixties when he did that, which shows the sort of spirit he was blessed with. I can also remember him wrapping himself in cabbage leaves to stay warm in the winter when he rode his BSA Bantam motorcycle to work. He'd come home stinking, but at the time it didn't seem particularly out of the ordinary; it was just something my dad did, and he didn't give a monkey's what other people might think. It certainly never bothered me either, because I was always much more interested in the bike itself than what my dad wore when he rode it.

He got a Norton Dominator after that, which was his dream bike, but unfortunately he only lived the dream for a few weeks. Dad was starting it up one day when it kicked back, catapulting him over the backyard wall. He ruptured his Achilles tendon in the process and so he was forced to downgrade to a Puch electric scooter – he could no longer kick up a motorcycle to start it – and this was the only bike he could operate with his damaged tendon. Not having a bike at all was unthinkable; nothing would keep Dad off two wheels.

From as far back as I can remember, Dad would sit me on the saddle of his motorbikes so I could pretend to ride them. I loved the smell of oil and machinery and rubber; just one whiff would set my pulse racing. Right from being a very small boy I was bike-mad and wanted to ride like my dad one day.

'We'll get you a bike of your own when you're old enough,' Dad would say, and I had dreams about saving up enough money to go out and buy one myself, just in case Dad couldn't afford it. That was my ultimate goal in life: to get a job and a motorbike.

In the meantime, once I was big enough, Dad would put me on the back of the Puch electric scooter and take me on rides all around the local area. We were incredibly lucky with what was on the doorstep. Within twenty minutes' ride there were the sand-hills up at Roanhead, plus Walney Island on the Irish Sea side of the peninsula, Roa Island at the tip and Morecambe Bay on the other side. For a really big adventure we'd go further afield, up to the Lakes, which took about an hour.

'Hold on tight!' Dad would say, and I'd squeal with delight as we hit the road, free as birds. We did wear helmets, but safety was much less of a concern then than it is today. The ones we had were cork-lined pudding basin jobs and we kept the same ones for years, whatever knocks they'd taken.

In the summer, Dad checked the tides daily and took me out at high tide, so that he could teach me to swim. He always put on swimming trunks himself and waded into the freezing water with me, encouraging me to be brave, lift my legs off the bottom and put my face underwater to look for little fish and cockles. Mam hand-made my swimming trunks, and there's a photograph of me as a young lad in a silvery grey pair that look like they've been made out of an old ironing board cover.

After our swim Dad would buy a bag of cherries or shrimps and we'd sit on the sandhills together tucking in. We did plenty of walking too, and in time we got to know a whole lexicon of walks all around the hills and down the coast road.

Once, when we were heading home on the scooter with our skin tingling from the seawater, a policeman flagged us down.

'Excuse me, sir, but did you know it is an offence to carry a passenger whose feet do not extend to the footrest?' the officious bobby barked.

'I'm afraid I didn't, sir,' my father said convincingly.

'Well, it most certainly is. You are breaking the law, and I must forbid you from carrying this passenger on your scooter until he has grown to a suitable height.'

My apologetic dad was fined two pounds for his misdemeanour and I was devastated at the prospect of waiting until my legs grew longer; I was only about six years old and they must have been at least a foot too short.

'There's nowt to worry about, son,' Dad whispered conspiratorially as soon as the policeman went on his way. 'I'll sort this out, quick as a wink.'

True to his word, Dad went straight to the paper mill and asked one of his workmates to make brackets to attach to the footrests of the scooter. My feet reached them easily, and so our adventures continued unabated.

Kenneth, my much older half-brother, sometimes came to Morecambe Bay with us, which was always very exciting as he had a car and liked to have a pint of beer. My dad was teetotal and I never saw him touch a drop, ever, but he'd accompany Kenneth into a pub on the way and enjoy a few cigarettes with his dandelion-and-burdock or ginger beer. Dad smoked forty fags a day all his life, which wasn't out of the ordinary then but shocks me now, not least because I wonder how on earth he afforded them. I'd be given a bottle of lemonade with a straw and a packet of crisps to have in the car, which was an amazing treat. I tasted cheese-and-onion crisps for the very first time in my life while sitting in Kenneth's car outside a pub, and I'll never forget the sensation on my tongue. I savoured every last crumb that fizzed and tingled in my mouth; it was amazing.

Once we reached the bay Kenneth, being nearly forty when I was around six or seven, patiently taught me the art of longline fishing

'Right, David,' he explained, 'when the tide is out we have to walk out to sea for a mile and put three stakes in the sand with a long string between them. That's what we'll put our hooks on.'

'How many hooks?'

'About a hundred. Then we'll run back to the beach and wait.'

'So how do we get our fish?'

'We watch and wait patiently, and when the tide sweeps in over our longline we need to be ready to run back out between the waves and collect our catch, before the seagulls get to the fish first!'

It's actually a dangerous practice as you can be cut off by the tide, but as a child I simply thought it was dead exciting, and by the time I was about twelve I used to go longline fishing on my own.

Anyway, that first time I watched eagerly as Kenneth taught me the tricks of the trade, and I was very excited as we waited expectantly for two long hours for the tide to come in. We caught about twenty plaice, and when we got home Dad put them in cold water in our bath, which was shoehorned into a tiny space over the stairs. Incidentally, we had no inside loo and the only toilet we had was in the backyard. We had no heating either, other than a fire in the front room that was only lit once a year, at Christmas-time. It probably sounds a bit Dickensian today, but it really didn't seem that way at the time. I didn't know any different and, as I say, my parents were generous with their time and love, which were all the riches I wanted as a small boy.

Mam and Dad pushed the boat out as much as they could at Christmas. We celebrated with the biggest turkey and best piece of ham they could afford, and we had all the trimmings, crackers and a tree in the front room, decked with strings of shiny beads. One year Uncle Norman, who was married to one of Mam's sisters, Auntie Edie, turned up with two pieces of fresh salmon wrapped in greaseproof paper parcels. Mam poached the fish in milk and it tasted delicious; before that I always thought salmon came in tins.

Mam and Dad always made a big effort on Bonfire Night too.

I'd have loads of fireworks, indoor as well as outdoor, and Dad would make toffee apples with a big, thick puddle of home-made toffee on top. Sweets were the only thing he really made in the kitchen, and his handwritten recipes for treacle toffee and butter-scotch, neatly copied out in fountain pen on yellowed rectangles of paper and stapled together, are now prized possessions of mine.

There was often music ringing though our house. Mam and Dad would play Cliff Richard and the Shadows, Adam Faith and Elvis tracks on the old turntable, usually from compilation LPs like *Music for Pleasure*, which Mam bought from Woolworths. The transistor radio also provided a soundtrack to my childhood. Both my parents liked to listen to classical concerts and I can remember Mam swooning with delight when anything by Mantovani was being broadcast. She would talk to me about composers and music, and as a result I soaked up quite a precocious knowledge.

'Who plays this song?' one of the teachers at my school, Abbotsmead Infants, asked the class one day.

'Greensleeves' was chiming from the record player at the front of the hall, and so I shot my hand up without hesitation. I was naturally extrovert and, up until the age of seven or eight, I didn't hold back.

'It's Mantovani, miss!' I shouted out enthusiastically, which took my teacher by surprise.

'That's very true, David,' she blustered. 'But, er, the answer I was looking for was actually "the ice-cream man". He plays "Greensleeves" too, doesn't he? And what do we *not* do when we hear "Greensleeves"?'

I wanted to say: 'Turn off Mam's radio, because she'll be swooning in raptures and she won't be happy', but of course, the answer was: 'We don't run across the road without looking'.

Another time, when we were putting on a performance in that same hall, it was my job to play the xylophone. I didn't really get the hang of it and hit all the wrong notes, and the rows of parents who'd come to watch started laughing. 'Stuff the lot of you!' I thought, before throwing my mallets into the audience and stomping off very theatrically. When I think about my performance on *Strictly*, I can see things haven't changed much! Anyhow, Mam had to come backstage and sort me out and apparently I was quite upset, and also full of righteous indignation. Who did the parents think they were, laughing at me like that? The cheek of them!

There were plenty of other times when I wasn't exactly angelic, or the easiest child to deal with. Once I rigged an old speaker through to my parents' bedroom and made spooky breathing noises down it to freak them out when they went to bed. Another time I knocked a tin of red tile-paint on the carpet and, realising it wouldn't come off, I decided the best thing to do was paint the entire floor. Poor Dad had to replace the whole carpet.

Breaking both my thumbs was another memorable 'Oh, David, whatever next!' moment. It happened when I was six years old and trying to launch an aeroplane off our six-foot high back wall. I'd built the plane from a big box and it was large enough for me to sit in. I was convinced it would fly, but of course when I launched myself and the plane off the wall I plummeted to the ground instead of soaring through the clouds.

As soon as my smashed thumbs had healed, Dad caught me heading outside with a hammer and a bag of nails.

'What are you doing with those?' he asked.

'Building a boat!'

'Oh no you're bloody not. Get inside, now!'

Unfortunately, the bags of confidence and reckless abandon I possessed at that young age were about to take a hammering, by the chain of events that began with my mother falling out of bed with a thump, and my dad crying after I made the cheese-and-potato pie for his tea.

More about that later, though, after Simon has told you about his early childhood.

2

Si's

Boiled Egg and Soldiers, Callard & Bowser Butterscotch and Flat Rib Beef Broth

I cannot believe that all of what Dave has just described happened before I was even born. It would be another year or so, when Dave was nine, before Mam pushed me out into the world in the main bedroom of our council house in Kibblesworth, County Durham.

My big sister Ginny, who was eighteen, had to help the midwife hold Mam's legs because the labour went on so long, while my dad was despatched in his Ford Anglia, along with my thirteen-year-old brother Will, to fetch more gas and air as Mam had gone through a whole canister.

When I finally arrived, on the evening of 20 October 1966, I was strong and alert and had a fine pair of lungs on me. My grandfather burst into tears and cracked open a bottle of whisky when he heard me cry. He had been spitting tacks when he found out my mam, Stella, was expecting me. She was forty-four years old, which in those days was considered dangerously old to be having another bairn. Apparently, the whole family had worried throughout the pregnancy that I might have Down's Syndrome because of Mam's age, and to make matters worse my dad, Graham, was forty-seven, and not in the best of health himself.

'Eee, what were you thinking of, having another bairn at this stage in your lives?' my grandfather had harrumphed. 'Ginny and Will are teenagers, practically off your hands. It's bloody madness! You're not gonna be around to bring the bairn up.'

'We didn't exactly plan it this way . . .' my dad said to his father-in-law. 'But we'll manage, we always do. Stella will cope fine. You know she's made of strong stuff, we both are.'

My grandfather was an incredibly tough bloke. He'd been the winder in the pithead in his day, which meant he was held in very high esteem in the North Durham mining community in which he lived and worked. His wife Nancy, my grandmother, had been a grafter too, and she spent her life skivvying after all the men in the family who worked shifts down the mines. She expected my mam, as the only daughter, to do the same.

'But I'd like to be a nurse,' Mam said.

'Well ya can't,' Nancy told her.

'Why not?'

'Need and necessity, Stella, that's why not. The men support us, and we have to support them.'

Mam dutifully stayed at home, helping her mother keep the house and look after the breadwinners. The experience made my mam into the sort of woman who was used to coping as best she could with whatever life chucked at her, even a new bairn in her mid-forties.

When I arrived, Grandad was the only one of my four grand-parents still alive. I have just one memory of him, sitting in the kitchen of the house I was born in. There was an old-fashioned range with two cookers either side of the fire, and Grandad was playing table-top skittles and eating a boiled egg.

'Eat up,' he ordered, and I did as I was told and dipped my soldiers in my egg. I was two years old, and I wasn't going to argue with my big, gruff Grandad. His hands were like shovels; no wonder he was the winder in the pit.

My father was from a different world altogether, having been born and bred in the heart of London. His dad, my Grandad King, had a horrendous childhood, spending time in the work-house before joining the army as a drummer and serving as a Corporal in the 8th Regiment during the First World War. He was a postman when my dad was born in 1919, but he deserted my grandmother when my dad was a small boy, though nobody really knew the reason why.

When my dad grew up he decided to join the navy rather than the army.

'Why didn't you join the army?' I asked Dad innocently once. 'Did you not want to be a soldier like your dad?'

'I wanted to join the navy and sail the world,' Dad said, which was true, but I learned later that the other reason was that he didn't want to follow in his wayward father's footsteps.

Dad worked on minesweepers in the Russian Convoys during the Second World War, but after one tour of duty he returned home to find his mother had been killed in the Blitz, and the family home in Stockwell completely obliterated. After that Dad signed up for another tour of duty with the 'white caps'.

'What are the white caps, Dad?' I remember asking. 'Did you wear a white hat?'

Dad smiled. 'Simon, we were called the white caps because of the ice-cold conditions we worked in.'

'How cold was it?' I asked. 'As cold as Newcastle when it snows in the winter?'

'Ooh, a lot colder than Newcastle, son. It was minus thirty-five degrees, and one of my jobs was to chip ice off the outside of the ship. The salt water would freeze on the bulwark of the ship, and if you didn't chip it off the ship would topple over and sink.'

'Ooh,' I said, eyes like saucers. 'That's scary.'

'Yes, son, it was. And it was so cold that if you fell into the water your survival rate was thirty seconds.'

I marvelled at Dad's story, imagining him chiselling away at the ice at breakneck speed. I was incredibly impressed, and when he showed me a photo of himself on the ship in his uniform I was bowled over, and thought he was the toughest, bravest dad in the world.

Unfortunately, Dad survived the freezing temperatures only to suffer a terrible injury towards the end of the war, when he fell down a hatch on board a ship and was left with damage to his kidneys. After that he joined the Merchant Navy Reserve Pool, working as a fire man or 'stoker' on ships and ferries all round the British Isles. It was when he docked at Newcastle upon Tyne in 1947 that he met my mam at a dance, in the popular Oxford Galleries ballroom in the city. Coming from 'the smoke', Dad was a snappy dresser who wore a pinstriped suit, had a trimmed moustache and drank pink gin, and at first glance Mam assumed he was an American sailor, because the place was full of them.

'I know you buggers!' she chided when he asked her for a dance. 'You Yanks – here one minute, gone the next. It'll be "wham, bam, thank you mam"! Then I'll never see you again.'

Not only was she straight-talking but Mam was a very bright

and beautiful woman who loved to sing and dance. My dad was smitten, and he used every ounce of his southern charm and sophistication to win her over. A year later, they were walking down the aisle at St Joseph's Catholic Church in Birtley, Gateshead, and on New Year's Eve 1948 my big sister Virginia – known to all as Gin or Ginny – was born at home in Kibblesworth, just like I was, eighteen years later.

The intervening years, before my noisy arrival, were quite tumultuous. My dad got a job working on a ship sailing from Southampton and, after a period spent apart, Mam and Ginny eventually went with him. It was a tough move for a young Geordie lass like Mam, who'd barely travelled outside the North East before.

'I wasn't too keen on the folk,' Mam said to me once.

'Why not?' I asked, because I really like the people in Southampton, and they've always been very friendly and welcoming to me.

'They were too cold,' she said. 'I didn't really warm to them. Maybe it was because it was post-war. I just didn't like them.'

I think the truth was that Mam found it incredibly difficult to be away from everything that was familiar to her, and she simply couldn't settle outside the North East. In the end, Dad found a steady job as a typesetter for Thompson House, which published the *Chronicle* and *Journal* newspapers in Newcastle, and the family moved back to Kibblesworth when our Gin was still a toddler.

Dad did extremely well in his new job, going on to win an award for not making one spelling mistake, ever, despite reading upside down to typeset the letters.

However, within the family there was heartache in store, as Ginny contracted polio at the age of three and had to be placed in isolation in hospital. Mam and Dad were devastated, but instead of sinking into despair they both came out fighting, full of determination to help our Ginny recover. That was typical of the pair of them. Mam was ingrained with her parents' working-class instinct for survival, and Dad's upbringing had given him the belief that if you want something done you have to roll your sleeves up and do it yourself, because you can't rely on any other bugger to do it for you.

Dad bought a caravan at Bamburgh, sixty-odd miles away on the Northumberland coast, and once Ginny was out of hospital he walked her up and down the beach at every opportunity for two years. He could have gone to the coast closer to home, but he considered Bamburgh the family's 'spiritual home' as he and Mam had gone there together many times, and continued to do so in years to come, taking all three of us kids with them. Dad's dedication to Gin's recovery was a labour of love that paid off. Not only did Ginny make a full recovery, but when she was older she made our parents extremely proud by running for the county and dancing in international competitions for the Tyneside Irish community. Mam shed many a tear when Ginny won trophies.

'Can you credit it?' she would say, looking back at the photographs. 'It just goes to show that if you put your mind to something, you can do it.'

'Did you ever think Ginny wouldn't get better?' I asked when I was old enough to understand what had gone on, because it sounded absolutely terrible to me.

'Nah! It wasn't going to beat us,' Mam said, wiping a tear from her eye. 'Not in a million years!'

Mam always seemed to be able to detect when I was feeling worried or vulnerable, and she'd give me a hug at exactly the right time, just as she did when I asked about Ginny. You couldn't have wished for a better mam.

There's no question that my dad was a very good parent too, and he was undoubtedly a kind man. He had not been raised a Catholic like my mam and would not have claimed to be religious, yet he had a very strong moral compass and was always willing to put himself out for others. When I was very young I can remember going with him to deliver loads of food to the Little Sisters of the Poor and the Little Sisters of Mercy nursing homes in Low Fell.

'If you have enough for yourself you should try to share, Simon,' he told me as I helped him carry armfuls of fresh turkeys, big sacks of onions and trays of eggs into the home. I've never forgotten that.

He loved football and also volunteered as an FA coach for many years, and in one of my happiest memories of Dad I am playing with a ball on the beach and paddling in the sea with him, during a holiday to Cornwall. I was five years old and Mam and Dad had taken me to Penzance. My brother Will was eighteen by then and studying to become an engineer, and Ginny was twenty-three and training to become a social worker, so it was just me, Mam and Dad on the trip. Dad put our Ford Cortina on the train in Newcastle, as you could then, and we all shared a sleeper carriage. It was the biggest adventure of my life. The bed was like a hammock and I tucked myself in all cosy but, best of all, Mam had brought dead posh Callard & Bowser butterscotch and liquorice sweets for the journey.

'Let us hear ya crunch!' she'd say every time I took a butterscotch. 'I don't want ya to choke, Simon!'

The sweets were individually wrapped in fancy paper and were absolutely massive. I was in heaven. When we finally arrived in Penzance we stayed in a B & B, which blew my mind.

'Mam, we're in somebody else's house! It's weird! Are we allowed?'

Mam laughed. 'Yes, love, it's like a hotel, only different. It's a bit more homely, like.' With that she produced what she called her 'curler pillow', which she always slept on at home after putting rollers in her hair.

'Thank God you've remembered that!' Dad said. 'I couldn't have gone home for it from here!'

'Oh, give over!' Mam said, rolling her eyes, because my dad was remembering a recent camping trip, when Mam had forgotten the pillow and he was forced to drive home to fetch it, despite the fact he'd only just put his head on his own pillow when she realised she'd left it behind. Dad knew there was no debate when it came to Mam's hair, though. She was one of those women who wouldn't even put the bins out if her hair wasn't done properly, and even when we went to the beach on holiday her blonde curls were perfectly set as she paddled in the sea and floated on a lilo.

Dad took me swimming and I couldn't get over how much warmer the water was in the English Channel compared to the North Sea, and how much bigger the waves were. We hired a blue-and-white beach tent and then Mam really made my day by producing a home-made Victoria sponge, which she'd brought in a tin, all the way from Newcastle to Cornwall.

'Eee, I really love the cream teas down here,' she said. 'But nothing beats a taste of home, does it, pet?'

She was right there. I loved my food, and especially the food Mam made. She was a superb cook, and for a working-class family on a low budget we really punched above our weight when it came to food. Before I was born Dad had sailed to exotic places like Brazil, Singapore, Uruguay and Vietnam, and he used to always bring back herbs and spices from wherever he'd been.

'Most men traded their rum ration to get their wife a bottle of perfume,' Mam told me once. 'But not your dad. He'd trade his for star anise or cayenne pepper. I wasn't complaining, mind!'

Mam loved it, actually, and she was always ahead of her time in the kitchen, making proper good curries, spicy casseroles and chillies.

'Eee, Stella, what's that, it stinks!' the neighbours would call out.

'Aye, but it tastes better than mince and boiled spuds!' she'd chide back.

One of Mam's signature dishes was flat rib beef broth, which was absolutely delicious and is still one of my all-time favourites. It filled the house with a wonderful smell and I can remember the mouth-watering anticipation of dipping home-made bread into it, and having big lumps of beef melt on your tongue. Mam was a dab hand at transforming a shin of beef into a curry that blew your socks off, and when Vesta curries first came out and her mates nervously tried them, Mam really took the mickey, because she'd been making better curries herself for donkey's years, and at a fraction of the price.

Once he'd stopped sailing Dad sourced his herbs and spices in backstreet shops around Newcastle and always found the best suppliers. He also knew all the best places to buy good value cuts of meat and really fresh fish at the lowest prices, so between the two of them my parents made sure we ate like kings, even when money was tight. They were very proud of this fact, and sitting down to eat together, practising good table manners and appreciating our food was a very important part of family life. Manners in general were very important, in fact, and my dad always encouraged us to speak 'the Queen's English' and engage in intelligent conversation.

Despite being raised in a mining community Mam did not have the thick Geordie accent some of her peers had, because she made a conscious effort to 'speak well' as she said, and she was very far from being a stereotypical working-class housewife. The fact she was forced to stay at home skivvying after all the men in the family might have scuppered her dreams of being a nurse, but it didn't change the fact she was a very clever woman who was always interested in current affairs and was quite politically engaged.

'What are you doing?' Dad snapped one time, when I reached for the salt and started sprinkling it all over my dinner. 'Where do you think you are, the NAAFI?'

I had no idea what the NAAFI was, let alone that Royal Navy sailors like my dad considered members of the Navy, Army and Air Force Institutes to be a bit rough and ready by comparison to them. He slapped my wrist angrily and told me in no uncertain terms that the correct thing to do was to put a pile of salt on the side of my plate.

'You bring the food to the salt, not the other way around,' he scolded.

I've never forgotten that, and this is one of my earliest memories of my dad being uncharacteristically narky with me. I didn't realise it at the time, but his health was failing rapidly, and one of the side effects of this was that he became very bad-tempered.

Dad's kidneys had never recovered from the damage he did to them when he had his accident on the ship, and by the time I was six years old he had become so ill he needed kidney dialysis three times a week, which made him miserable and angry. I was too little to recognise the stages of his decline, and so in my mind he went from being an easy-going dad with a huge heart to a narky git practically overnight, and I didn't really grasp why.

Looking back, the day Dad's dialysis started marked a point of no return in my life. Things irrevocably changed for me, and not for the good.

3

Dave's

Braising Steak with Bay Leaf, Sole Véronique, and Tyne Brand Mince with Smash and Processed Peas

My mam went into hospital for tests after she fell out of bed, and she ended up being there for three weeks. One of the procedures she underwent was something that Dad said was called a 'lumbar puncture', and I heard Mam describe it as 'the most bloody awful experience of my life', which really upset me, though there was much worse to come.

It turned out that Mam's fall was an early sign of the onset of multiple sclerosis. My parents never hid anything from me and they sat me down and explained that 'MS' had caused Mam to fall out of bed, because it affected how she controlled her body, or something like that.

At seven going on eight, I was far too little to comprehend the magnitude of the diagnosis. I knew it was serious, because Mam cried just like Dad had when she fell out of bed, but at that stage I had no idea MS was incurable, or that it was a condition affecting the nervous system that would get progressively worse, randomly causing different parts of Mam's body to let her down.

I do have some clear memories of the early stages, though, and of seeing my indomitable, energetic mother start to buckle. In my very first recollection, I am sitting down waiting for my tea at the age of seven, and Mam walks in with a tray full of gorgeous-smelling, piping-hot food. She is smiling and laughing one minute, and the next she is losing her balance, the tray is falling and our tea is flying everywhere. Gravy and spuds are tumbling through the air, and Dad finds the whole thing funny and teases her about it, because at this point he thinks it's just a silly accident. Mam knows it's not. Her body has not done as she's asked it to do, and she bursts into tears of frustration.

In my next memory, which comes after she went to hospital for her tests, the three of us are on holiday in the Isle of Man, to see the TT Races. It was only the second holiday we ever had – the first was a short stay in a guesthouse in Southport – but this one was well worth waiting for. It was a dream come true for a bike-mad little boy like me. I was completely enthralled by the noise and speed of the bikes, and the spectacle of the leather-clad riders whizzing before my eyes, leaving dust clouds and the marvellous whiff of hot engines and burning rubber in their wake. I'd never seen anything like it in my life before, and riding in the TT Races one day was my ultimate ambition, after I'd got my first bike. I badgered every rider I could to sign their autograph in my little pocket race book, which I still have to this day.

Anyhow, back in 1967, me, Mam and Dad stayed in the three-star Metropole Hotel, which was the poshest place I'd ever been in. For my tea I ordered braising steak that arrived with a fresh bay leaf on top. Mam only ever used dried bay leaf and I thought it was probably a bit of privet off the hedge outside that someone had accidentally dropped on my plate, so I pushed it to one side and thought I'd better not eat it. It amuses me that I have such a clear memory of the food on my plate when I was in the midst of the TT Races, but I think that says it all. Bikes and food were vying for my attention, even then.

Before the holiday Dad had taken early retirement from the paper mill. He was sixty-four years old, had worked there for fifty-two years and got a lump sum of about two hundred-odd quid, the equivalent of about half a year's salary as he earned eleven pounds a week. He splashed about a hundred pounds on the Manx holiday, and I can remember him gleefully telling me about the adventure we were about to embark on.

'We'll have the time of our lives!' he said. 'You're going to ab-solutely love it, David. And what's more, so am I!'

'What about Mam?' I asked, knowing she wasn't particularly interested in motorbikes.

Dad winked. 'She'll have a ball. She likes nothing better than us all being together.'

I knew this was true, and I have old cine films that clearly show this. The silent home-movies taken by my dad capture us playing in the park together, with my mother in a dress and cardigan, swinging on the kids' swings with me beside her, lapping up every moment.

Looking back, the Isle of Man must have been a very bitter-sweet trip for my parents. I realise now that Dad retired a year early because of my mam's diagnosis, and it must have been bloody diabolical for both of them, wondering how her illness was going to play out. I can remember that Mam was already walking with a bit of a limp when we were on the way to the Isle of Man, and I take my hat off to both my parents for seizing the opportunity to go on holiday and splash a bit of cash when they had so much worry and no idea what the future held.

After the holiday Mam's condition steadily worsened and it became hard for her to stay on her feet for any length of time. Dad tried his very best to look after her and me, run the house and maintain some sort of normality, but things were never the same again.

I still went out on the back of Dad's bike from time to time and we got in a bit of fishing whenever we could, often going to Roa Island, as we liked it there. We couldn't go on longer adventures up to the Lakes like we used to, but we did still manage to get around the peninsula.

One time I remember we caught some fabulous plaice at Morecambe Bay which Dad, God love him, decided warranted some special treatment. He rifled through Mam's cookbooks, announced he was going to cook the classic old recipe Sole Véronique, even though we had plaice rather than sole, and bought a bunch of grapes from the greengrocer. The recipe also required white wine, which I'd never seen or heard of but, Dad being Dad, he added Mam's old Christmas trifle sherry instead, which ruined the flavour. I tried to help salvage things by carving up some tomatoes into rose shapes for Mam, and I boiled some eggs, sliced them thinly and displayed them in a fan to fill our plates.

Mam tried to appreciate the effort we both went to but she found it very frustrating that she was spending less and less time in the kitchen.

'What are you doing?' she'd call from her chair in the front room when she heard a pan-lid clatter or smelt something she thought might be burning.

'It's all under control!' I'd reassure her, but that was not what she wanted to hear. The back kitchen had been her engine room, and now she'd lost her grip, quite literally.

'I wish I could help you!' she'd cry.

'There's no need, mother!'

'Well, I still wish I could. It's God-awful being stuck in here!'

On Friday nights I was allowed to stay up late, watch telly and have chips, but instead of Mam making the chips for me like she used to I was given two potatoes and made them myself, copying the method she'd taught me while Dad kept a watchful eye on the hot fat. I really enjoyed it, and I took great pride in peeling the potatoes, chopping them as neatly as I could into even-sized chips and frying them until they were immaculately golden. There was a kind of ceremony about it, and I always stuck fastidiously to the same routine. I was incredibly pedantic in fact, working out exactly how many chips I could fit onto my slice of bread so it was perfectly covered, and sprinkling on the salt really evenly. Before I tucked in I'd eat any mis-shaped or leftover chips that didn't fit into my precision-made butty. Only then would I be ready to bite into the work of art that was my Friday night chip butty – and it was bliss! I would savour every last mouthful, and to this day I still think chips made at home like that are the best you can have.

Anyhow, Mam's limp had got a lot worse and she was becoming less mobile, but at this stage she was still just about managing to get out and about.

One day she gave me the money to go up to Ernie Gummersall the barbers.

'Ask for a short-back-and-sides,' she instructed. 'Your hair needs a really good tidy-up, David.'

I was eight years old and did exactly as Mam told me, because I didn't want a repeat of what had happened when she sent me to another barber in the town one time.

'You look like a prosperous young man!' this other barber had remarked, but I didn't know what 'prosperous' meant and so I ran all the way home, leaving him scratching his head.

Since then I'd always gone to Ernie Gummersall's, and that day I sat obediently in his chair after glancing at the sign on his wall that always puzzled me. It had prices for gents, boys and OAPs, and I really wanted to know what an 'oap' was, but was too afraid to ask.

Anyway, when I got home Mam went nuts.

'What the 'ell has he done?' she screamed, lifting herself to her feet, limping to the front door and putting on her coat.

'Come on, David, you're comin' with me!'

She hobbled up to the barber's as briskly as her failing legs would carry her, with me in tow, wondering what all the fuss was about. My hair had looked fine to me when Mr Gummersall took the black towel off my shoulders and I looked up from my comic and gave a cursory glance in the mirror.

'What the 'ell have you done?' Mam screeched at the unsuspecting barber as she pushed me through the door, setting his bell clattering loudly. 'Look at my David's head! What 'ave you done to him?'

The other fellas in the shop shuffled in their seats and looked at their feet as Mr Gummersall wheeled me and my mother to the back of the shop.

'I'm very sorry, Mrs Myers,' he said. 'But, here's the thing. I did exactly the same trim I always do.'

'How could you have? Look at the state of 'is head!'

'The thing is, Mrs Myers, I didn't put the bald patches there. They were . . . well, they were already there. Do you follow me?'

I was flushed red with embarrassment by now, but Mam was the opposite. She'd gone as white as a sheet as she ran her fingers through my thin and patchy dark brown hair. There were several scruffy-looking bald spots, mostly around the top left-hand side of my head, but it was clear from Mam's expression that she was no longer blaming Mr Gummersall for giving me a bad haircut.

'I see,' she said as politely as she could muster. 'Well, thank you for your time. Come on, David, we'd best be off.'

Mam couldn't get out of there quick enough. She relayed the whole story to my dad, and then to our local doctor, who nodded sagely, made reference to the shock I'd doubtless gone through because of my mother's illness, and promptly prescribed tranquilisers. The assumption was the pills would help me deal with the stress and upset I'd endured, and once I'd calmed down and come to terms with Mam's health problems, my hair would grow normally again.

Unfortunately, it didn't work out like that. I'd moved up from the infant school to Cambridge Street Primary by now and was top in everything, but all the tranquilisers did was hamper my performance in class.

'Why do you want to take the edge off his creativity and energy?' I overheard one of my teachers say one day. I stopped taking the pills after that and just had to put up with the hair loss as best as I could.

It wasn't that bad at first, and I didn't really see what all the fuss was about. At that age I was more interested in bikes and fishing and what I was having for tea than how I looked. It was boring and a pain in the backside more than anything, and I just tried to ignore it. Inevitably, I got called 'baldy' from time to time, which did upset me, but in the beginning I was too young to be properly vain about it, and on a good day it wasn't that noticeable anyhow.

'Is anything bothering you at school, son?' Dad would ask.

'Nowt,' I'd say, which was nearly always true. 'I like learning.'

In fact, I was fascinated by all the interesting things the teachers taught us. Doing maths puzzles, reading fantastical stories and learning about volcanoes erupting, or kings and queens and bloody battles, totally engrossed me. Rather than fretting about my hair I poured my energy into lapping up everything the teachers chucked at me.

Mam's problems far outshadowed mine, in any case. She went from limping to walking with a frame within six months, and six months after that she couldn't walk at all. I realised how bad she was when she went to bed one night and couldn't get herself up again. She screamed in anger and frustration.

'Why me?' she wailed. 'Why is this happening to me?'

I felt a tightening in my throat when I heard her like that, and Dad looked terrible, like a man condemned. He tried to pacify her, but there was no answer.

'Will Mam get any better?' I asked.

I knew the MS wouldn't go away, but I guess I wanted to know if she would have good days and bad days. It was all I could think of to find a bit of light in the situation.

'No, son, I'm afraid not. It just gets worse, you see, this MS. It doesn't get better.'

'Oh,' I said. 'That's not very good, is it?'

The following night Dad explained that I would have to help him get Mam into bed as she couldn't manage to climb the stairs. As he spoke gently and quietly to me, Mam was sitting in the armchair, shouting and crying and raging against the world for all she was worth.

'I used to drive cranes!' she howled. 'Look at me! I climbed ladders to drive cranes, and now I can't climb my own flamin' stairs!'

I know now that the drugs she was on affected her personality. The doctors had given her Valium and other tranquilisers to calm her down, and barbiturates to help her sleep. She began to suffer from mood swings and lethargy she wasn't able to control, and it's not an exaggeration to say it was like my old mam had been replaced by somebody I barely recognised. Even her physical appearance started to change. Her chestnut hair, which she used to take pride in styling, lost its bounce and shine. Her skin became puffy, and it wasn't long before she started to gain weight because she was so immobile.

'I'll take her arms, you get her feet,' my dad instructed as we helped her from her armchair that first time.

It was an awful experience, because Mam yelped and complained as we struggled to lift her, and we more or less bounced her up the stairs.

'Well done, David, you're doing a grand job,' Dad said. 'I've got her weight, just lift her feet. And again . . . well done, David.'

It was hard work, and when Mam's back or legs bashed against the thin stair-carpet she didn't hesitate to vent her disapproval with both barrels. She never hid her emotions, ever, and from then on we'd go through the same ritual every night, with my mam crying and moaning, or spitting feathers about her fate. Of course, it got harder the heavier she became, and it was a task all three of us dreaded on a daily basis.

Dad asked for support from the local authority and Mam got a wheelchair, when I was nine. We also got help once a week with the cleaning, but that was it. Dad and I became Mam's carers, muddling through each day. He took charge of washing Mam and lifting her onto her commode, and I did whatever I could manage.

Fetching shopping was my main job. Dad would give me a list of things to buy from the local shops, but he wasn't used to cooking and for ages we lived on tinned Tyne Brand mince, Smash and cans of processed peas. Once, Dad just mixed the whole lot together and piled it on two plates.

'What's that?' I asked suspiciously, as it really didn't look great.

'Same as we had last night.'

'Oh! Why's it like that?'

'I thought it would make a change. I got bored of looking at the same meal.'

I was too young at that stage to have any say in what I bought from the shops and I'd just get what Dad told me to buy, which besides the mince, Smash and peas typically consisted of the same basics every week, including cheese, eggs, bread, milk, potatoes, carrots, onions and perhaps a bit of ham, braising steak or chicken.

Sometimes I got out the Be-Ro or the *Radiation* cookbook and made a pie or a stew out of whatever ingredients we had in. Cheese-and-onion or -potato pie was always a good option as we were rarely short of cheese, onions or potatoes, or I'd follow a recipe for beef stew, say, and substitute whatever meat we had in the house. My dishes weren't always perfect but I'd watched and helped Mam enough times to have a headstart on most of the recipes.

'Mix until it looks like runny cream,' she'd always taught me whenever she made Yorkshire pudding, and I'd hear her voice as I cracked the eggs and measured out the milk and flour for the recipe and tried to make it on my own.

I cooked because I wanted to, and not just because I was fed up of Dad's meals.

Cooking was never a chore; chopping and mixing and watching the gas stove work its magic when scones were rising or a pie was browning was a source of wonder for me. It was like being let loose in the science class and being able to mix chemicals together and watch them react, but without a teacher there to spoil the fun.

Cooking became my new hobby, really, because, not long after Mam got the wheelchair, Dad and I stopped going out for rides on the scooter together. For a start we couldn't leave Mam for hours on end like we used to, and then somebody broke into our back-yard and slashed the tyres on the scooter, and Dad didn't have the money to replace them. He said it would take a very long time to save up, if he ever could.

We lived on Dad's pension money, which was paid on a Monday but invariably ran out on a Friday. This meant we often had to get by with just potatoes and vegetables over the weekend. Dad and I were both appalled when that happened; not being able to ride to the sea and catch fresh fish was a double whammy of misfortune.

I was one of the kids at school who qualified for free school dinners, which I really hated, but not because of the grub. I had tinned tuna for the first time at school and liked it; it came with two ice-cream scoops of mashed potato and a ladle of tomato soup. We also had chips once a month and puddings like Manches-ter tart, which was delicious, and the not-so-delightful prunes and custard. Once, a load of us all saved our prunes and gave them to one boy, who ate seventy-odd prunes in one sitting. Anyhow, the food was alright on the whole, but I dreaded dinnertime because I had to produce my free meal tokens every day, which marked me out as a poor kid.

My patchy hair loss, which I now knew was called 'alopecia areata', hadn't improved one bit and the name-calling had got worse the older I became, so the very last thing I wanted to do was stand out any more than I already did. I was totally stuffed by the tokens; being poor as well as the class baldy was irresistible to the bullies, and I had the piss taken out of me something rotten.

I complained relentlessly to my dad and he decided to pay for the dinners in the end, which was a hell of a thing to do, given our circumstances. Nevertheless the damage was done, and the token system had caused another blow to my confidence. Even though I was naturally quite extroverted, all I wanted to do was keep my head down and avoid being in the spotlight as much as possible.

Anyhow, outside of school it was obvious to me that earning a bit of money could only help matters, and so I asked the local newsagent for a paper round. I was ambitious even then and he must have seen how keen I was, because he gave me a huge round of one hundred and ten papers. I took it on without hesitation and used my old push-bike as a trolley, strapping the papers to the seat. That way I delivered papers all over the neighbourhood, Monday through Saturday, and all for one pound a week. Some of the local kids took the piss out of me for that too, but I didn't care.

Despite my attempts at boosting the family income, Dad's motorbike never did get fixed, and in hindsight I can see that lack of funds was only part of the problem. Dad's spirit had really taken a battering. He was getting ground down by the pressure of looking after Mam morning, noon and night and, slowly but surely, my dad was giving up. One of the many tragedies of the situation was that he had done it all before, having nursed his first wife for twenty-five years. Now his second chance at happiness had turned to ashes at an alarming pace. Dad must have been wondering what on earth he had done to deserve such bad luck, though to his credit he never said as much to me.

I spent a lot of time drawing throughout my childhood, be-cause with Dad working in the paper mill there was always a plentiful supply of paper in the house, even after he left work. I'd spend hours copying pictures of trains out of the Hornby cata-logue, enjoying picking out the fine details, though this led to an unhappy accident one time, which landed me and Dad in even more difficulties.

I was about ten years old, and after I'd finished sketching on my bedroom floor one day I stood my pencil up in a chunky Helix rubber. The next time I went into my room I bounded in without thinking, stamping heavily on the sticking-up pencil. It disappeared inside my foot, and the pain was absolutely horrific.

'Help!' I bellowed in agony. 'I've trodden on me pencil! Dad! Can you come and pull it out? Arrghhh!'

My dad ran up the stairs and yanked hard on the pencil – so hard, in fact, that he unwittingly left the lead embedded in my heel.

'I'm sure that'll be fine now, son,' he soothed, before shouting down the stairs to my mam, who was calling out in frustration at not being able to come to my aid.

'He's alright, Margaret. No need to worry!'

Six weeks later I needed an operation to remove the embedded lead, which was lodged a full two inches inside my foot and had caused a nasty abscess to form. I stayed in hospital overnight, but that was a trifle compared to the fix my father now found himself in.

Without me at home, Dad simply couldn't manage. Mam was incontinent now on top of everything else, and just meeting her basic needs had become a very difficult full-time job for my father. Getting her up to bed without my help was impossible, so when I was in hospital she had to spend the night in her armchair.

Even once I was back home our problems weren't over. It was weeks before I could put pressure on my foot and walk properly, which meant Dad had two invalids to look after. I couldn't do the shopping like I normally did, and carrying Mam up the stairs to bed was an almighty kerfuffle, with me hopping on one leg and Mam getting bumped around all over the place, which needless to say didn't leave her best pleased.

Once I was fully back on my feet I volunteered to push Mam to the local park in her wheelchair, to give my dad a break. I could see he was struggling to get through the days; he was tired out and his natural spark had well and truly dimmed. Mam's state of mind seemed to have worsened since my hospital stay too. She'd become even more emotionally unstable than before, which obviously took its toll on Dad.

'Come on, Mam,' I told her. 'This'll cheer you up. Let's go to the park!'

I didn't get much response as Mam seemed to be in a particularly black mood, but I carried on regardless, putting a blanket over her knees before wheeling her across Devon Street and up to the park.

'Shall we have a walk round the lake, Mam?' I asked as I pushed her through the gate.

'No!' she snapped.

'Oh, well then, where shall we go?'

'How do I know? What does it matter?'

I was too young to spot the warning signs, and Mam's reaction came right out of the blue. In a fit of frustration at having her ten-year-old son take *her* to the park, Mam just let rip. She was screeching and bellowing and flailing her arms around all over the place in a terrible temper, and people started to stare.

'Mam! Stop! Just calm down!' I hissed.

'No!' she screamed. 'No I won't!'

'It's OK. Shall I take you home?'

'No! Don't bother!'

A couple of lads from school spotted the commotion. 'Look, it's that bald kid!' they sniggered, pointing at me.

'Please, Mam,' I begged, pulling my hood up and turning my back on the bullies. 'Just be quiet. Pleeeeease!'

Whatever I said seemed to make matters worse. Mam's screams got louder and she was getting herself in such a twist I was worried she might fling herself right out of the wheelchair. I decided there was only one thing for it – I had to run home and get Dad. I knew I couldn't leave Mam in the park where she was in case she wheeled herself into the lake, but I had a bright idea. Checking to see that the park-keeper wasn't on the prowl, I decided to push Mam into the middle of the biggest flower bed I could see.

'Argghhh!' Mam bellowed as I mowed down a swathe of bluebells forming the border to the flower bed. 'Where are you taking me?'

'In there, mother, it's for the best.'

'What on earth! Get me out of here! Argghhh!'

She let out another ear-splitting screech but I kept going, ploughing the wheelchair into the centrepiece of the flower bed, which was – or had been – a wonderful display of red and pink roses. I then let down both tyres on the wheelchair before legging it home as fast as I could. Absurdly, I felt quite triumphant as I fetched Dad and told him what I'd done.

'It was all I could think of to do!' I puffed as we both ran back to the park.

'You did the right thing, son,' Dad said gratefully, but his face fell when he spotted the park-keeper, who was now in the flower bed ranting at Mam and complaining about the damage to his roses.

'Irreparable!' he was saying. 'Months of hard work DESTROYED!'

This made Mam even more hysterical and we could have really done without him carrying on, as Dad was now struggling like mad to pump up the tyres with Mam still thrashing around in the chair.

'I can explain,' Dad apologised, but the park-keeper was red in the face and was having none of it.

'The greenflies I've killed! The pruning I've done! I've a good mind to report you to the council.'

The park didn't need a bandstand with my family there, providing the sideshow.

I can laugh about it now, but it was no bloody joke at the time. There's no two ways about it: the Myers family was in deep trouble. We needed help, and we needed it fast.

4

Si's

Stuffed Turkey Hedgehog Buffet, Minced Scrag-end of Lamb and Millionaire's Shortbread

'Don't ride on the road!' Dad shouted at me from his bedroom window one day, after Mam had walked me home from primary school. 'Simon! Do you hear me, son? Ride on the path!'

I was seven years old and pootling around on my bike on a quiet, safe patch of tarmac outside our council house at Fellside in Birtley, which was the house we moved to after leaving Kibblesworth.

'Alreet, Dad,' I shouted up at the window obediently, but he carried on nagging me.

My dad's shouting and complaining quickly became a regular, constant part of my life. I disliked him for it, and I began to feel very hard done by being the baby of the family; it was like I was the one who'd got the shitty end of the stick. In retrospect, I can see that it was his condition I didn't like, not my dad. I loved him dearly, of course, but at the time I wasn't old enough to make this distinction, and I felt robbed of the father he'd been before he got so ill.

'It's alright for you,' I'd think when our Ginny drove off in her little Fiat 127, or when Will came in all merry from a night out with his mates. They'd had Dad when he was fit and healthy and now they were old enough to have lives of their own outside the house. It wasn't fair at all.

Unbeknown to me, there had been a big debate in the family about whether Dad should have his treatment at home or in hospital. It was the early seventies and the dialysis equipment filled a whole room and was scary to look at, even for adults. Mam and our Ginny, who was by now in her twenties, decided it would be too frightening for me to see my dad on dialysis at home, not to mention incredibly demanding for Mam. This meant Dad went into hospital three times a week and recuperated at home, but in my memories he might just as well have been in a hospital ward.

I remember Mam and Dad's bedroom being stacked with medical equipment, and our garage became piled high with huge bottles of yellow liquid. I really hated those bottles. Our three-bedroom house was built on a sloping hillside and had two storeys on one side and three on the other, incorporating the garage. Before Dad was ill I associated the garage with cars, and I always got excited when I was allowed to go in there and explore. Dad had a bronze-coloured two-litre GT Capri with sports wheels and a black leather interior. It was mint, though I'd usually end up asking Dad about motorbikes he had ridden in the past, as I thought they were much more exciting than cars. Dad had worked as a despatch rider in his younger days, after his injury on board ship confined him to 'lesser duties', as they said in the navy.

'There's no better way to travel!' he always said when reminiscing about his bike-riding days.

Before I came along Dad rode a Bantam with a sidecar, which was what a lot of working-class men had in those days, but as the family grew the car became his mode of transport of choice, and we always had a car of some sort, like his trusty old Ford Anglia, a green Cortina we once owned and the blingy bronze Capri that I remember the most.

My uncle George, who was a close family friend, was the one who was really bike-mad when I was a bairn, and I aspired to have motorbikes like him one day. He and my auntie Hilda lived in Lamesley, near a big crossroads that was notorious for crashes, often involving lads on scooters and motorbikes riding up from the Team Valley estate. Auntie Hilda always had old bedsheets ripped up ready to use as bandages, and Uncle George would pick up pieces of broken bikes off the road and put them in his back garden, which I loved to investigate.

Hearing about all the accidents didn't put me off at all; quite the contrary. I simply could not wait to ride a motorbike. It wasn't just the thought of hearing the roar of the engine and zooming down the street ten times faster than I did on my push-bike. I loved everything about motorbikes and scooters, even when they were standing still. It was a thrill for me just to smell the oil and petrol or touch the shiny spokes on the wheels of Uncle George's bikes.

I wished my dad still rode bikes, but the truth of it was that he was becoming so ill he would soon be unable to drive the car. Very sadly, the bigger I got, the sicker my dad became, until we had more bottles of yellow liquid than cans of Castrol motor oil in our garage.

The treatment made Dad progressively more exhausted and foul-tempered and he was forced to give up work, which meant Mam was struggling not just to help care for him, but to pay the bills and keep the house running. I know she did her utmost to maintain some sort of normality for me, but it was very tough for her and she was under constant strain.

I can honestly say I have practically no good memories of my dad from when I was about six or seven. The only happy occasion I can really remember was when my parents celebrated their twenty-fifth wedding anniversary when I was nearly eight, and friends and family came round to the house for a party.

Mam really excelled herself by producing a classic seventies buffet. The dining table was covered in a posh cloth and loaded with sticks of celery, bowls of gherkins, vol-au-vents, trifle and a big square iced cake, but it was the turkey centrepiece that really stole the show. Mam had de-boned this huge bird, stuffed it with nuts and roasted it with all kinds of goodies, then reconstructed it and spiked it with long cocktail sticks so you could help yourself to a diced portion. It looked like a giant dead hedgehog, but it tasted absolutely sensational.

Mam kept her recipes in a little black recipe book in the kitchen that had been passed down through several generations of her family. I started taking an interest in it around this time, when Mam was on her own in the kitchen, and Dad was in bed.

'Can I have a read of it, Mam?' I'd ask, intrigued to see exactly what went into her meatloaf, rhubarb wine or ginger snaps. There was a recipe for kibbe in there too, and I really wanted to read for myself how to create one of those torpedo-shaped fried croquettes, stuffed with minced lamb and onions.

'Can I just have a quick look? I won't rip it or anything, honest! I just want to see inside!'

'No! Ya bloody can't! It's my recipe book. You'll get your turn with it when the time is right. I'll be passing it down to our Gin and then Will before you, mind, so you might have a long wait!'

'Awww, Mam!'

'I said no and I mean no! Now just sieve that flour and shut your face!'

Though I wasn't allowed to have the book, Mam always encouraged me to help out or watch and learn in the kitchen. She had all kinds of gadgets that looked like instruments of torture and fascinated me. Her heavy silver metal mincer, the type that you clamped to the kitchen worktop, was used a lot as Mam never bought mince but would always get a scrag-end of lamb, for instance, and mince it herself. I'd sit at our white table on one of the two bench seats we had that were covered with wipe-clean blue cushions and watch in amazement as she turned the handle and minced meat plopped out into a bowl beneath the machine.

'What's this?' I said when she produced a weird kind of press one day. 'It looks a bit scary, Mam!'

'It's just a tongue press, son,' she laughed. 'Next time I get a nice ox tongue I'll show ya how it works.'

The cheese wire was another weird and wonderful-looking device, not least because the handles had broken off and Mam had replaced them with a couple of wooden clothes pegs. I loved it when she let me cut the cheese, and I always volunteered to slice the hard-boiled eggs too, because we had one of those slicers that did it all in one action as you pulled half a dozen wires down over the slippery egg.

Not only did the gadgets draw me into the kitchen to learn about cooking, but the truth is I was also a very willing apprentice because I liked to eat the results, especially when we made home-made bread, cakes and biscuits. I don't suppose it will come as a big surprise if I tell you I was a fat kid. There was never a time when I wasn't 'on the chunky side'. In infant school I was routinely called 'fatty' or 'fatso' by the other kids, and by the time

I was at St Joseph's Roman Catholic Junior School in Birtley I was commonly referred to as 'fatty', because I was by far the tubbiest boy in the school.

My primary school days were crap; I don't know how else to describe them.

Not only was I bullied because I was fat, but I didn't make any friends because nobody wanted to be associated with the red-faced lardy-arse who struggled in PE and had to wear uniforms three sizes bigger than theirs. One of the few friendly faces I saw at school was Helen Lee's. I'd known Helen since I was about three or four as she was a neighbour and her dad John ran the mobile shop on our estate.

'Give us a kiss to be your friend!' she'd said when we were tiny bairns, because Helen always had a penchant for kissing and play-ing 'catchy kissy'.

'No! I'll be ya friend but I don't want a kiss!' I always said, run-ning away from her.

We became good mates – still are to this day, in fact – and I was always glad to see Helen at school, because she would not be nasty to me like the others.

The name-calling and bullying increased along with my weight, making my life progressively more crap. I put on a stone every year, and my weight typically corresponded to my age. To save you the trouble of working it out, this meant I weighed eight stone when I was eight years old, while the average weight for a boy that age is around four stone.

I wasn't interested in learning, and playtime was always a night-mare. I was left out or picked on in the yard, and if I did manage to join in a game I got puffed out very quickly. Dinnertime was terrible too. I felt like all eyes were on me as I carried my tray to the table, and to this day I avoid self-service restaurants like the plague, because they remind me of the shame I felt when the other kids looked at what was on my plate, and sniggered behind my back.

I can remember walking home feeling close to tears one afternoon, because life at school was just so hard and lonely. When I got home Dad was in bed, as he generally slept until about half past four after his treatment, and I asked Mam if I could go up and see him.

'Yes, love, go on up,' Mam said. 'He's quite poorly today but I'm sure he'll be pleased to see you.'

Dad was lying on his side in bed and, not wanting to make any noise that would annoy him, I quietly got under the covers beside him, because I wanted to have a cuddle. Dad opened his eyes just as I went to put my arms around him, and then he opened his mouth and spoke.

'Not like that,' he said sternly. 'Back to back.'

It was a devastating rejection to me, and I had to choke back the tears. I was too little to understand how ill he was and it pained me for years and years afterwards, and still hurts when I think about it now. It baffled me why he found it so hard to give me a hug; it didn't make any sense at all.

I didn't say a word to Mam when she asked me how I was afterwards. I could see she had a lot on her plate trying to hold the family together with Dad the way he was, so I just carried what happened around with me.

The week after Bonfire Night in 1974, a police car came properly screaming up our road, with lights and sirens flashing and blaring. I'll never forget it. It was like a scene from Z Cars as the car screeched to a halt outside our house and two frantic-looking policemen leaped out.

I didn't know it at the time, but my dad had been on the waiting list for a kidney transplant for six months, and now a motorcyclist who was a suitable match had died on the A1 in Leeds, and his organs were on their way to the Royal Victoria Infirmary in the centre of Newcastle.

'Simon, you're going to Auntie Hilda's,' our Ginny said. 'And dad's going to hospital. Now.'

Apparently, Dad refused to get in the police car outside our house, even though this was his big chance of survival and there wasn't a second to lose. In the event, Ginny drove Mam and Dad to hospital with the help of a speeding police escort, while I was despatched to Auntie Hilda and Uncle George's house.

I don't think I knew Dad was actually going to have a transplant, and there was no time to ask questions. In any case, I really liked it at Auntie Hilda and Uncle George's, and I was happy to go there. As well as being into motorbikes, Uncle George liked to brew his own beer. He'd sit in his garden on an old bus seat he'd acquired, drinking home brew with his mates and chatting about the war. He'd always let me have a little taste, and every time I'd ask if I could have a 'big, full one'.

'No, you bloody well can't,' Auntie Hilda would say if she caught us. Then she'd bring us out some home-made soup, or send me on an errand to keep me out of trouble.

'Simon, you can go and pick me some crab apples. Get the ones that are sour, they make the best jelly.'

I wasn't sure how I was meant to know a sour crab apple from a sweet one, but I always enjoyed picking fruit in Auntie Hilda's garden. I thought she was loads posher than us because her garden was big and really well-stocked with all kinds of soft fruits and giant stalks of rhubarb. Rooks and crows were always trying to get into the soft fruit cages Auntie Hilda used to protect her crops, and I'd often be sent down the garden to free them when they got themselves stuck in the wires. My reward would be a slice of Auntie Hilda's millionaire's shortbread, which was so lush I'd have freed a hundred of those flamin' rooks to have a single mouthful. If I could eat it while I explored the latest fender or shiny exhaust that Uncle George had recovered from an accident outside his door and put in his back garden, I was in total paradise.

Anyhow, that's where I was when Dad was in hospital having his kidney transplant. I stayed with Auntie Hilda for three days and, according to our Ginny, for the first two days I visited Dad twice a day. The very first time I went in he was in a private room, looking like his old self. He talked about his mam, who died in the Blitz, and he told a story about drinking beer in London, which was weird because he always drank pink gin; he even had his own gin glass down at the local club.

I know now that Dad was actually in intensive care, but at the time I had no idea. There was a positive atmosphere around him for the first time in ages, and Mam seemed really relieved and happy.

'Are you OK at Auntie Hilda's?' Mam asked.

'It's great!' I replied. 'I've been there ages!'

I can still picture her smiling at me, and Dad smiled too. I honestly thought he was as right as rain and was going to be coming home any day soon.

On the third day I visited Dad during the daytime, though I can't remember much about it, and that night our Ginny came to pick me up at Auntie Hilda's. I thought this meant Dad was coming home, but as soon as Ginny walked in the house the atmosphere completely changed. It was like a switch had been flicked and everything turned cold and grey. The next thing I remember is being back at our house, and Will was there too, who must have been twenty-one then.

All eyes were on me, and I wasn't sure why.

'I want you to be really brave,' Ginny said, her voice cracking.

I was standing next to the cooker, feeling very anxious now, and then Mam spoke.

'I've got something to tell you, Simon,' she said.

There was a pause as she took a deep breath. Then she said: 'Son. Dad's died.'

I learned much later that Dad had been one of the first patients to have a double kidney transplant in the UK, and the anti-rejection drugs available in those days were nowhere near as good as they are today. His body rapidly rejected the new organs, and there was nothing anybody could do to save his life. On his death certificate it says he died of chronic renal failure, malignant hypertension and failed renal transplant. It was 15 November 1974, and he was fifty-five years old.

Mam's words were in my head but I couldn't take them in. 'Son. Dad's died' was such an unbelievable sentence to come out of my mam's mouth, and I just stood there in stunned silence, not knowing what to do or say. I didn't cry immediately, and I can remember that I wanted to be strong for Mam. She cried, and I gave her a big hug. I think I felt her loss more than mine in that moment. I knew she needed me to be brave and responsible and, even though I was just a bairn, I felt that very strongly. That was the way life was going to be from now on, I could tell.

5

Dave's

Meatpaste Butties, PG Tips and Cheese-on-Toast Doorsteps

Coping with crap is in Si's blood and bones, and makes him who he is today. It's also one of the reasons we get on so well. If all we had in common was beards, bikes and food, I think we may have drifted apart years ago.

The experiences we both had as kids have left their mark, and in many ways we're made of the same mettle because of what we went through.

Dad and I were in desperate need of help in dealing with Mam, who was in a wheelchair and becoming increasingly hard to care for. After more than a year of constantly badgering Social Services for help, Dad was finally told that we were to be given one of four ground-floor flats designed for the disabled on a new council estate nearby, called The Griffin. A gushing official told my dad: 'It'll be like fairyland, compared to what you're used to.' It wasn't; I thought it was crap.

We moved in when I was about twelve, and I was gutted. We had no backyard and there were blowers on the walls instead of the real fire we had in Devon Street. The fact we rarely lit the fire wasn't the point; the new flat had no character and seemed soulless by comparison to the old two-up-two-down. Its one saving grace was that we no longer had to carry my mother up the stairs to bed, because there weren't any.

The cheap wall-heaters riled me not just because they looked like they belonged in an office rather than a home, but because I missed the supply of soot from our old fire. I'd found a good use for it whenever the bald patches on my head became particularly noticeable. I'd collect a bit of soot from the back of the fireplace, mix it with Vaseline and stick it on my head to disguise my hair loss. Then I'd use Mam's hairspray to fix the gooey mess in place. She'd go mad at me afterwards, not because I used her Elnett, but because I ruined all the pillowcases.

'DAVID!' she'd scream. 'Look at the state of that! It'll never come out in the wash!'

I didn't argue with Mam. She had very little else to focus on, because she was stuck in the house nearly all of the time, and a pillowcase drama was about the most exciting thing that happened to her most days.

She did get out once a week by now, thanks to my dad's persistence in nagging the council for any support we could get. Every Thursday Mam was collected in a little council van and taken out to a community centre, which was for my dad's sanity as much as hers. Mam didn't always get into the van willingly. She'd yell and protest and berate the care workers; I don't think a day went by when she didn't curse her fate.

The MS was cruel enough, but God knows what it was like for my mam to see her cherished little boy walking around looking like he'd actually torn his own hair out with worry over the state she was in. It must have been bloody awful for her.

The alopecia had become a constant, on-going struggle for me.

From the first time the bald patches appeared when I was eight, they would come and go in random fashion, usually affecting the left-hand side of my head, and mostly on the top and side. Some weeks and months were better than others, but the condition never, ever went away, and the older I got the more of a problem it became to me.

I passed my eleven plus and started at Barrow Grammar School for Boys around the time we were moving to The Griffin estate. Dad did his best to sort out some treatment for my hair before I started secondary school, knowing full well that adolescence is hard enough when you fit in, let alone when you feel like a freak.

We tried all sorts, ranging from lotions and potions rubbed into my hair to a course of steroids, injected through my scalp. That was terrible. The course of treatment required dozens of hypodermic injections into a two-inch patch on my head, to deposit the steroids between my skull and scalp. I'd come home from the local hospital bleeding and sore, but the worst of it was that nothing ever worked. In fact, by the time I was thirteen it got dramatically worse, as I woke up to find clumps of hair clinging to my nylon sheets.

Over the space of about three weeks I lost all my remaining hair, my eyebrows and my eyelashes. The bullies at school started to call me Uncle Fester, after the *Addams Family* character. One particularly nasty lad called me 'cue ball'.

Even when the weather was warm I'd pull the hood up on my anorak to hide my head, and I didn't even bother hoping I might get a girlfriend like some of the other boys at school. Nobody would want me looking the way I did, I was absolutely convinced of that. I'd come home at lunchtime whenever I was allowed, because the more time I was away from school the better. This meant I'd often end up with boring meatpaste butties instead of a hot dinner, but despite the fact I loved my food the sacrifice was worth it if I avoided the bullies for an extra hour a day.

One weekend I was dreading Monday morning so much I decided to take drastic action, and I went out armed with my air pistol. Don't worry, it's not what you think! I didn't try to shoot my bullies; I attempted to shoot myself in the leg, in the desperate hope I'd be able to stay off school for a while and recover. Unfortunately, the pellet hit the seam of my bell-bottom jeans and all I ended up with was a nasty bruise that didn't warrant any time off at all, or even a trip to the chemist. It would have been funny if I hadn't felt so rubbish about myself. I couldn't even shoot myself, that's how much of a loser I was.

The one ray of sunshine in my school life was my art teacher, Mr Eaton. Without a shadow of a doubt, Mr Eaton changed my life. He was a graduate from the Royal College of Art and was more flamboyant than all the other teachers. The school was very old-fashioned and traditional, the kind where most masters wore gowns and mortarboards, but not Mr Eaton. He wore a sharp suit and snappy shirts and ties, and he also drove a sports car, which impressed me no end. It was his refreshing style of teaching that really hooked me, though.

'Why is *The Planets* playing, sir?' I asked him one day, when I walked into his classroom and heard the powerful music bouncing off the brick walls.

'We are going to try to paint Mars today,' he said. 'Holst's music should inspire us!'

It certainly did. I always looked forward to my art lessons, and I excelled in the subject. Thanks to the reams of paper my dad had always supplied at home I'd enjoyed drawing and painting throughout my primary school years, but Mr Eaton taught me to really appreciate art. He realised I had a bit of talent for it and encouraged me at every opportunity, especially in his extra-curricular art club, which he held a couple of times a week.

'You have a good eye, David,' he'd say. 'Don't be afraid to let rip with the colours!' It was comments like that that buoyed me, and kept my spirits up when the rest of my school life was rubbish. Mr Eaton arranged lots of trips to art galleries in Manchester and Liverpool and, thanks to him, I became obsessed with the Pre-Raphaelites, which incidentally was my specialist subject when I went on *Celebrity Mastermind* a few years back.

Another huge benefit of attending Mr Eaton's art club was that I made friends with several boys from different year groups, including Graham Twyford and John Carling. They were a bit arty and alternative and we got on really well, which was another lifeline that kept me afloat at secondary school.

One time I designed a pack of Tarot cards that I painted with intricate designs and bright colours. Mr Eaton was impressed, and in typical style he turned a blind eye when he discovered what I went on to use them for.

'Roll up, roll up, come and get your tips for the 2.10 at Doncaster!'

John Carling took 50p off every boy we coerced into using the Tarot cards to divine for the horse racing, and we even started to believe our own sales pitch after I put a 50p treble on a horse that came in. I collected my £106 winnings from the local betting shop in my school uniform, and spent it on my first ever music stacking system, complete with record deck, radio and twin cassette players. I loved music, and I'd shut myself in my bedroom with a mug of PG Tips and some cheese-on-toast doorsteps and blast out tracks from Black Sabbath, Bob Dylan and Pink Floyd. The music was my escape.

6

Si's

Garlic Sausage Omelette, Communion Wine and Two Packets of Bourbon Creams

After Dad died, not only was Mam grief-stricken but she was practically penniless, too. Dad left no money at all, not a bean. All we had to live on was Mam's widow's pension of £47 a week, and we received housing benefit. Mam was ashamed of our predicament and, despite being newly bereaved, she wanted and needed to get herself a job as quickly as possible. She'd worked as a florist for a while, during Dad's illness, and she was really good at it because she was incredibly creative. Now, though, all she could find was uninspiring shop work, first in a chemist's and then in a local pound shop called Purse Care.

Our life seemed to be ruled by finding fifty pence pieces to feed the meter.

'What's the meter doing, Si?' Mam would shout.

'It's on red!'

'It's always in the red, son, but how far?'

When the telephone bill arrived there would be a particularly horrible panic about whether or not we had enough to pay it. Getting cut off and not being able to make calls would only be half the problem as far as Mam was concerned; explaining to friends why Birtley 2498 was unobtainable would be too shameful to bear.

'What happens inside our four walls stays inside our four walls,' Mam said, which was a phrase I heard many times throughout my childhood. I can remember her having terrible panics about the fact we didn't have a TV licence for our little portable black-and-white TV, both before and after Dad died.

'If anyone asks, we haven't got a telly,' she would say. Hilariously, she kept the TV in the airing cupboard when we weren't watching it, in case a 'detector van' was in the area. If there had been a sighting of a van and she was feeling especially vulnerable Mam would put the telly in the garage or under the stairs, with a cloth over it. Honest to God, that cloth was like the telly version of the Turin Shroud. Only when Mam felt confident we wouldn't get caught would she bring the telly out and put the ornaments back on top, I guess to make it look like it was always part of the furniture, in case someone we knew popped in. We'd watch stuff like *The Two Ronnies* or *The Wheeltappers and Shunters Social Club*, which was a variety show set in a fictional northern working-men's club. Because the telly had been crammed in a cupboard or hidden away we always had to spend ages fiddling with the aerial to get any sort of signal. Sometimes I'd actually have to stand there holding it in the right place throughout a programme, and it was really annoying because after all that effort Dad would invariably send me straight up to bed as soon as the strippers came on *Wheeltappers*.

Despite not being able to afford it, Mam would always push the boat out at Christmas.

Me, Gin and Will would get a big sack each, on top of whatever Father Christmas would bring, and Mam would take great delight in carrying them into the front room.

'Ting!' she said one year, arriving in a sparkling tutu, struggling under the weight of three huge sacks. 'Your Christmas fairy is here!'

'Oh no!' I thought. 'Mam's got into hock again! How long is it going to take to pay this lot off?'

She would always be adamant the house had to be nicely decorated, and she absolutely loved fresh holly, or what she called 'berried holly'.

'Eee, Simon, can you go out and get us some berried holly?'

'Aw, Mam, do I have to?'

'Yes, ya do. They've got some at that bungalow up by the roundabout. Don't get caught mind!'

I'd be despatched on a raid, typically after dark, so I could snaffle us a lovely big bunch of fresh holly.

One time Mam sent me to Lambton Lion Park, because they had loads of holly bushes in the grounds. I dutifully climbed over the wall with a pair of secateurs in my back pocket, but unfortunately the groundsman spotted me straight away.

'You little bastard!' he cried before firing shots of salt and bacon rind at me from his pellet gun.

After school I'd walk to the shops and wait on the street outside Purse Care until Mam finished her shift. Then the two of us would go down the high street together, buying whatever cuts of meat were cheap and whichever fruit and veg were on special.

When we were a family of five, Mam used to be very proud of the fact she'd 'never be one of them who has to put cardboard boxes in her freezer' to keep it full, but now it was just the two of us we didn't need the freezer at all. We bought whatever we could afford fresh every day, and then we got home and went straight into the kitchen together. Mam still used her little black book all the time and her flat rib broth, stews and oxtail soup were regular staples, because she could make them really tasty with cheap cuts of meat. She seemed to start all of her savoury dishes by finely chopping carrots, onion and celery to make a mirepoix, as I know it today, though Mam wouldn't have used 'fancy language' like that. We also made and ate all kinds of bread, sausage rolls, cakes and biscuits – everything was freshly made, and throughout my childhood Mam never ever bought a packet of biscuits or a cake from a shop.

In hindsight, however, after Dad was gone, me and Mam started comfort cooking, and comfort eating. Mam would shed a tear in front of me sometimes and talk about how she missed my dad, and for a long time she kept his glasses on the side, as well as a cedar wood box containing his cigars, which had been something he treasured. She would encourage me to talk about my feelings, and she told me not to be worried about sharing any-thing I wanted with her. She was lovely and warm like that, but I can't say I really took her up on it very often. I think I was more concerned about looking after her than being another problem she had to worry about, and so I just tried to be brave and say the right things. That feeling of responsibility I had immediately after Dad died stayed with me; I felt I needed to be strong for Mam, because it was obvious she was very sad and life was hard.

Despite being a naturally chatty, lively person, Mam was never one for going out much, even before she was widowed. She lived through her kids, and I elongated that process for her, coming along late in her life as I did. Mam became quite anti-social after she lost Dad, though, and all she seemed to do was get me to school, go out to work, come in and cook and then fret about

'Welcome to our youngest ever member!' the friendly lady in charge beamed. 'This is Simon, and he's going to lose a bit of weight before he goes to the big school!'

I looked up and saw a sea of smiling ladies, but I didn't feel as daunted as I'd expected. They all seemed really nice, and when we queued up to get weighed on the old-fashioned scales, which had a slide measure like at the doctor's, they all said encouraging things and told me how much weight they'd lost since joining the club.

'It'll fall off you, Simon!' the course leader said. 'Now then, what weight do you think you should be? Do you have a goal?'

Having never encountered a young boy in her class before, the leader had no idea what I should be aiming for. Mam and Ginny were sitting on the side and we all looked at each other, clueless. In the end, after a bit of educated guess-work, it was decided my target should be to lose two of my eleven stone, for starters.

Thankfully, the prediction that the weight would 'fall off' proved to be fairly accurate. I attended the classes for months and months, mind, every Wednesday after school, but sure enough, the numbers on the scale reduced steadily each week. Knowing I was going to be weighed in front of the lovely ladies, who all fussed over me, made me think about what I was putting in my mouth every day.

Mam encouraged me to eat fruit instead of cakes and biscuits and I'd fill my plate with vegetables rather than spuds or Mam's home-made chips, which was the biggest sacrifice of all, because her chips were the best. Mam stopped buying pop that the Barr 'pop man' delivered to all the houses on the street, and I avoided the mobile shop, which was run by Helen Lee's dad John and sold my favourite salt-and-vinegar Chipmunks crisps at two pence a packet. When she worked a half-day on a Wednesday, Mam would make me the most fantastic garlic sausage omelette with diced pepper ready for when I got in from school. She'd never really counted calories in her life, but Mam was a natural at knowing how to trim down the fat and carb content of food and make up for it with tasty flavours and lovely textures.

As I lost weight I found I was going at a brisker pace when I walked the two miles up and down to school through the estate every day, and that spurred me on. I felt fitter and healthier, and I didn't want to go back to feeling so lardy ever again. I started making a few friends once my weight went down too, which was another incentive to keep on track.

One of my new mates was a lad called Paul, and on hot summer days we'd go up to the beach at Bamburgh together with whoever we could cadge a lift from. Sometimes Ginny or Will took us and occasionally Mam would come, if she was off work, and she'd float on her lilo in the sea to cool off.

'Eee, I've made us a lovely picnic,' Mam would say.

'What have ya got, Mam?'

'Oh, just the usual!'

'Oooh, great!

Mam's 'usual' was not the sort of cheese-and-pickle sandwich and bag of crisps type picnic you might expect to have on the beach. No, Mam's picnics typically included a whole freshly roasted chicken, home-made sausage rolls and cakes straight from the oven, and I loved every morsel.

Paul and I would tuck in like there was no tomorrow, then we would muck about in the water and play war games in the long grass, pretending to be Japanese soldiers being shot by German snipers, and vying with each other to make the 'best fall' into the grass.

Thankfully, by the time I attended St Robert of Newminster,

a Catholic comprehensive in Washington, which was bleeding miles away on a bus, I'd managed to trim down considerably. I was never going to be slim, but at least I'd reached the point where you would have described me as a 'big lad' rather than a 'fatty'.

'Mr King, come here!' the Religious Education teacher, Mr Johnson, bellowed down the corridor one day. He was quite an imposing character, and I wondered what the hell I'd done wrong.

'You're playing rugby, for the school,' he told me, which was very unexpected, particularly from the RE teacher.

'Am I?' I said, amazed.

'Yes, you are. Don't back answer.'

I did as I was told, and I actually found that I loved the game. For the first time in my life my size was something positive, and I thoroughly enjoyed being in the team.

In the school summer holidays, when I was twelve years old, Ginny organised a two-week camping holiday to the south of France for me and Mam, plus herself and one of her friends. I'd never been abroad and it was dead exciting getting in Gin's little red Citroën 2CV and heading to a foreign country. Mam was excited too; though she loved her home comforts she was looking forward to the trip away, even if it did mean squashing in a small, hot car for several hundred miles, and then sharing a tent with me.

'Eee, Mam,' I said when we went into a cafe on the way to our campsite. 'Look at that man. What's he doin'?'

Mam explained that the Frenchman was drinking something called pastis with his cup of coffee, which was very common, and I watched in fascination as he poured water in and the clear liquid went a milky colour.

'That's so cool!' I said, making a mental note that I wanted to try this for myself.

I was also blown away the first time I went into a French supermarket, and I could cheerfully have spent the whole afternoon in there, looking at the amazing salamis and the well-stocked fish counter, and trying to work out what was in all the interesting little tins with pictures of unusual beans or fish on the sides that I'd never seen before.

It was a great holiday and I was sad to leave, but at least when we got back I had a couple of reminders of my time there. I'd bought a giant salami, and I'd also managed to smuggle back a bottle of pastis! When Dad was alive he encouraged me to try a very watered-down glass of wine with my food like the French kids, even when I was very young, so I figured I hadn't stepped out of line too much. Besides, I don't remember getting past the first glass: it tasted like lighter fuel to me.

Back at school, Mam was incredibly proud when I was put forward to train as an altar boy with the Guild of St Stephen Altar Servers. Having had a staunch Catholic upbringing herself, Mam had sent me to Sunday school at an early age, though I didn't like it much and didn't stick with it for long. She didn't mind; she didn't often go to church herself. 'I'm not dressing up on a Sunday,' she'd declare. She wasn't the sort of person who would go to church just to be seen, and to her mind her religious and spiritual beliefs were private, maintained perfectly well 'inside the four walls'. We had crucifixes on the walls of all the bedrooms and there were pots of holy water dotted around the house. Mam was never without her rosary beads either, but she never tried to push her beliefs on anybody, and she seldom even talked about them.

Interestingly, Dad had always said he was an atheist, though he converted to Catholicism before he died. I was too young to be involved in any discussions about how he came to that decision, but what I do know is that Mam's faith helped her a great deal after he was gone. She'd sit with her beads in quiet contemplation, and because of her beliefs she still felt spiritually connected to Dad. Thanks to Mam's influence I always carried rosary beads too, and I still do so to this day.

Anyway, I felt quite honoured to be asked to be an altar boy and I liked that it pleased Mam. I was thirteen when I started the training and I always liked being in church. It gave me a sense of place, and it was somewhere I felt safe. I enjoyed dressing up in the robes and serving at Easter and all the big festivals.

Mam would sometimes come and watch me serve Benediction, and I always tried to be on my best behaviour when she was there, which, to be fair, wasn't always how I was as a young teenager. Nicking Communion wine was one of the perks of the job, and I soon learned exactly when you could get away with taking a great big slurp of the sweet red stuff without getting caught.

One Sunday some of the other lads didn't turn up, so I ended up doing four masses in a row, as it was Easter-time. Every time I went into the vestry I had a glug of wine, and by the time Mam showed up for the last mass I was hammered.

'That's the last time you're doing four in a row, our Simon!' she said, escorting me from the church.

'Sorry, Mam,' I hiccuped.

She never said another word about it because Mam was very lenient like that, and she knew I wasn't actually a bad lad. Some of the other lads thought it was a great laugh to water down the wine when the priests weren't looking, but I would never have been that naughty. To me it was just too much hassle to do anything so dodgy; the last thing I ever wanted was to cause my mam any more grief than she already had.

I can only recall one time when I properly fell out with Mam, to be honest. It was around this time, when I was a young teenager, and for some reason I decided I was going on hunger strike. I refused to eat meals for what felt like about three days and I put a lock on my bedroom door, though I can't for the life of me remember why.

'Simon!' Mam yelled. 'Open the bloody door or I'm breaking it down!'

'No, Mam! Go away!'

'I'm telling ya, Simon, open the door.'

'No! Leave me alone.'

'Eee, ya've left me with no choice!'

The next thing I knew Mam had booted the bedroom door open, kicking it as hard as she could until the lock I'd lashed up flew off.

'Don't be so disrespectful,' she said when she'd composed herself. 'Eat it.'

With that she handed me a plate of home-made chips and an omelette, which of course I gratefully devoured before eventually apologising to Mam.

Occasionally, I went on religious retreats organised by my school to Ushaw College in Durham, which was a really lovely, peaceful place, set in rolling acres of land. The Jesuits who looked after us were a hoot, and I liked being there.

At one point I was asked if I would like to consider training for the priesthood, which I thought about very briefly and then swiftly dismissed. I think by that time I had discovered girls.

I got into rock music around this time too, which I knew didn't go hand in hand with a life in the priesthood either, so that was the end of that. I can remember saving up my one pound a week pocket money for two whole months to buy the Thin Lizzy *Live and Dangerous* double LP. I went to town one Saturday afternoon with a lad I knew from school called Anthony Howarth, handing my hard-saved eight pounds to the girl behind the counter at Pet Sounds. I was chuffed to pieces, but when Anthony and I got to the bus stop later I realised I didn't have a penny left to pay my bus fare home. Anthony had to lend me some cash to catch the 725 back to ours, which was a bit embarrassing, but at least I didn't have to wait another whole week to get my mitts on the LP. It was mind-blowingly brilliant, and I turned up the volume as loudly as Mam would allow, at every opportunity. I also started to dream of learning to play the drums as well as Brian Downey.

The next lot of pocket money I saved went on Thin Lizzy posters for my bedroom wall, and tins of emulsion and gloss so I could paint my blue canvas rucksack with an image of the album cover, which I traced and copied. What I really wanted, though, was a drum kit of my own. How the hell I was ever going to afford one was completely beyond me. As for lessons, I knew there was absolutely no chance. I'd have to teach myself if ever I got a drum kit.

I can remember our Ginny introducing me to one of her mates, Lesley, when I was about fourteen, and being blown away by her because she had the biggest record collection I'd ever seen in my life. On top of that Lesley wore tight leather pants and lived in a squat behind Newcastle City Hall, where Bronski Beat and UB40 had been known to hang out before they got really famous. 'You're awesome and I love you so much!' I thought to myself when I looked at Lesley, even though, like our Ginny, she must have been in her early thirties. When I was older, I wanted a record collection and an exciting lifestyle like Lesley's, and I desperately wanted a girlfriend who wore tight leather pants like Lesley too.

I think it's fair to say I had a lot of aspirations as a young teenager, but absolutely no means with which to achieve them.

If the school was organising a trip somewhere, or even if the other boys were planning to go to a match at St James's Park, I swerved the conversation. I loved football and was a big Newcastle United fan, as I still am today, but there was no point in even talking about going to the game because we simply didn't have the money to pay for anything beyond the rent, food and day-to-day essentials.

My old friend Helen Lee would come over and I'd cook her a curry sometimes, because that was something I could do that didn't cost any money, and I enjoyed doing it.

'What's that big red thing?' she said the first time, eyeing a fresh chilli.

'That? Oh, it's a, er, pepper.'

'Is it hot?'

'Nah,' I lied, chopping up the potent chilli and chucking the whole lot in the pan. 'It's nothing to worry about!'

When Helen tasted the curry it nearly blew her head off.

'I'm gonna kill you!' she shouted, calling for water.

'Drink this milk!' I said though tears of laughter. 'This'll help!'

Mam came in the kitchen as a red-faced, sweaty-browed Helen glugged the milk as if her life depended on it.

'That was a horrible thing to do, our Simon,' Mam tutted, giving me a disapproving look, but I was still too busy laughing to apologise just yet.

By now cooking had become a pleasant pastime, and for the time being it was one of the few hobbies I could afford to do. Getting a drum kit was my aim in life, but one that was still beyond my reach. I also longed for a motorbike. I couldn't fathom how

I would manage to buy either, but I knew I was going to have a damn good try as soon as I was old enough.

There was a lad called Alan Smith who lived a couple of doors down from us and had a bright yellow Suzuki TS250, and I'd watch him tear off down the road on it. 'How jammy is he?' I'd think, longing to have a go.

'Can you ride?' Alan asked me out of the blue one day, when he saw me admiring his bike.

'Yeh,' I lied, caught up in the thrill of the moment.

'Want a go?'

'Wey aye, man!'

Alan was a neighbour and, with me being a big lad, he clearly had no idea I was only fourteen years old. I wasn't going to enlighten him, and I got myself on the bike and rode it up the street and back again before he could change his mind. It was bloody terrifying and electrifying all at once. God knows how I managed to stay upright because I didn't have any clue what I was doing and the bike weighed a ton, but somehow I survived with my pride, and Alan's bike, intact.

'Thanks!' I beamed, giving Alan a grin as wide as the Tyne bridge. 'That was mint!'

I was totally bitten. Feeling the power of the engine and breathing in the smell of oil and fuel just blew my head off. Skint or not, I was going to get a motorbike of my own one day, but for the time being I had to make do with buses.

In the summer, when I was fifteen, I saved up a few quid to take myself off to the Lake District. I did this by doing odd jobs for Auntie Kath, who was a relative of Hilda's and married to Uncle Stan. I'd go to their house every Monday and do stuff like tidying the garden or fixing the guttering. I'm sure Auntie Kath found me plenty of jobs she didn't really need doing because, like my mam, she was a canny woman with a big heart and a great sense of community. My dad's ethos of helping others if you've got enough for yourself was certainly shared by Auntie Kath too.

At this time we had a shaggy black hound called Pippy, who I called Pippda, and Mam said it would be alright if I took the dog away to the Lake District with me because she had to stay at home and work. I packed a tent and got two buses cross-country for several hours to Stonethwaite in Borrowdale, where I pitched up in a farmer's field. It probably sounds a bit lonely, but I was used to feeling pretty isolated at home, and I was very independent by this age. It was nice to get away, and at least have a change of scene.

The first day was fantastic. I walked Pippda up the valley to Black Moss Pot, which is a dramatic little gorge with a waterfall. It started to rain on the way back to the tent, though, and it didn't stop. I'd heard people say that the Lake District was the wettest place in Britain, and now I was finding out why. It rained non-stop, and then to put the top hat on it I got a belly bug after swimming in the water at the gorge. It was absolutely terrible. I was doubled up in agony, and I couldn't leave the campsite for the next two weeks. I survived on the two packets of bourbon creams I had with me, and when the farmer came round to take my money I think he felt genuinely sorry for me.

'Can you not get yourself home, son?' he asked.

'I would if I could,' I said. 'But I'm from Newcastle, ya see. It took me three hours to get here on the buses, and I don't think I could make it back like this!'

I only left the tent to go to the toilet and fetch drinking water, and even that was a struggle because I was literally doubled over with stomach cramps. The only positive was that, thanks to the

'Borrowdale Belly Bug', I lost about half a stone without even trying.

I was the thinnest I'd been, so even if I couldn't get a motorbike just yet, maybe, just maybe, I started to think that I might be able to get myself a girlfriend like Lesley, or at least a younger version of Lesley. I was optimistic like that, and being a big lad certainly never stopped me having an ego.

7

Dave's

Vesta Curry, Fiery Poached Eggs and 30p Pub Grub

Ninety miles away from Newcastle, over on the opposite coast of England, I was also trying to figure out how I was going to achieve my dream of owning a motorbike. Just like Si, earning money was something I had to do if I wanted to have anything over and above the basics my dad could afford to provide for me.

When I was doing my O levels I applied for a job as a photographer on the local evening paper. Some of the boys in the year above me had left school, got jobs at the shipyard and, most importantly, were now driving round on motorbikes. It seems incredibly short-sighted when I look back now, but the reason I wanted to leave school at sixteen was so that I could earn money and get my first motorbike.

Mam and Dad didn't get involved in my decision-making. Dad was in his early seventies now, and looking more careworn than ever, and Mam continued to become increasingly infirm and detached from daily life. I didn't get the job and was gutted, but I kept my feelings to myself, figuring I'd just have to think again about what to do after my O levels.

We had a home-help now who came to help bath my mother, and Mam had an electric wheelchair. I had completely taken over the cooking at this point. For a few years I'd been making all the stuff Dad recognised from the days my mam did the cooking, like stews and hot pots, and ham, egg and chips, but now I became more adventurous. Dad wasn't very happy; he was the sort of man who thought garlic was the food of the devil and he often said as much, but I did manage to get him to try a few new things.

When I did the family shop I would pick up wonderful, exotic foods like dried Vesta curries – Si's mam would have laughed at that – and chow mein noodles that puffed up like magic when you put them in hot oil. I was also a dab hand at making my own beefburgers and savoury mince-pies. The pastry was always just right, but I suppose it should have been as I'd been perfecting the art of 'rubbing in' since I was seven years old.

The Galloping Gourmet was on telly, and I'd watch Graham Kerr make amazing recipes like Jamaican soup, Mexican red snapper, spicy kebabs and flamed rum babas. We couldn't afford all the fancy ingredients needed for some of the recipes, but I had a go at what I could, learning as I went. It didn't always go to plan. The first time I used garlic I put three whole heads in a recipe instead of three cloves because I didn't know the difference, but that was a minor blip compared to a couple of other mistakes.

Our cooker in the flat was cheap and nasty, and one time I was on my own in the kitchen, stark bollock-naked, when I decided to light the gas hob to make some poached eggs for breakfast. I was rushing around, and I whacked the gas up really high before igniting the flame. Suddenly, there was an almighty fiery whoosh and then a horrible burning smell. I couldn't believe it when I looked down and realised I'd set my pubes on fire. I'd only just grown them too, which I had been triumphant about because of my alopecia!

I never found another job that caught my eye, and with Mr Eaton's encouragement I started in sixth form after passing all my eleven O levels, opting to study Art, History, English and General Studies at A level. At the weekend me and my mates would drink beer in each others' houses, and in whichever pubs would let us get away with it.

I soon learned that after a drinking session all the lads invariably ended up looking for a late-night snack to soak up the beer.

'How about we start a little takeaway empire?' I suggested to a mate of mine, Pete Thompson.

Like me, Pete wasn't shy of seizing a business opportunity and the two of us started cooking whatever 'one-pan wonders' we could come up with in my mam and dad's kitchen, often with the help of Graham Twyford.

'If we charge 30p a portion, we'll clean up!' I said.

'What are we putting in it?' Pete asked.

'Let's have a look!'

We'd buy a few bits and I raided Mam and Dad's cupboards for extras, and the result was usually a cross between a paella, a biryani and pilau rice.

'Curry powder?' Pete would say.

'Oh aye, chuck it into the rice.'

'Can of tuna?'

'Oh, that'll do.'

'Sausages?'

'Why not? Chop 'em up and throw 'em in.'

After sinking a few pints in The Victoria on Church Street or The Farmers Arms in Baycliff I'd invite the lads back to ours.

Typically, there would be about ten of us, including one poor lad called Jamie who was vegetarian and never got fed!

All the others thought it was the bargain of the century to have a massive plate of our 'pub grub' for less than the price of a fritter from the chippy, and Pete and I always earned our next pint out of it. Incidentally, Pete went on to become a director of BT and a few years back we teamed up at a charity dinner and relived the 30p pub grub days, although this time I did a lush *Hairy Bikers* chilli recipe with dark chocolate, which was infinitely classier than the stuff we used to feed to our mates!

Another sideline of mine at school was to use my calligraphy pens to make fancy football posters which I sold for 30p each, and I'd also copy album covers to sell as posters. Mr Eaton encouraged me to keep visiting art galleries, which I did, and I'd go round to my mate Graham's and paint with him. He was in the year above, and when I finished the lower sixth, Graham went off to study art at university.

'You have the talent to follow in Graham's footsteps, David,' Mr Eaton told me. 'Have you thought about it? I think you'd be very good.'

Barrow Grammar School was a fantastic institution, giving working-class lads like me terrific opportunities we wouldn't otherwise have had, and about two thirds of boys went on to university. No other Myers had ever gone on to further education, though, and if it wasn't for Mr Eaton's support and guidance I probably would never have even considered it. He really did change my life.

'Do you think I'll get the grades?' I asked him anxiously, which provoked a broad, knowing smile.

'I have every faith in you, David. You're one of our brightest boys.'

A compliment like that was absolutely priceless to an insecure teenager like me.

My alopecia was still the bane of my life. When I dug out an old school photo recently, from my days at Barrow Grammar, it confirmed how difficult things were for me. This was not a minor issue for an adolescent. I went through what I called 'ugly phases' when the alopecia was particularly bad, and when the photo was taken I looked very odd, with thick brown hair on the right-hand side of my head and nothing but smooth skin on the left. Si gasped when he saw it for the first time a few months ago, even though I had told him all about it. 'Fooking hell, mate,' he said, looking shocked and actually very sad. 'You must have had one hell of a hard time.'

'I did, mate. I certainly did.'

Entrenching myself in the world of art really started to appeal to me, not only because I was interested in art and had a talent for it, but because of the like-minded friends I had made through Mr Eaton's art club. It was a world I believed I could be accepted in, which was a massive attraction for me. I applied for a foundation art course at Preston Polytechnic's art school, which was based in Lancaster, and I resolved to get the best grades possible in my A levels.

Six months before I was due to take them, I came home from school one afternoon to find my dad slumped in his chair and Mam screaming in her wheelchair. She'd wet herself and was in a terrible state, and my dad couldn't move properly and wasn't making much sense. He'd clearly had some sort of collapse and was in shock. I phoned the GP who told me to give Dad an aspirin and put him to bed, which I did, with difficulty, because one side of his body wasn't working properly. Then I cleaned Mam up, tried to get her to eat some cheese-and-pickle sandwiches for tea and put her to bed too.

'What the hell do I do now?' I thought, standing alone in the front room.

I didn't really know the answer, and in the end I just took myself to bed.

Fortunately, we had a lovely district nurse called June Jolly at that time, and she turned up early the next morning to bath my mother.

'There is no way you can cope on your own like this,' she said, as soon as she saw what was happening. Both my parents were still in bed. I couldn't manage to get either of them up, dressed and fed on my own, and so June swiftly arranged for a doctor to visit and assess the situation.

My dad was just about compos mentis after his night's sleep, but he looked very frail and poorly and it turned out he'd suffered a stroke, which explained the paralysis on one side of his body. The fags had finally done for him, as well as all the stress he had to deal with looking after Mam.

'Which one do you feel better able to cope with?' the doctor asked me.

'Come again?'

'You can't look after both your parents like this, David. We need to make alternative arrangements for one of them. Which one do you suggest?'

In a heartbeat, I knew it had to be Mam.

'Me dad'll get better, won't he?'

'He'll need to make adjustments, but as long as he doesn't have another stroke then, yes, his condition should improve.'

'Dad should stay here then. He'll get better, my mother won't.'

I felt a horrible churn of guilt in my guts as I said those words, but I knew it was the right decision. Mam needed full-time care, and I just couldn't give it to her, not with my exams looming and Dad the way he was.

'How long do you think we'll need her to be away for?' I asked anxiously.

'I can't answer that question,' the doctor replied. 'We'll have to see how things work out, for all of you.' It didn't sound good at all, and in my heart I knew that Mam might be away for a long time.

It was bloody awful when the doctor began to explain to Mam that arrangements were being made to move her out of the house. She cried and protested, but all I could think of saying was: 'Mam, it's for the best. It won't be forever.' I wasn't sure I believed the words myself.

Mam was eventually moved into Roose Hospital in Barrow. It had previously been a workhouse and mental institution, and my mother was convinced she'd been locked up in the poorhouse or confined to a 'loony bin'. Even though she was only just sixty, she was placed on a geriatric ward as there was nowhere else to put her. The only saving grace was that, despite being a very difficult patient to deal with, Mam was very well looked after by the nursing staff and I could visit whenever I wanted to, which I did as much as possible.

In the meantime, I did my best to look after Dad and the house, which wasn't easy. In the last three months before I took my A levels I didn't go to school because he still had restricted movement and just wouldn't have coped. When I went to sit my exams, in the summer of 1975, I refused to wear my uniform. I was eighteen years old and had been a carer for more than a decade. I certainly didn't feel like a school-kid any more.

I failed History and English but scraped an E in Art and a B in General Studies. Thankfully I'd been offered an unconditional place on my foundation course at Lancaster and they let me in. Moving away wasn't an option, though, as I needed to be around for Dad, and so I began a year of commuting to college every day. The round trip was two hours by train.

Dad muddled along and even got a bit better, but Mam got steadily worse. After a year on the geriatric ward she became prematurely geriatric herself, and she never left hospital from the day she was admitted. Forty years on, I still feel a tremendous amount of guilt about that.

8

Si's

Sticky Ribs, Tandoori Chicken and Sherry Trifle

I've just worked out that Dave's dad must have had his stroke within weeks of my dad dying, which is uncanny. We were both in the mire at the same time, just not together; not yet, anyhow.

I do consider myself to be very fortunate in comparison to Dave, though, because at least I had my mam by my side, and in fact strong females were my main role models throughout my childhood. Auntie Hilda, with her supply of bandages for the lads who came off their bikes, was a feisty, no-nonsense woman, as was Auntie Kath, whose generous and regular supply of odd jobs provided me with some much-needed pocket money.

In my last year of school Mam was still working in Purse Care on the high street, and the only real difference in our circumstances and routine was that instead of walking to meet her after school like I used to when I was younger, I'd sometimes pick her up in a little car that Gin had bought me for £50 from one of her mates. It was a VW Beetle 1303 S and I restored it so it was road-worthy. I was only sixteen and didn't have a driving licence, but Will had given me two lessons in his mustard yellow Austin

Princess before deciding he didn't have the stomach for being a driving instructor to his little brother any longer.

'Never mind, I'm alreet now!' I said optimistically as I bunny-hopped out of the car park we practised in.

After that I pretty well taught myself to drive on the streets of our estate. It stressed Mam out, but she turned a blind eye to the illegality of it; she was made up to get a lift, especially when it was cold and raining. We were a proper team by now, me and Mam. We'd help each other out as much as we possibly could, sharing out all the jobs that needed to be done. It was like being in a relay race. We'd pass the baton to each other, always picking up where the other left off.

I went through the motions of taking my O levels but nothing had changed since primary school, and education was lost on me. I still hated studying and didn't excel at anything, and on results day all I got was four O levels in English, Geography, Commerce and Ceramics – the latter thanks to a creative teacher called Mr Kelly, whom I quite liked. Mrs Hancock, my commerce teacher, was absolutely delighted with my result in her subject; I think I must have far exceeded her expectations!

Mam had never pushed me. Even though it was now seven or eight years since Dad died she was still grief-stricken, and really quite miserable a lot of the time. She always tried to give me the best life she could, but by now I understood that she had been on Mogadon for years, to help her sleep, and had been taking the antidepressant Prothiaden for a long time too. Kicking my backside through secondary school on top of everything else was too much to expect of Mam; feeding me and keeping the roof over our heads were much bigger priorities. That said, when Mam realised just how badly I'd done in my O levels she was adamant I had to stay on in the sixth form for a year, and retake my exams.

'But Mam,' I moaned, 'I've just spent five years trying to get out of the place. Why would I want to go back?'

'Ya should have thought about that before,' she told me. 'You're gonna have to, Simon. What are ya gonna do with four O levels? And one of them's in bloody pottery!'

I had no answer to that and I didn't have a clue what I wanted to do with my life.

A bloke called Fred had just moved in next door with his wife Linda and in the summer holidays he took me on as a labourer for his construction firm, which had the contract to flag Gateshead High Street. I was still sixteen and my job was to lift these massive one and a half metre wide flagstones off a flatbed truck and carry them to the fella who was laying them. The more flags we laid, the more we were paid, but it was such hard work I hardly earned anything, and I hated every second of it. After a week or so of that I decided Mam was probably right. I'd better go into the lower sixth and try to pass a few more exams.

I hadn't really learned any lessons, though, and to be honest once I started in sixth form all I actually wanted to do was meet girls, play drums and listen to Led Zeppelin, Thin Lizzy and AC/DC.

My brother Will, who at this time was working in Saudi Arabia as an engineer, knew how desperately I wanted to play the drums, and he surprised me by buying me my first drum kit. It was an acoustic drum kit and the best present ever. It completely knocked my socks off, and nearly blew the roof off our house too. As our walls were paper-thin you could not only hear me all over the house, but halfway up the street.

There was a knock on the door one day and it was Alan Smith's dad from three doors down.

'Er, hello!' Mam smiled, mentally preparing an apology for the noise blasting from our house.

'Hello, Stella!' Mr Smith replied. 'I just wanted to say that your Si's sounding smashing on them drums. He's doing canny! Tell him well done from me!'

I'd practise at every opportunity, very loudly, very often for five hours on end. Led Zep's drummer, John Bonham, was my absolute hero; I wanted to *be* him.

At the same time I grew my hair and started wearing a bandana and ripped jeans. I figured girls might fancy me if I looked like a bit of rough. To my utter delight, the hippie image actually did seem to work wonders with the girls. At first relationships didn't interest me at all; but things changed when a girl called Karen Marshall came on the scene. She was what I would call a 'flippy floppy hippie chick' and I fancied the pants off her. Karen became my first proper girlfriend, and we dated for two years on and off.

I was having a bloody good time and my confidence improved no end. I was still big, but I got away with it now, because it kind of went with the image.

For my eighteenth birthday Mam decided to throw a party at the house for close family and friends. I'd taught myself to play the drums quite well by now and had started doing some gigs with various different friends who had bands. I loved the craic, and earning a bit of money from it was very useful indeed. I arrived home for my birthday party after being at a gig at Buffs in Birtley, where I'd started to do Saturday nights with a band called Pandora's Box. I was feeling pretty knackered and absolutely ravenous. The miners' strike was on, and that night I'd heard some blokes from another band talking about the number of musicians who were suddenly on the market, looking for gigs and session work.

'Thanks to Maggie Thatcher we've gone from a three-piece to a twelve-piece, complete with a friggin' brass section!' one of them said. The economy in the North East was shot to pieces, and people were literally going hungry and crying out for work.

I was thinking about that conversation when I walked through the front door of our house, but you'd never have guessed how bad the economic climate was if you'd seen the spread Mam had laid on that night. She had made all of my favourite things, and the table was groaning under the weight of a mad, spectacular mix of food. There were curries and tandoori chicken, sticky ribs, pork pies, pastries, an iced birthday cake and one of Mam's best-ever home-made sherry trifles, which was my favourite. I felt a surge of gratitude for Mam when I saw the spread, and it was amazing to see the front room filled with friends and family, all smiling at me and enjoying themselves.

Mam really showed what she was made of that day. She was an absolute trouper, and she pulled out all the stops to make sure I had an eighteenth birthday to remember, and one she could be rightly proud of. I really appreciated the trouble she'd gone to, and I savoured every single mouthful of the food. It was made with love, and it was epic.

With the cash I earned from gigging and helping Auntie Kath, plus some birthday money, I eventually managed to save up enough to buy my first motorbike, a customised Yamaha XS 650 Twin that was brush-painted black. I say 'motorbike', but really it was just a knackered old scrapper that needed all kinds of work before I could ride it. Nonetheless, I was over the moon when I got it going and sped off round the neighbourhood, or up to Hill End with my mates Stevie and Martin Proctor and David Howe, aka Howie. The sense of freedom and achievement was bloody brilliant.

Dave

Left: Me mam and dad on holiday in Switzerland, 1956. Big trip, big beer and, 9 months later, big baby. Me mam said it was the Swiss air that did it.

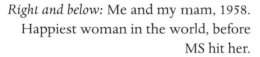

Right and below: Me and my mam, 1958. Happiest woman in the world, before MS hit her.

Right: Dad and me in the backyard. He was 55 when I was born in 1957 and was an epic dad. Never too old to change a nappy.

Left: On my very first motorbike, Dad's BSA Bantam. He used to put me on the tank and let me ride it holding the throttle. Bonkers. He was great.

Right: Me, aged 2, in home-made silver trunks. Similar clothes were worn on *Strictly*, some 50 years later.

Left: On holiday with me dad on Walney Island in 1962. Both beautifully co-ordinated in blue. That was his best suit – even to go to the beach. Best suit, tie and Old Spice. Pure class.

Dave

Left: Me and my mam in 1963. Men in space and The Beatles were born – life couldn't get any better.

Above: Christmas tea at the Myers' in 1963. Happy days. Best china and me dad in his bow tie and bobbly jumper. He was lovely, me dad.

Dave

Left: 1972 was not a good year for me. I lost my hair, eyebrows and eyelashes. Pubes and pits always remained intact, in case you're wondering!

Below: My 1980s Harley Davidson FXRD. This was the bike that had to be sold when I moved North to Scotland.

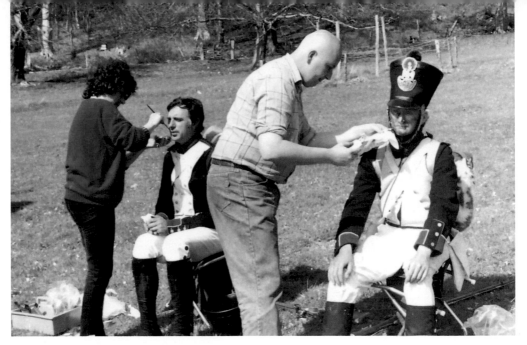

Above: Me with make-up designer Marion Richards on the BBC series *Soldiers* in 1985, making-up the Battle of Waterloo wounded. Big belly and big, bald head.

Left: Due to alopecia, I was asked to stand in as a Mohican in a film in 1985. They didn't say that a stunt man was going to jump out of a tree and cut my throat. I wore no sunblock, so at the end of the day I had a big white stripe on my head and looked like a skunk. I did all that for a crate of beer.

Right: Creating a pig prosthetic for the *Sam Pig* pilot in 1986. Even the ears could wiggle with radio controls. That's the pig's, not mine!

Left: Lil and I go courting in the early days. I look like the cat that's got the cream.

Right: My wedding day in 2011. Kingie was one of the best men. Lil realised that in one way she married both of us.

Left: First day of training for *Strictly* in 2013. Karen was a great mate from the start and I owe her for one of the happiest experiences of my life.

Right: Costume fitting for *Strictly*. I glimpsed the future.

Below: The Halloween special on *Strictly*. I was meant to be Beetlejuice but ended up just looking like a panda with homicidal tendencies.

Right: Heading down the corridors at Elstree 2 for *Strictly*, to perform my American Smooth. Made-to-measure suit, made-to-measure tan. Never been fitter or thinner.

Left: On Week 6 of *Strictly* we did the salsa to 'Cuban Pete'. Craig said, 'Dave, you have to keep time with the band.' I replied, 'It's not my fault they can't keep up!' *(BBC Photo)*

Right: Having embraced *Strictly*, I took on another new adventure, a Christmas panto in 2014 as Baron Hardup. Oh yes I did!

I didn't keep the scrapper for long because, as much as I loved it, I realised I could make a few quid by doing it up and selling it on, and we needed the money. My mates knew how skint me and Mam were and chipped in with parts for the bike. Mam was washing clothes in the sink at the time as she couldn't afford to have her twin tub repaired, so it wasn't a hard decision, and I was very grateful to my mates for helping me repair and re-spray the scrapper for next to nothing. Doing up bikes became another little money-spinner for me from then on, and I was always buying old wrecks, tinkering with them in Mam's garage and flogging them on for a bit more than I paid for them.

After lower sixth, armed with a few more O levels despite my worst efforts, I went to Gateshead Tech and studied for three A levels in Communication Studies, Politics and Economics. It was 1984, the year Band Aid recorded 'Do They Know It's Christmas?', but I was more preoccupied with what was going on in Britain than in Africa. I'd grown up seeing the North East economy decimated through the Thatcher years. She was the daughter of a shopkeeper and in my opinion she'd sold industries like British steel and North Sea gas and oil down the river. Now I was witnessing first-hand how the miners' strike was grinding down families and eroding away the communities I'd grown up in.

I attended lots of demonstrations and got myself beaten up a few times. Mam worried about me and hated it when I came home battered and bruised, but she supported me nevertheless.

'Ah well, never mind, son,' she said, dabbing my swollen cheek-bones with cream from her First Aid tin. 'I'm reet proud of ya and your dad would have been proud too, but I wish you'd be more careful.'

Mam was always very interested in politics and the state of the country in general. Like my dad, she had a very strong sense of right and wrong and of fighting for the rights of the community.

'There's a greater community spirit in people who have nowt,' she said to me more than once, and never have truer words been spoken. I've seen it on my travels with Dave many times, and I always think of Mam.

Through Gateshead Tech I heard about a project called Media Action, which ran a Community Programme course that involved putting together radio adverts to give advice to local people hit by unemployment. It sounded right up my street and, very fortuitously, Ginny's partner at the time worked for Media Action, and helped get me on the programme.

I was paid £43 a week to write scripts for the adverts, and after I finished college I was invited to stay on. I'd failed my Politics and Economics A levels miserably, but passed Communications Studies, which I think was indicative of the direction my life was taking.

Before long I started volunteering at Newcastle Arts Centre, which was a not-for-profit organisation based at Bells Court Studios near Pilgrim Street, a run-down part of the inner city. The studios hosted all kinds of funded art projects, many aimed at disadvantaged kids, and I started to volunteer whenever I could, alongside my radio script work.

I loved it from day one. The projects brought in youngsters who didn't have a bean, from the arse ends of West and East Newcastle, and we did things like creating musical instruments and making pop promos with them. The joke of it was I barely had a bean myself, although I did manage to get some paid work there eventually, as a session drummer in one of the other studios.

A fax came into Media Action one day that really caught my

eye. It was from the Mariners' Club and it explained that they were looking for crew for several ships that were taking part in the famous Tall Ships Race, which Tyneside was hosting in 1986.

It seemed like the opportunity of a lifetime as it involved working on one of the ships for several months, travelling around the coasts of Germany and the North East and docking at various ports. I needed to raise £325 for my keep, though, and when my brother Will heard what I was trying to do he got MTM Chemical Engineering, the company he worked for, to sponsor me for the full whack, for which I was incredibly grateful.

It was dead exciting. I was put on the *Irene*, a stunning ship owned by Dr Leslie Morrish, an eminent psychiatrist who had spent fifteen years restoring her. I was absolutely buzzing when we set sail for Heligoland, a small German archipelago in the North Sea. I was totally out of my comfort zone, but that added to the excitement. I met people from all walks of life, I didn't know what tomorrow held and I was learning new skills on the ship every day, performing all kinds of different duties on board. What was not to like?.

One day we docked in Bremerhaven and I took myself off to a 'waschsalon' because my clothes were minging. I didn't take a spare outfit off the ship with me, though, and so I stripped off and sat in the launderette in my boxers while I waited for the washer and dryer to finish, just like the guy in the jeans advert I'd seen on telly. However, unlike the model with the six-pack, I was a pasty, flabby Geordie with a trucker's tan, but I didn't give a monkey's what anybody thought. I look back on stuff like that now and realise it was actually all good practice for some of the improvising and silliness Dave and I have got up to as the *Hairy Bikers*.

Back home, I discovered I'd been 'let go' from the remainder of my Community Programme with Media Action, having gone AWOL to join the Tall Ships. I was a bit disappointed, but my experience on the *Irene* had given me the confidence to be more ambitious.

There was a television production course at the North East Media Training College (NEMTC) that I fancied getting onto, which my sister's partner was also involved in, and so I went in to ask about it one day.

'There's no spaces on the course, but we could do with somebody to drive a minibus for us,' I was told.

'Brilliant, I'll do it,' I replied, never having driven a minibus before and not knowing anything more about the job.

It turned out I needed to ferry around the cast and crew for a very politically correct, left-wing film. This proved to be simple enough, as long as I minded my Ps and Qs, and so for a while I scraped by with the driving job, as well as gigging again.

I joined a well-established band called Cyan around this time, as I was really good mates with one of the guitarists, Simon Harrison, who I'd gone to school with. The band did everything from Led Zep and Thin Lizzy to Guns N' Roses, Bon Jovi and Van Halen, which was all the music I'd played for years and absolutely loved.

The others guys, brothers Kev and Joe McNesty and Simon Holden, the lead singer, were all good lads to work with and it was lush when we went on the road. One night, however, we were booked to play in a pub in Hetton-le-Hole, but when we arrived the floor was covered in vomit and there were fights kicking off all over the place. It felt like a tinderbox about to ignite. We all looked at each other with trepidation, knowing we should get the hell out of there, but not wanting to lose the gig. Someone threw a punch as we were tentatively setting up, still contemplating whether to stay, and there was literally blood splattered all over Simon's keyboard.

'Sod it, let's just play,' one of us said, and we launched into 'Sweet Child o' Mine' by Guns N' Roses. The place started absolutely rocking, and it turned out to be one of the most fantastic gigs we'd ever done. I loved being in the band and I'd have played for free if I didn't have to take every penny going, because it was such a good vibe whenever we got together.

Another night, when we were on a night off, we went to the City Tavern pub in Newcastle.

'Oooh, he-llo!' I said to Simon Harrison, though I wasn't looking at him. The focus of my attention was a tall, elegant blonde I'd spotted across the bar.

'Who's *that*?' I said.

'Oh God,' Simon replied, rolling his eyes. 'You're off again are you, Kingie?'

I'd developed a bit of a reputation for chasing girls, and Simon knew this girl well and was a bit wary. He told me her name was Jane Dodd, and that she lived in the same part of town as him, which was the posh end.

'She's got a boyfriend,' he cautioned, because he's a gentleman like that, but I didn't give up, and I got him to introduce us nonetheless.

It turned out Jane was in the last year of a degree at Liverpool Poly, though she definitely looked like more of a rock chick than a student. Her style was very individual, which I liked, and not only did she have a stunning face and figure, she was lovely to talk to. She told me she was studying Home Economics, and I told her I was the drummer in Cyan, hoping she'd be impressed by this, but she wasn't! My blond hair was longer than hers, plus I had a trimmed beard and was wearing a red bomber jacket, skin-tight pants and white trainer boots. When I eventually left the pub I said: 'I'd better get back for me Mam', which Jane thought was really sweet, though I didn't find that out until later.

Not long afterwards the band got a massive gig at a concert celebrating the anniversary of the Blaydon Races. It was the gig of our lives, playing to a crowd of 1,100 in a 'battle of the bands'. All the lads brought their mates along to watch, and it made my night when I saw that Jane had turned up. Better still, I found out she was no longer with her boyfriend, and so I asked her if she wanted to stay for a drink after the gig.

'I can't,' she said. 'I'm going straight off to stay at my mum and dad's caravan in the Lakes. Most of the boys in the band are coming over for the weekend, actually. Would you like to come?'

I didn't need asking twice, and the next day I set off to Keswick in an old red Renault 4 called Mo, which was short for 'Mercurial Muriel'. Kev, the guitarist, hitched a lift with me, and because Mo had no stereo Kev strummed tunes all the way to the Derwent Water Caravan Park. We were really chilled when we arrived and the atmosphere at the caravan was great.

Jane was flitting around looking stunning and I really enjoyed being there, having a great craic with everyone. At one point I decided to have a dip in the water, and Jane said: 'I'll come with you.' We walked and talked, and then I gave her a kiss. I'd never felt anything like it before, and when Jane looked at me with her big, doe eyes, I was captivated. That was it, completely; I just knew she was the one for me.

Jane was staying in a room on her own and I was sharing with Simon Harrison, who was feeling very protective of his old friend, having been the one who introduced us and all.

'If you move, Kingie, I'll effing kill you,' he told me.

I promised him I'd behave myself, but it wasn't long before Jane and I did get together. We fell in love very quickly, and we absolutely adored each other and felt destined to be together. I was twenty-two years old – the same age as Jane – and I couldn't believe my luck.

9

Dave's

Drop Scones, Thirteen Latkas with Salt Beef and Steamed Christmas Puddings

'Look, Dad, I don't have to go to university, you know. I could get a job at the shipyard.'

'What would you want to do that for?' my dad baulked. 'You get a job in the shipyard and I'll break both your bloody legs!'

Dad wanted me to do well in life and was very keen that his and Mam's circumstances didn't hold me back, so when I finished my foundation course at Lancaster and was offered a place on the Fine Art degree course at Goldsmiths he was genuinely pleased for me.

He was coping well at home in the circumstances, and managing to make regular visits to Mam in hospital. For my part I had a full grant and a student railcard at my disposal, which was more than I'd ever had before, so I figured that even if I was living in London I would be able to come home and keep an eye on Dad whenever I wanted.

I'd only been to London once before my move, and that was

for my interview at Goldsmiths several months earlier. I absolutely loved the buzz of the city, right from the start. Smoking a pipe and wearing green cords, a pink denim jacket, red Kickers and a Rupert Bear scarf, I was stopped by the police before I even got out of Euston station. They searched my tin of St Bruno tobacco and, when it really was what it said on the tin, eyed me suspiciously as they let me go on my way. This didn't faze me one bit. It was all part of life's fantastic adventure; an endorsement, in fact, for an aspiring Pre-Raphaelite artist like me.

My old school pal Graham Twyford was already at Goldsmiths, doing the same course a year ahead of me, and when I embarked on my course in the autumn of 1977 we started sharing a flat together on Asylum Road, Peckham. I think it's fair to say that at this early stage I was more taken with the art of being a student than with the art on my degree course.

Graham and I began brewing our own beer at the flat and one night, after a particularly heavy session, Graham crashed out on the sofa. He had the hairiest legs I'd ever seen, and in my drunken haze I decided it would be a great idea to shave circles around his legs, so it looked like he was wearing rugby socks.

'I'm glad I'm not living at home,' he said the next day, when he eventually saw the funny side. 'Can you imagine what my dad would say?'

Graham's father was a police inspector with a reputation for drumming caution into the heads of 'young people'. 'Graham and David,' he'd told us once, 'I've just seen ten O levels, three A levels and a university degree splattered on a fence!' It was mainly motorbikes he was worried about, to be honest, and Graham was forbidden from riding one, but we laughed about how he would not have been impressed by our childish home brew escapades either.

The next day there was a loud knock on the door and Graham rushed to answer it in his dressing gown. A police officer was standing on the step, and his gaze fell immediately on Graham's strangely shaved legs.

'I can explain, officer . . .' Graham began, going into automatic mode, thinking he was about to be told off by a copper, maybe even one sent by his dad to check up on him . . .

'Are you David Myers?' the police officer asked.

'No, he's not in, I'm afraid,' Graham replied warily.

'Well, can you give him a message? His dad's not well. He's in hospital.'

I was on a train from Euston to Barrow-in-Furness as soon as Graham got hold of me. Dad had suffered another stroke. It was more than two years since the last one, and for the whole length of the four-hour journey home I told myself that it would be another setback for him, but one he could cope with. Mam had been ill for so many years, I just expected them both to go on and on.

'What the hell are you doing here?' Dad said when I arrived at the hospital, which confirmed he was still his doughty old self.

'Well, you've had a stroke, Dad. I wanted to see you.'

'What for? I'm being perfectly well looked after in 'ere.'

Five days later, on 20 January 1978, Dad was dead. He had developed pneumonia in hospital but, strange as it may sound, even then I had no indication he was going to die, and nobody warned me. Dad was stoical to the end, and one of the last things he said to me was: 'Can you tell your mother what's going on? She'll be wondering why I've not visited.'

I did as he asked, but the very next day I had to return and tell her Dad was dead.

'You know I told you Dad was in hospital, Mam?' I said as gently as I could.

Mam was sitting in a chair on the geriatric ward, surrounded by translucent-skinned old ladies and the smell of cleaning fluid. She looked eighty though she was only sixty-three, and she said nothing and just stared straight at me.

'I'm sorry, but it's not good. I'm afraid Dad was very poorly, and, the thing is, Mam, Dad has died, in hospital.'

I will never forget her reaction. Mam let out a piercing scream that sounded like something out of a horror film. It wasn't always easy to work out what she understood and what she didn't, because she was always so drugged up and rarely spoke, or at least not coherently, but she certainly understood this.

'I'll sort everything out,' I heard myself saying, though I didn't know how. 'Don't go getting too upset, Mam.'

Looking back my words seem so inadequate and I was quite unemotional, but I think that is how I'd come to deal with Mam's situation. It was upsetting being with her even on a good day, and I coped by playing everything with a straight bat and focusing on practicalities rather than feelings.

The funeral arrangements fell to me and my dad's brother, Uncle Turner. Graham and my other good friend John Carling both travelled up to Barrow to support me, and John came with me and Uncle Turner to the funeral parlour.

'Have you ever been in a chapel of rest?' John whispered as we stepped inside.

'No, mate,' I said. 'I'm not sure what to expect . . .'

The local undertaker was a suitably macabre-looking woman called Mrs Sawrey who didn't waste any time with pleasantries. I'd imagined she'd sit us down to discuss the arrangements or ask me if I wanted her to explain anything before I was taken through to see my father's body, but there was none of that. Seconds after arriving at the funeral parlour, a grim-faced Mrs Sawrey was marching me officiously through a dark doorway to the chapel of rest.

'Come on, son, follow me,' she said matter-of-factly.

I'd never seen a dead body before and I could have done with Mrs Sawrey giving me a few minutes to gather myself together, but instead she led me straight over to the coffin, where my father was laid out with a handkerchief over his face.

'Here's your dad, son,' Mrs Sawrey announced, whipping the handkerchief away with a swift and efficient hand movement, one she had clearly performed many times before.

'Oh,' I gasped.

It was horribly, horribly upsetting and I just stared at Dad's lifeless features in total shock, not knowing what to do or say.

'Thank you, Mrs Sawrey,' I stuttered.

'You're welcome, son,' she said flatly.

I couldn't believe my dad was dead. This was the man who scaled barbed-wire fences to pick mushrooms and braved the Irish Sea in a pair of trunks to teach me to swim. To this day I can still see him clearly, lying there in that chapel of rest, and it's an image I'd rather not have of him.

'Shall I cover him back up?' Mrs Sawrey asked.

'Yes, please,' I said, wanting to get out of there as quickly as possible.

Once we were back in the main funeral parlour with Uncle Turner and John, Mrs Sawrey suddenly changed gear.

'Now then,' she grinned, 'I baked some drop scones especially for you this morning!'

I thought I'd misheard her at first because her words were so unexpected, and I looked at Uncle Turner and John aghast. They were both looking back at me with alarmed expressions on their faces.

'Drop scones?' I stuttered. 'Did you say drop scones, baked especially?'

'Yes, don't look so worried, they're lovely and fresh. They won't kill you, and if they do, you're in bloody good hands!'

Absurdly, we all smiled politely and sat down and ate the drop scones, in incredibly British style. It's a scene I found hilarious eventually, and in time John and I laughed our heads off about it, but on the day itself it was just weirdly unsettling.

I can barely remember Dad's funeral. I know I took out a student overdraft with NatWest to pay for it, and I also bought myself a three-piece suit in Burton and had my hair cut short. In my efforts to look Pre-Raphaelite I'd grown my hair as long as I could, or at least it looked long. There were bald patches underneath that I tried to cover up by combing the long strands over them, which meant I probably had the world's worst comb-over at the tender age of twenty. It looked a bloody mess, and so for Dad's sake I attempted to spruce myself up with a short-back-and-sides, though I'm not sure which look was better.

Mam wasn't well enough to go to the funeral of course, and she spent the day in hospital, just like every other day. I was grateful for my good mates Graham and John, who were there for me on the day; I had a great infrastructure of mates like that.

After the funeral I remember standing alone in the family flat and thinking: 'What now?' There was no way Mam was ever going to live there again, but I didn't want to let it go, not just yet. I couldn't have faced telling my poor mother she no longer had a home on top of everything else, and so I left everything as it was, took over paying the £3.50-a-week rent to the council and headed back to London.

Before I left, I found £500 in the bottom of Dad's wardrobe, which I assumed was to cover the funeral costs. I could have paid off the student overdraft with it, but do you think that's what I did? Did I 'eck as like!

Back in London, I went to a second-hand wheeler-dealer in Peckham and bought my very first motorbike for £350. It was a blue Cossack Ural Mars MK 3, which was a Russian wartime motorbike with a sidecar, built to the same pattern as the German Second World War ones that had a machine gun on the side. Mine had a gold imperial eagle on the tank, which I reckoned added to its street cred, and a powerful 650cc engine, but I could still ride it on a provisional licence because of the sidecar.

I moved from Asylum Road to Monsoon Road, just off the Old Kent Road, for the rest of my first year at Goldsmiths. The most memorable thing about Monsoon Road was that it was where I properly lost my cherry, to a girl I'll call Marie, though her name has been changed to protect the innocent! I met Marie at a riverboat party on the Thames. I'd had a bit of a fumble with a girl I met when I was in sixth form, but nothing as exciting as this. Marie and I ended up on a pile of cushions on the lounge floor of Monsoon Road and, after the terrible year I'd had, I finally felt that things were, well, picking up.

Marie was quite a quirky character who was half Sri Lankan, very middle class and wanted to be an opera singer. I fell head over heels in love with her although, looking back, I was trying hard to fit in to what I perceived to be 'normal' society. Marie and I both wanted to be all grown up and so we'd have dinner parties and cook for each other. When I'd lived with Graham we were the archetypal 'spag bol' boys, but he had a mate who played the tuba and cooked really good *moules marinières*. I was always jealous and aspired to be more like him.

Being with Marie spurred me on to be more experimental and adventurous with cooking. By now I'd already discovered my first southern Indian food at the Sree Krishna restaurant in Tooting, and that had been a revelation and an inspiration to me too. I loved it so much I even took to lining the top box of my motorbike with polystyrene so I could take curries and dosas home sometimes. There was also a really good kosher restaurant called Blooms in Whitechapel, which was a grand old place that fascinated me. I'd been going there for a while, and often went in on my own before I met Marie. The waiter had a handlebar moustache and I always tipped him ten per cent, but when he found out I was a student he told me to sit by the kitchen in future, so he could slip me free food. I did, and on my next visit I gorged myself on thirteen latkas with salf beef.

Anyhow, partly thanks to Marie and partly because of my sheer gluttony and love of food, I was really starting to enjoy myself in the kitchen. Being Sri Lankan, Marie's mam had all the spices and made proper authentic biryanis, and we tried making loads of Indian and Asian foods. I wasn't afraid to give anything a go and was forever clipping recipes out of magazines and sticking them in scrapbooks.

One time Marie and I tried to make Christmas puddings, but that didn't go to plan at all. We left them steaming away on the hob in the kitchen while we were engrossed in *Quatermass and the Pit* on telly and sitting on cushions in the lounge – not the same cushions I lost my cherry on, I hasten to add! All of a sudden we heard a horrible rushing sound.

'What's that?' Marie asked, looking around in confusion.

'I don't know,' I said. 'What the hell?'

I suddenly looked up and saw that the lounge ceiling had started falling in because of all the steam filling the flat.

'Get out!' I shouted.

'Why? What are you doing, Dave . . .?' Marie said as I grabbed her, just about managing to throw her out of the door before she was hit by falling chipboard and bits of plaster.

In the summer Marie worked at Patisserie Valerie in Marylebone and I'd lined up some work at the steelworks in Barrow, cleaning out the furnaces during the annual shutdown. The foreman was my uncle Harry, who was married to one of my mam's sisters, Auntie Marion, and the pay was one pound an hour and double-time on Sundays, which I thought wouldn't half supplement my student grant.

I didn't have a clue what I was letting myself in for. On the first day I turned up in a pair of Doc Martens which Uncle Harry chortled at along with my new colleague Big Brian. I didn't understand why. The furnaces were forty feet across and lined with two-metre wide bricks that had to be stripped out by hand, and the work was filthy dirty. It was also very hot in the chimneys, and when I stepped inside in my DMs I realised what had made Uncle Harry chuckle. The soles of my boots started to melt off my feet, and someone had to fetch me a pair of wooden clogs to put on. Honest to God, I looked like something out of a Hovis advert, but once I got going again I absolutely loved the job; I'd never been so dirty and so happy in my life. The blokes I worked with were really lovely people, and there was a great sense of satisfaction and camaraderie when we went to the pub at lunchtime to rehydrate. I'd sink a couple of pints of bitter and eat a great big French stick with cheddar cheese and raw onions, and after work we'd have another couple of pints in the working-men's club. There was always a lot of beer involved, but after each honest day's work I felt so fit and alive. It was bloody great.

In the evenings I visited Mam. I'd sit by her bed or her wheel-chair, telling her what I'd been up to.

'I'm not sure what they'll say back at university, when they see the state of my hands!' I'd say, showing her my black-rimmed fin-gernails and trying my best to get the conversation going. 'Fine art and furnaces don't really mix, do they, Mam?'

Mam was never very responsive; her depression made her either very quiet or provoked an outburst of anger. She'd dete-riorated more since Dad died, but I suppose it was only to be expected.

I'd ring Marie most nights at her flat in Streatham, feeding ten pence pieces frantically into a phone box each time the pips threatened to cut us off. I was going to say I missed Marie, but that's only half true. I think it's probably more accurate to say I was lonely.

Marie and I ultimately didn't last the course, although we did stay together for a fair while longer. I moved into her flat, but things were never exactly brilliant between us. Marie was a very civilised sort of person who liked classical music as well as opera, while I had discovered punk rock at uni and was going to see bands that had names like Headbanger and the Nosebleeds or Buster Hymen and the Penetrators.

For most of the time I spent living with Marie I was engrossed in creating my final degree show, which took the best part of a year to put together. None of the professors or lecturers were very keen on my fine art paintings and so I'd elected to do most of my degree by writing about art history, and for my final show I also steered clear of painting. Instead, I designed a fifteen-foot-wide merry-go-round and filled it with gnomes, blue fibreglass Martians, vampy ladies and little blue gully men. Some of the figures were five foot tall, and I added timers and light bulbs that made the set whirl and flash chaotically when you touched a button that said 'please press'.

'Are the figures facets of your personality?' the examining tutor asked.

'Yes,' I said, hoping that was the answer he was looking for. 'The vampy ladies represent my feminine side and the little blue gully men, well, they show my experimental side . . .'

I was awarded a 2:2 and stayed on to do a post-graduate diploma in Art History, as I really didn't know what else to do with myself. I chose to write my thesis on the Northern Renaissance and, thanks to a benevolent Cumbrian education official called Mr Tiddy, I received a grant that got me a ticket to the wonderful research room at the British Library. I'd always try to sit at Karl Marx's desk to do my research, reading blue leather-bound books on folk like Erasmus, handed out by gentlemen in top hats.

I remember it very fondly as one of the happiest years of my life, though looking back at the dates, it was during the first term of my post-grad that Marie and I went our separate ways. She left me on 8 December 1980, and I remember the exact date because it was the day John Lennon died. I was absolutely gutted . . . and I was quite upset about being dumped an' all!

I presented myself at the university accommodation office with my belongings in holdalls and a fibreglass gully man under my arm, and when the staff had finished laughing at me they sent me to live with a lovely couple called Jeremy and Pat Harvey, who had a room to rent in their very arty household at Glenton Road, Blackheath. Fortuitously, their other lodger was a beautiful French au pair called Patricia Murrish, who I called 'French Pat'. I think she thought I was a right tosser.

In the New Year I got myself a job sitting in a night security box at an NCP car park, and one evening I started reading an old

Guardian newspaper that the fella on the previous shift had left behind. With just a few months to go on my course, I was starting to wonder whether to apply for another grant and try to stay on at uni, or look for a job. With this in mind I flicked through the media pages, and there were two positions advertised that caught my eye. One was for a trainee picture-frame restorer at the National Gallery, and the other was for a trainee hair and make-up artist at the BBC. I applied for both jobs, figuring they sounded quite quirky and interesting, and I was eventually called for two interviews in the same week.

My first interview was at the National Gallery, where I was taken behind the scenes and shown various different picture frames I had to put a date to. It was fabulous having a peek 'backstage' at such a prestigious gallery and I think I did all right, but it wasn't half as exciting as my BBC interview. Before I went to Television Centre, I got French Pat to help me prepare. She tipped out the contents of her make-up bag and showed me how to apply foundation, face powder, blusher and eye shadow, and she demonstrated how she pinned her hair in a bun and a ponytail. It was all new to me, but it seemed simple enough. 'I'm sure if I can paint a picture I can paint a face,' I said. Unbeknown to me, the thinking within BBC make-up was that they could teach a fine art graduate to do hair, but it was not so easy to teach a hairdresser to be creative with make-up. I don't actually agree with this, but at the time it stood me in good stead.

On my way to the interview I walked past the Blue Peter ship and Dr Who's Tardis, which was incredibly exciting and seemed much more up my street than the crypt of the National Gallery. I also met a girl who was just off to work with the Two Ronnies on the *Canberra* in the Caribbean for six weeks, so there was no contest really. This was the job I wanted.

For the practical part of the interview I had to do 'straight' make-up and 'age' make-up as well as apply a hairpiece to a model. For the first I used a pancake base, even though I technically should have started with a liquid foundation, and for the age one I just used a bit of common sense and applied dark shades and shadowing. The hairpiece was a doddle; I just pinned it tight, so it wouldn't fall off, which was the acid test.

'Why did you use a pancake base?' I was asked.

'It seemed appropriate.'

'Why did you pin the hairpiece in that way?'

'I've helped brick up chimneys at the steelworks, so I know a bit about construction, and how to keep things in place.'

My answers weren't textbook and my referee was from the British Steel Corporation, but I think that's what got me through. I was honest and a bit different, and that obviously went in my favour. More than three thousand people had applied, and I was given one of nine jobs on offer. Not only that, I was the first male make-up artist ever to be taken on in London.

The job was due to start on 1 September 1981, and when I finished uni that summer I took French Pat up to the Lake District to celebrate, along with a couple of her au pair mates. There was nothing going on with any of them, but the four of us spent a fantastic weekend together, hiking and rambling. Unfortunately, by the time we were travelling home on the train I'd developed a terrible hacking cough which turned into pneumonia and then pleurisy, and I was very poorly indeed

I was in hospital for two and a half weeks, and when I started work at the BBC I still hadn't fully recovered. I looked really moth-eaten, as clumps of my hair had started to fall out again, worse than they had for a long time.

On my first day at Television Centre I was summoned to the

personnel office and told that, because of the state of my hair, I would be required to wear a wig.

It was made clear it was not acceptable to have bald patches when working in close proximity with 'the talent', as the actors and presenters were called, as my looks might offend them.

'Go to Ray Marsden, he's one of the best wigmakers in the country,' was the polite but very firm instruction.

I was taken aback, to say the least. It had never occurred to me to hide my alopecia with a wig, and it was a bit weird to have this BBC person telling me how to present myself. I didn't want to argue, though, because I had to pass an interview after the first three weeks' training, and if things weren't going well I could be asked to leave. Reluctantly, I visited Ray Marsden at his wig studio in the East End, explaining my dilemma.

'Do you know what you're getting into?' he asked, before explaining that I'd have to cut off all my hair, apart from some strategically placed 'anchor points' that the wig would be attached to. I'd also have to buy two wigs, for when one needed washing.

'How much are they?' I asked anxiously.

'£350 each,' came the alarming reply.

My salary was £290.97 a month. 'Sod that!' I said. 'I'd rather shave me 'ead!'

Later that same day that's exactly what I did, and it was actually very liberating seeing all the wispy tufts of hair fall to the floor, knowing I was ridding myself of something that had caused me so many years of torment and hassle. I contrasted my newly bald head with a neatly trimmed beard and, though I say so myself, the combination didn't look half bad. Compared to my moth-eaten look it was a massive improvement, and for once I felt OK about myself when I looked in the mirror.

I had much better ways of spending my money than on wigs,

and as soon as I got paid I treated myself to a nearly new Honda 185 Benly, which I bought on hire purchase. It was a sensible commuter bike – nothing like the monster chopper or Harley Davidson I dreamed about riding one day – but it got me to and from work every day, and I was well chuffed with it.

Life was looking up. I also moved from Blackheath into a new flat on Connington Road, which was just round the corner from Television Centre in Shepherd's Bush. My flatmates were two party animals, James and Howard, who thought I was great because I was always bringing other make-up artists back, all of whom were young and female. I even got myself a new girlfriend.

The BBC training was second to none, and after three months I was working 'in brackets' on my very first show, *Blake's 7*. The phrase 'in brackets' meant my name appeared in brackets on the call sheet, by the way, indicating I was still a new trainee. Roy Kinnear, who played the caterpillar in *Blake's 7*, was one of the first actors I spotted around, which I thought was very cool. I'd imagined I might be kept well away from the big stars and exciting dramas until I'd earned my stripes, but here I was with my name on the same call sheet as Roy Kinnear, and making up a whole band of aliens; I knew painting those Martians and gully men would come in handy one day!

'Ooh, there the *Blake's 7* spaceship!' I said to one of my colleagues excitedly on the first day. 'I'm going to have a closer look!'

Imagine my disappointment when I discovered the spaceship I'd admired on television was actually constructed from tin-foil roasting trays that were staplegunned to 8 x 4 pieces of plywood.

'The magic's gone!' I jokingly lamented afterwards. 'Even the control panels are a let-down, they're made of yoghurt cartons!'

By the spring I'd come out of 'brackets' and l was looking forward to getting my teeth into some of the big shows I'd grown up watching, like *Top of the Pops* and *The Generation Game,* and hopefully some period dramas where I could learn more about special effects and prosthetics. I'd have to tell Mam next time I saw her, I thought. I was never sure how much she could understand these days, but I always told her what was going on, and the visits were always easier if there was news to pass on, and particularly good news.

10

Si's

Sunday Roast, Lamb Kibbe and Pub Curry with a Pint

'I'm pregnant,' Jane said.

My heart thudded. We had been together for less than a year, and having a baby was not in the plan at all. I had no money, no proper job and no clue how we'd be able to support ourselves, let alone a bairn.

'Well, there's a quick and easy road or there's a long road,' one member of the family said once the news had sunk in, but even as the words were still hanging in the air I knew what we would do.

Jane and I loved each other and were incredibly happy together, and there was no way in the world I would have encouraged her not to have the baby, or done a runner, for that matter. We chose to take the long road together, and I don't regret a single second of it.

I'd recently moved out of Mam's house and was renting a small flat at 47 Westbourne Avenue in Gateshead. I'd been scraping together the rent from gigging four or five times a week, earning a few quid from driving the minibus at NEMTC and doing whatever odd-jobs I could, including doing up old bikes and selling them on. Jane had moved in after finishing her degree in Liverpool and didn't have a proper job either yet, and so we were not in a great position at all.

Mam was brilliant, as you'd expect. 'Never mind, we'll work it out,' she said.

Ginny and Will were very good to us, offering lots of emotional support and, in Will's case, giving me odd-jobs to do up at his house whenever he could, so I could earn extra cash. He had moved back to the North East and was married with two daughters by now, Kirsty and Louise, plus his third child, Samantha, was on the way, so he had his hands full too.

Jane's mother and stepfather were both hard-working teachers and very decent people, and they also helped us a lot, for which we were incredibly grateful. They were a massive lifeline; I don't know how we'd have managed without their help.

I was constantly on the look-out for new opportunities and any openings at all that would bring some more money in and help me and Jane stand on our own two feet. I did several other voluntary jobs to gain experience and make contacts that might lead to the break I wanted, into any job at all in the media. I had my eyes peeled all the time I was at NEMTC and, one day, I saw a notice on the wall that immediately caught my eye.

'Runners wanted for the pilot of a new BBC children's TV series,' it said.

It sounded great. You didn't need any formal qualifications, and the chance to get my foot in the door at the BBC was very appealing and exciting. I applied straight away, and shortly afterwards I was called for an interview with a producer called Matthew Robinson, in his office on the first floor of the BBC in Newcastle.

'That's smashing, Simon,' Mam said when I told her about it. 'Nothing ventured, nothing gained.'

I'd grown up hearing that phrase and I totally agreed with Mam's attitude, but it was still incredibly daunting going into the 'Pink Palace', as the BBC building was known, and meeting a producer like Matthew. I found out he'd been the lead director on the launch of *EastEnders*, among many other things, and so I knew this new show could turn out to be a very big deal, and I was anxious to impress.

Jane had everything crossed for me, but I certainly wasn't counting my chickens when I walked in and shook Matthew's hand. I was well aware that getting a job at the BBC, albeit on the bottom rung, was no mean feat. People who were qualified up to the eyeballs and had fancy degrees applied over and over again for jobs there, at every level. My only hope was that I'd win on my experience with kids and on my personality, because I couldn't compete on any other level.

Matthew told me that the show he was recruiting for was called *Byker Grove*, a new drama about a group of Geordie kids who were members of a youth club. He wanted runners for a month or so, for the pilot, and he explained there was the possibility of more work in the future, if the show went on to be commissioned. I told him about my radio course and all the volunteering I'd done with the kids at Bells Court and so on and, thank God, he seemed to be impressed.

The sun was shining that day, and I think my guardian angel was looking out for me, because I was taken on as one of two runners for the initial pilot. The cherry on the cake was that I was to be paid £150 a week on a freelance basis, which was an immense sum to me. Honest to God, when I got the news I felt like the BBC had saved my life. Jane was heavily pregnant by now, and this could not have come at a better time. Everyone in the family was delighted for us, and Mam especially was brimming with excitement.

'Simon, I'm so proud I can't tell you!' she said. 'A job at the BBC! Perhaps I'd better start paying the licence fee!'

'I'm quite proud of meself, Mam,' I said, which was something of an understatement. I was absolutely beside myself. This was it; I was on my way at last.

I worked my nuts off on *Byker Grove*, and I absolutely loved it. It was great to be in on something right at the beginning; when I first started it was even before Ant and Dec had joined the cast as young lads. It was my job to get call sheets, pick the child actors up, get them onto set and generally help out with whatever needed doing. I was flying, and I really cared about my work and what people thought of me. I desperately wanted to make a good impression, because even at that early stage in my career I was very aware that, as a freelance, you are only ever as good as your last job.

My hard work paid off. Matthew Robinson said I looked like I'd been doing the job for years, and when the first series was eventually commissioned he asked me what job I would like to do next. There was a guy called Paul Paxton on the crew who looked confident and in control on the set, though I wasn't sure exactly what he did.

'I want to do his job,' I told Matthew Robinson and, sure enough, when filming began on the first series I was taken on as a first assistant director, like Paul. This meant more responsibility, such as scheduling the working hours of each day and making sure every individual scene had the right cast in the right place at the right time, in front of the right camera. I absolutely loved it and developed an air of quiet authority under Matthew

Robinson's watchful gaze. He helped me no end in the early parts of my career; then again, there were so many others I could name.

I'd take home about £400 a week if I was booked every day, which was lottery numbers to me back then. The pay rise was obviously great, but as I was freelance I also took on any other work I could, to keep the money coming in.

When Jane went into labour I was doing night-time security on a shoot for a drama. It was when mobile phones were still very new, and I can remember taking the call on a black battery phone the size of a house brick, getting cut off then making frantic calls from a phone box in the middle of nowhere. Then I was piling it down the A1 to the Queen Elizabeth Hospital in Gateshead.

'Are you Simon King?' a nurse asked as I legged it to the maternity ward.

'Yes!' I gasped, before being frogmarched into a delivery suite by one stern midwife and a frantic-looking nurse.

As Jane went through labour, a deeper connection formed between us that neither of us quite understood. This was it; Jane and I were going to be a mam and dad at the age of twenty-three. We were setting out on life's journey together, because that day Jane and I were to be in receipt of a miracle.

I made it with seconds to spare to see Alex being born. I stopped and stared; when Jane held him in her arms she looked so angelic it was something to behold.

'This is it,' I thought in that moment. 'This is going to change our lives forever.'

The date was 27 September 1989. I didn't sleep a wink that night, and when I returned to the ward for visiting the next day Alex wasn't there, and Jane was looking pretty dishevelled.

'Where's me son?' I said to a nurse. I was feeling gaga through lack of sleep, and when the nurse told me that Alex had been taken away and was in an incubator I immediately started to lose it.

'I want to see him!' I demanded, feeling close to tears. 'Where is he? Please God, don't let there be something wrong with him!'

I was taken to another room where Alex was surrounded by consultants and students, and then I properly lost my temper when one of them asked me who I was.

'I'm the father!' I growled. 'Tell me what's wrong with my son, now!'

In the end a midwife explained that Alex just needed 'a little bit of help' as he'd had fluid on the lungs, and that he was going to be fine. I cried with relief, and the huge responsibility of bringing a bairn into the world began to dawn on me. I still feel the power of the emotion when I think about it today. It was remarkable that Jane and I had created this little human being together. Alex was the manifestation of the love and commitment we had between us, and his birth was simply miraculous.

We were ecstatic to be parents, and that winter was absolutely brilliant. In the previous few months I'd managed to save a little bit of money so I could afford to take some time off without worrying too much, and the three of us just hung out together in our little house, having Mam and Jane's folks over for Sunday roasts, and inviting other close family and friends to come and visit.

It was a blissful time, and Jane and I were so happy we soon started talking about having another baby.

'I think Taglet needs a brother or sister,' we started saying, as this was one of the nicknames we had for Alex when he was very small.

The name came about because as soon as Alex started eating solid foods he adored pasta, and especially tagliatelle. I'd been desperate to get him on to proper foods, as the baby mush he had seemed so bland.

'Can't we make the baby food tastier for him?' I'd say to Jane.

'No, Si! You can't put salt in it, or spices for that matter. He's a baby. His little body can't process anything fancy yet!'

I knew this really, but I couldn't wait to start making proper home-cooked food for my son, just as my parents had for me. I was delighted when Alex started tucking into pasta and all sorts of other goodies I cooked for him, and when he got a bit bigger another nickname we had for him was 'fruit bat', because he adored fruit, as I do. The two of us would sit in front of the fire with a big fruit bowl, tucking in as we listened to some music together, and I loved every minute.

Jane is an only child and there had been so many years between me and Will and Ginny that I'd felt pretty much like an only child too. Jane and I both felt it was important to have a sibling of a similar age to grow up with, and so we decided we'd try for another baby as soon as we could afford it. We also vowed to get married once we had enough money to do so properly. This was clearly going to take some time, as we'd also agreed that Jane was going to stay at home full-time. It was what we both wanted.

My work was sporadic, to say the least. I went back to being a runner on *Byker Grove* after my stint as first assistant director, purely for the continuity of work. That was when Ant and Dec had joined the cast as PJ and Duncan. They were real pros even then; good, hard-working lads to have on the set. In hindsight it was a terrible career move for me to go back to being a runner, but I was offered loads more shifts doing that job and so I felt I had no choice. Earning regular money was what mattered more than anything else, because it really was a question of putting food on the table for Jane, Alex and myself.

Whenever I had the time I'd cook in the evenings, because to me it was a way of relaxing and getting back into the flow and pace of family life. I never thought of it as a chore. I'd make some of the old favourites I'd learned from Mam, like lamb kibbe or a spicy beef curry. I also did a lot of couscous and hearty soups and I had a reputation for making great belly pork; it was thanks to Mam that I knew how to make plenty of really good, tasty meals without going over budget.

'Can we have egg and soldiers?' Alex would ask on a Sunday morning.

'Not pasta this time, Taglet?' I'd joke.

'No, egg and soldiers, egg and soldiers!'

He would sit there dipping his toast in his boiled egg just like I had as a toddler, when I was under the watchful eye of my grandad. Alex was absolutely adorable, and I was never happier than when I was doing normal everyday stuff with him like this.

'Don't like them,' he said one time, turning his nose up at some mushrooms or grilled tomato I'd given him alongside his bacon sarnie.

'Don't tell me you don't like it before you've tasted it,' I said, repeating what my dad had said to me as a child. 'You can only say you don't like it after you've tried it!'

It was very important to me to bring my kids up to be good, adventurous eaters. I was very grateful I'd been raised the way I was, and feeding the family well was something I wanted to do properly, right from the start. Jane agreed with me and we never skimped on food; it was a priority to eat well in our house, whatever our circumstances.

The drive to provide for my family was very powerful, and Alex motivated me to do whatever it took to give him and Jane the best life possible. Thanks to the network of contacts I was building up, I got a call one day from a Tyne Tees TV producer who asked me if I fancied working on locations for a drama called *Wallpaper Warriors*. Of course I didn't hesitate in saying yes.

Just like with my first break on *Byker Grove*, this one couldn't have come at a better time, because we'd just found out that Jane was pregnant again. This was a bit of a surprise, as it happened within weeks of us deciding to try for another baby. We used to joke that if it wasn't for contraception Jane and I would have needed to live in Blenheim Palace to house all our kids, because she fell pregnant ridiculously easily. Anyhow, we were dead chuffed and couldn't wait for Alex to have a brother or sister.

James was born on 15 June 1992, also at the Queen Elizabeth. I was blown away by his arrival. He weighed more than ten pounds so it wasn't the easiest delivery, but despite this there was a serenity around his birth, and it was joyful, quiet and contemplative, like his existence.

Right from the start he was really pleased to be here; a very laid-back chap who was full of happiness. I always say he's an old soul, someone who'd been here before.

Alex was two and a half, and I'll never forget how his lovely little face lit up when he registered he had a brand new brother. He absolutely adored James, and our family of four was complete.

'We've cracked it,' I said to Jane when we were all back home together.

'Two beautiful healthy boys,' Jane agreed. 'How lucky are we?'

It really did feel like our world was perfect. We were blessed to have the boys, and now all Jane and I had to do was look after our sons and love them. Even though money was tight, there was never a moment when the kids were an inconvenience or we wondered what on earth we'd done. Jane was a magnificent mother. I knew we would survive and manage, however uncertain our financial future, because nothing mattered more than our two little lads. Me and Jane would both do anything in our power to provide them with all they needed.

I've mentioned my guardian angel before, and I think she visited me again around this time, because I had another very lucky break in my career, just when I really needed it again. Thanks to the work I'd done for Tyne Tees, I got a call offering me work on the Catherine Cookson period dramas, which were filmed on location in the North East and were incredibly popular in the nineties.

I'd been round the block on all kinds of productions by this point, and I'd started to make a name for myself as someone who was capable, enthusiastic, hard-working and reliable; all the qualities I'd learned in the school of life, rather than the classroom. I also had an encyclopaedic knowledge of the North East, which weighed heavily in my favour at Tyne Tees.

I was taken on as a freelance second assistant director on *The Cinder Path*, which starred the young and very beautiful Catherine Zeta-Jones. The first assistant director was a guy called Nael Abbas, who I'd worked with on *Wallpaper Warriors*, which shows you how important my networking and reputation were. This was a massive breakthrough for me, and I was over the moon. The Catherine Cookson dramas were shot in super 16mm film as opposed to Beta SP used for most TV shows, which meant they were effectively film-standard productions, and they were held in very high esteem in the industry.

Doing the job well became my raison d'etre. I was responsible for feeding the set, arranging artists' transport, organising daily call sheets and generally helping to make the filming schedules achievable.

One day I went to Catherine Zeta-Jones' dressing room as she was due on set. I knocked politely on the door and heard giggling inside.

'Come in!' the costume designer, Delphine Roche-Gordon, called.

I stepped through the door, expecting Catherine Zeta-Jones to be in full costume, but she was barely dressed at all. In fact there, right before me, was a sight I had not expected to see at all: Catherine Zeta-Jones' bare chest.

'Oh God, I'm terribly sorry,' I spluttered. I started apologising profusely, while desperately trying to focus on the actress's eyes rather than her breasts. 'I'll, er, tell Nael you'll need another few minutes.'

Catherine Zeta-Jones was a massive star even back then, having recently finished working on *The Darling Buds of May*, and I was mortified.

'Oh, you're alright!' she said with a kindly smile when she saw my shocked expression. 'Have you not seen a pair of these before?'

'Well, I have,' I replied, exhaling with relief at her laid-back reaction. 'But not a pair like that!'

My schedule was full on, every single day, and I worked all the hours God sent, but I was thoroughly enjoying myself. It was around this time that Jane and I managed to get a home of our own.

'Are you sure we're doing the right thing?' Jane worried.

'Of course we are,' I said, because I felt very strongly that, whatever happened on the work front, me and Jane would manage.

'We're a family of four and we need a proper family home,' I said. 'It'll be absolutely fantastic.'

Our new house at Brettenby Gardens in Ryton on Tyne was everything we'd dreamed of. It was completely lush – a proper three-bedroom family home in a Victorian terrace, not far away from our first house in Winlaton Mill. We didn't want to move far; we liked the area, and we'd also moved Mam into a little place over the road from us several years earlier. It was great to have her nearby and she offered to help out with childcare, though we didn't ask very often. Usually it was a case of Jane popping over with the bairns for a cup of tea and a biscuit, and Mam would be fabulous with the boys, involving them in baking cakes or doing a bit of gardening, or whatever else she was doing. Jane adored my mam and really appreciated having her so close.

Mam wasn't getting any younger, mind you, and her health wasn't as good as it had been. Over the years she suffered from several serious conditions but, Mam being Mam, she always bounced back.

Alex and James became what I began to describe as 'lumps in the duvet', and quite often Jane was in bed too by the time I got home from work. I reckoned it had been that way with nearly all of the jobs I had before the Cooksons. I couldn't see any way out of it, other than to work as hard as I possibly could. If I played my cards right, I knew the Cooksons could be a source of income for a long time to come, as the public loved them and there were loads more books to be turned into TV films.

In hindsight I became a workaholic, and Jane was operating as a single mum. I was regularly leaving the house at 5.30 a.m., putting in ninety-hour weeks and grabbing a pub curry and a pint to keep me going. I was constantly telling myself that the hard work would pay off and things would get easier the more my reputation grew. It was important to build contacts and network with the crew, and so sometimes I would be out three or four nights on the trot. Jane was utterly fantastic. She understood what I had to do and she never complained; she was magnificent.

The Cookson producers, Ray Marshall and Dom Bell, also completely understood what I was trying to do and were incredibly supportive; I'm very grateful to them too. After *The Cinder Path* they hired me for *The Glass Virgin*, and as well as being an assistant director, in time I began to work as a location manager. This meant roving around the North East with a very large chequebook, talking toffs into renting out their manor houses and country piles for film shoots.

'It's like having a wedding reception on your front lawn,' I'd tell them. 'One that lasts for three weeks . . .'

The landed gentry were always very amenable and good fun, willing to move in my direction. I tried to make the process as enjoyable as possible and I liked the fact I had to be something of a social chameleon to make things work, because it came naturally to me. Right from day one I found I could walk into a wood-panelled drawing room and know exactly which buttons to press to strike up a rapport with a lord or lady that would make things go swimmingly. It was like being a double-glazing salesman except I was selling actors and television crews instead of windows and doors, so it was a bit more interesting. The next Cookson was going to be *The Gambling Man*, starring Robson Green, and I really hoped I'd be hired, in any role at all. I had two bairns to feed and shoe. I had to keep getting the work or my family would sink very quickly indeed, and that was simply not going to happen.

11

Dave's

Chicken Curry, Packet of Digestives and Turkey with Jell-o and Marshmallows

I smiled when Si described how his mam, Stella, reacted when he got his first break at the BBC. That's what jobs at the BBC did to mams; it made them very proud indeed, and it was seen as real a badge of honour to work for such a great British institution.

As I was the only male make-up artist working for the BBC in London I was quite a novelty within the organisation, and as a result I was asked to appear on the cover of the BBC staff magazine, *Ariel*.

'I'd be honoured!' I said when the request was passed to me, and I thought about how proud Mam would be when she heard about this.

'What will I have to do?'

'Oh, not much. Just give a little interview and pose for a picture.'

I did – and ended up on the cover of the magazine with Hamble, the rag doll out of *Playschool*!

I was loving the job. I can remember being put on *Blue Peter* one week, when the legendary editor Biddy Baxter was in charge. This was a show I'd watched hundreds of times as a child, and I felt honoured to be a part of it. Mind you, on my first day there were a couple of lads from Birmingham pre-recording a novelty song about poppadoms, and one of them very embarrassingly got his lyrics in a muddle when he responded to a line about Bombay duck.

'That's the dunniest looking f*** I've ever seen,' he accidentally announced in his broad Brummie accent, at which point a furious-looking Biddy Baxter stormed into the studio and gave both lads the mother and father of a telling off.

We'd get our rotas three weeks in advance and it would always be a case of: 'Oh great!' or 'Oh no!' It was rarely dull and I enjoyed the variety of work; we never knew which personalities we would be working with next.

'Can you do Des O'Connor's hair?' I was asked matter-of-factly one day.

'Er, what does he need?' I replied, with half of me thinking: 'Help – this is Des O'Connor we're talking about!' and the other half thinking: 'Oooh, Mam will love to hear about this too!'

'Des needs his highlights doing.'

'Well, I've never done highlights before.'

'Oh well, don't you know the rule?'

'What's that?'

'Never admit you've never done it before!'

With that I was despatched to give Des O'Connor some copper streaks, which I was incredibly nervous about. I kept the dye light to limit any damage in case it went wrong, but in the event Des seemed perfectly happy, thanking me kindly and not suspecting a thing about my novice skills.

I'd just finished work at Television Centre one Friday night when the hospital rang unexpectedly, to tell me that Mam was dying. Even though she'd been ill for so long it still came as a horrible shock. I thought she'd go on forever, just like I did with Dad, I suppose. I rode the Benly from London to Barrow on all the A roads, as I still only had a provisional licence, and it took me about ten hours.

It was 4 a.m. when I finally arrived at the hospital, but thankfully I managed to see Mam before she died.

Despite the initial shock I'd felt when the hospital phoned me at work, ultimately I accepted her passing quite readily. Mam's death was matter-of-fact, a fact of life. It was 20 June 1982, I was twenty-four years old and Mam had been dying for many years. As I sat with her in hospital I tried to think about her as she was before she got ill, but I couldn't remember her walking normally. Even now I think I can only picture her out of her wheelchair because I have some old cine-films. It may sound hard, but when it sunk in that she was gone I was glad that, finally, she wasn't suffering any more.

The funeral is a blur to me now. Some of Mam's sisters were still alive and they made most of the arrangements while I put my mind to sorting out the flat. I'd been paying the rent to the council for the three years since Dad died, but after Mam's death they wouldn't let me keep the flat on. I had one day to clear it out, as I had to get back to London for work, and so some of my old mates came round to help me. It was bloody awful. A few bits and pieces I didn't know what to do with ended up in a mate's girlfriend's attic, most of the stuff was chucked out, and then I tied a bag and a box containing photos, the cine-films and a few other personal belongings to the back of my Benly. Honest to God, I drove the three hundred miles down to Shepherd's Bush looking like something out of the *Beverly Hillbillies*.

I still had a good infrastructure of mates in Barrow, but as I drove away I wasn't sure if I'd ever go back. It was frightening, actually, leaving the old flat for the last time. Living in London, I'd seen people on the streets because they'd lost their homes and families, and now the only safety-net I ever had was gone. Even though things were going well at the BBC, I knew that if I lost my job I could end up on the street too. I was expendable, and now I had no parents and no family home. I felt incredibly vulnerable, and it made me work my fingers to the bone.

Not long after Mam died I split up with the girlfriend I had at the time. She asked me to pick her up after work and take her to a party one night and I was absolutely knackered but foolishly agreed. Unfortunately, I was riding my Benly along Queen's Gate when I lost concentration and had my first motorbike accident, T-boning a Jaguar XJ6. A cloud of goose-down from the big padded coat I was wearing floated down the Cromwell Road, and my girlfriend ran out of where she worked to see the feathers flying and me lying in the road beside my smashed bike. My glasses had disintegrated and I was in a hell of a state, but as soon as she saw I was alive and could just about hobble to my feet, my girlfriend declared: 'Oh! I thought you were dead but you're not! That's good. I'll go to the party on my own then . . .'

Needless to say, that was the end of that relationship. It was also the end of my bike, which was written off. All I was left with was cracked ribs and lots of bruising, and I had to take three weeks off work to recover.

James and Howard were great and they put me in the garden every day, brought me tea and food and wouldn't let me go out. I decided that living in such a lively house wasn't doing me any good, though, and it felt like time to move on and get a place of my own.

I saved like mad and eventually bought a flat for £16,000 at Gipsy Hill, with a hundred per cent mortgage from the Chemical Bank. I bought some 4 x 2 planks of wood and built myself a bed frame, and everything else I owned came from junkyards and charity shops.

The cooker was second hand but I treated myself to a chicken brick and a new wok from Habitat, and one of the first ever Ken Hom cookbooks. Keith Floyd was very popular and my hero back then too; I think we all wanted to be him. Let's face it, having a slurp of wine in between chopping the onions for a chicken curry made cooking a very appealing pastime, didn't it? I always felt very much at home in the kitchen, and I suppose that's a throwback to my early childhood and cooking with my mother. It was a place I could be myself, be experimental and creative and, with a bit of luck, end up with a plateful of great tasting food.

There was always something very satisfying about getting a recipe just right that had gone a bit skew-whiff before, and I enjoyed the whole ceremony of cooking for friends, and did it whenever I could. I've got fond memories of that flat, because I entertained there a lot and even threw a black tie dinner party once.

I eventually worked on *Top of the Pops* and totally loved it. It was in the New Romantic days of Adam and the Ants, The Teardrop Explodes, Steve Strange and Spandau Ballet, and so the make-up department always had plenty of interesting work to do. Putting the white stripe on Adam Ant was always one of my favourite jobs as it was so iconic. When Jennifer Rush did 'The Power of Love' she liked the way I did her make-up and always asked for me, which was lush as she stayed at number one for six weeks. I met Elton once too, who came into make-up wearing a hat.

'Can you take your hat off for me, please?' I asked hopefully.

'No.'

'Oh. It's just that it's hard to do the foundation under the rim.'

'No.'

'Oh, right-o then. As you like.'

Wham! were massive then, and the first time George Michael came in he'd already made himself up, in a fetching shade of orange.

'Sit down,' I said. 'I'll do your hands to match . . .'

It was exciting times. One day I'd be doing Marc Almond's make-up before Soft Cell performed 'Tainted Love', and the next I'd be working alongside Deborah Kerr and Paul Scofield for a period drama. The first time I spotted Deborah Kerr I wanted to tell her my mam used to have all the records from *The King and I* but unfortunately I never got the chance.

'Can you go and get the sausage rolls in for the cast, Dave?' someone said, and the moment was gone.

One part of the job I really loved was working with prosthetics, making amputated feet for a sci-fi show or a false chin, eye-bags or nose for a drama. Making a fake nose look real is actually one of the hardest jobs of all, but I thoroughly enjoyed learning the craft. Doing a nose is a bit like baking a delicate sponge cake, in fact, except the kitchen stinks like rotten eggs afterwards because of the chemicals. You start by moulding the nose shape you want out of some foam rubber-type Latex, then you make a face cast of the actor with plaster, a bit like the way a dentist makes a mould of your teeth. Needless to say, this is not a pleasant process for the person on the receiving end, as having the plaster mixture applied to your face can be very claustrophobic. Anyway, after that's done you need to model the fake nose onto the face cast with clay, forming your finished mould. The next job is to mix up some foam rubber in a Kenwood Chef, in a similar way you'd mix egg white, then you place that mixture in the mould and bake it in the oven. After four hours you split the mould and then peel the foam rubber mask out – easy peasy! If you're lucky it's worked, but two out of three times it doesn't unfortunately, and so it's back to square one.

'I've got a great job for you, Dave,' I was told one day. 'Stanley Baxter is playing all of the characters from *The Wizard of Oz* in a Christmas special.'

'Oh noooo!' I exclaimed, thinking I was going to need the patience of a saint for this one, but in actual fact it worked really well, not least because Stanley Baxter was a very professional and charming man to have in the chair.

Lots of other stars were just fantastic to work with too. I loved Lena Zavaroni and Marti Caine because they were always very friendly. Michael Parkinson, Ken Dodd and Larry Grayson were always delightful to work with too, and I found it hysterical seeing the famous *Generation Game* conveyor belt in action, as there really was a man frantically piling hairdryers and dinner services on the prize-carrying belt as it moved into shot.

One time I made up Hank Marvin for an appearance on the *Des O'Connor Show* – yes, Des still let me near his show so his copper highlights really must have been alright! – and I can remember thinking: 'I wish Mam were still alive. I'd love to tell her I'm painting one of the Shadows!'

Vanessa Redgrave came into make-up once and was so down to earth and unpretentious that I didn't even recognise her.

'I'm terribly sorry but I think you're in the wrong place. I'll have to ask you to leave as I'm expecting Vanessa Redgrave any minute.'

'But I am Vanessa Redgrave!'

'Oh dear! I do apologise!'

Another time, the actor Richard Greene's name was on my list.

'It can't be him, he's dead,' I said, when I was told it was the same Richard Greene who'd famously played Robin Hood in the original series many moons before.

'No, he's not,' a colleague told me.

'He is!' I insisted. 'He's got to be dead!'

Just as I finished my sentence a familiar-sounding voice boomed behind me, which took me right back to watching *Robin Hood* as a boy.

'I can assure you I'm not dead!' Richard Greene said. 'I am *very much alive!*'

Thankfully he had a generous smile on his face, but I was so embarrassed I didn't know what to say other than: 'Oh, that's good!'

Princess Diana popped in to TV Centre for a private visit one day, and in typical style she didn't want any fanfare. All the big-wigs were dying to meet her, but she kept them waiting as she sat down for a long chinwag with the guy who emptied the bins. That story always gives me a warm glow.

In 1986 I was given a very prestigious job, working on *The Life and Loves of a She-Devil*, the TV mini-series starring Patricia Hodge and Dennis Waterman. It was a terrific opportunity. For one thing, I had to create a hairy mole for a top lip, which I did by buying one of those wallpaper flocking machines to make the hair stand up, like on 'hairy' wallpaper. Then I had to make a cast of Patricia Hodge's small but perfectly formed breasts, and one of Julie T. Wallace's whoppers. My job was to clone Julie's boobs onto Patricia's, as one lady changes into the other during the drama. It was a hell of a challenge, especially when Julie fainted halfway through the process. We got there in the end, and when all the filming was finished, just for a laugh I stuck Patricia's supersized boob cast on the back of the catering truck and watched it being driven off down the motorway.

On paper my career was going really well. I'd been at the BBC for five years, had received the most incredible training and amassed a wealth of experience. I was starting to get itchy feet, though. Working in films was beginning to really appeal. It seemed like the next step up the career ladder for me after *She-Devil* and so I took the bold decision to leave the BBC and go freelance.

I'd taken in a lodger called Lance, and he had a mate who ran a courier business in Chelsea and gave me a job as a despatch rider to tide me over while I got myself set up. Being paid to tear around London on a BMW K1100 RT motorbike, albeit one I had to buy myself on hire purchase, sounded like my idea of heaven. Of course, in reality, it wasn't. I think I was the worst rider they'd ever employed; I was a total disaster. Every night I'd get in after delivering dozens of packages on a carefully planned round, only to discover one left at the bottom of my bag. It would invariably be the most urgent one of the lot, destined for somewhere like East Grinstead, and I'd have to go back out and deliver it, effing and blinding as I did so.

I needed a holiday, and good old Lance stepped in again. He was bike-mad like me, and the two of us cooked up a plan to go on a great European road trip, ending up in Italy. Lance was very clean-shaven, had blond highlights and looked like he should have been in a boy band; I always felt like the ugly friend beside him!

Anyhow, me and poster boy set off to Italy on 17 June 1986. I had a big 850cc Moto Guzzi that I'd bought in bits from a fellow make-up artist's boyfriend. I did it up in their spare room, and on the day it was finished Lance and I rode it out of their house and straight down the Old Kent Road to Dover, then onto the back of the ferry. From Calais we rode around the *périphérique* in Paris, through the Mont Blanc tunnel and all the way down to Florence. Lance and I shared the riding, stopping off for some great meals along the way, like *coq au vin* and *saucisson* on the ten franc menu that came with a little jug of wine. We wore white trousers and Eighties-style cheesecloth shirts, the sun shone, the scenery was wonderful and, all in all, it was a thoroughly magical trip.

Not long after I got home I took a fortuitous call from an old colleague called Miri Ben-Schlomo. She had been offered the job of make-up designer on a period drama set in the fifties called *Sputniks, Bleeps and Mr Perry*.

'I can't do it,' she said. 'Do you fancy it, Dave?'

'I'd love to do it,' I replied without hesitation. 'The only trouble is I'm not set up on my own yet. I haven't even got a box of make-up.'

Miri said she could get me some supplies together and so I took the job, which was how my freelance make-up career started. I was made up! After the courier job and the holiday I was really up for it.

I loved the *Sputniks* set. It was a good craic, and the money was great. Soon afterwards I got offered a day in the studio on *Coronation Street* which really appealed to me, as it was a show I'd grown up watching. I was completely star-struck when I walked on the set at Granada TV in Manchester, and I think the head make-up designer, Linda Tully, must have taken one look at me and thought: 'Who's this wide-eyed bloke? Can I trust him with the *Corrie* stars?'

Linda now does make-up for *Loose Women* – including mine sometimes! We're good mates to this day and have laughed fondly about our time on *Corrie* together. The first job Linda gave me was to powder the bald head of Bill Waddington, who was the actor who played grumpy pensioner Percy Sugden. I was also bald at the time, and the next thing I knew Jean Alexander popped up from behind the bar of the Rovers in her Hilda Ogden cleaning-pinny and rollers, sprayed some Pledge on top of my head and gave it a cheeky polish. I laughed my socks off, felt immediately welcome and really hoped I'd get more work there.

Unfortunately, I managed to make things a tad difficult for myself despite this lucky break. On my way home from my very first day on *Corrie* I was knackered, and I fell asleep at the wheel of my car and demolished twenty-five yards of the central reservation on the M6. The police gave me the benefit of the doubt and put the crash down to the high cross winds, but I knew I only had myself to blame. Now I never, ever drive when I'm tired. Si and I have been known to deliberately lose the crew when we're on the road sometimes, and we'll curl up like two sacks of rubbish on a roadside and have a sneaky kip.

Anyhow, I was asked back to *Corrie* and before long Granada started to put me on the rota regularly. I was dead chuffed. It was a fabulous set to work on, and I loved the cast and crew. I was soon trusted with lots of big jobs, like Mavis's wedding, for which I was responsible for tweaking Deirdre's famous perm and wrestling with Gail's fringe.

'Barbara needs a new wig,' Linda told me one day, which immediately sent me into a tailspin. Even back then Barbara Knox was one of *Corrie's* biggest stars, and her character Rita was a stalwart of the street.

'Oh no, I'll have to go on a train with her to London and she'll hate me!' I said, because at the BBC you automatically visited a master wigmaker like Ray Marsden whenever you needed a wig, as I'd found out right at the start of my career.

Linda burst out laughing. 'Oh no, love! You just go to the wig man on Arndale market. He'll give you a bagful, you bring them back here and Barbara will try them all on and pick her favourite. You can take the rest back.'

Jill Summers, who played the old blue-rinse temptress Phyllis Pearce, would always instruct me to use two bottles of purple hair dye on her own hair when I made her up. She looked like an African violet, but she absolutely loved it. I started working at *Corrie* so often that I rented a room in Salford, and in the evenings I'd go fishing for fresh trout in the reservoir near Stalybridge. I'd take a couple of cans of beer with me and a packet of digestives, and I'd invariably catch more than I could eat. I was very fond of Jill, and so I took to gutting the trout and taking her in a packet of fish whenever I knew I was working with her the next day. This went on for ages, until I overheard Jill saying to a colleague: 'I haven't got the heart to tell the little f***er I'm living at the Midland Hotel.'

Jill took me out to dinner after that, to a wonderful Italian restaurant, and she was dressed up in diamonds and fur, looking every inch the music-hall star she had been in her younger days. I ordered extra bread with my meal, which Jill eyed mischievously. 'The little f***er does like to build butties out of his dinner,' she explained to the dumbfounded waiter.

Through *Corrie* I got work on other Granada shows, doing odd days on anything from *The Grumbleweeds* to *Lost Empires*. Granada was riding high, and the make-up room was massive and shared by everyone. It meant you could have Sir John Gielgud sitting beside punters being made up for *Stars in Their Eyes*. I enjoyed the glamour and fun of being part of that scene, and I felt very much at home there.

By 1987 I was established and very well connected as a freelance, and while I was still working for *Corrie* I got offered a job on the Granada TV movie, *Breakthrough at Reykjavik,* starring Timothy West as Gorbachev. One of my first tasks was to work out how to replicate Gorbachev's famous red birthmark so it looked exactly the same on the set each day. I did it by stippling the paint on Timothy West's head through a template I created, and I also had to source some glasses that looked like Gorbachev's, although there was a bit of a debate about whether this was my job or the costume designer's, who was an attractive lady called Kate.

Fortunately, Kate and I got on very well indeed, the work ran very smoothly and I thoroughly enjoyed the job. One night, Timothy West took us and several other members of the crew out for a celebration dinner at the famous Yang Sing restaurant in Manchester. We had a fabulous evening, and not long afterwards Kate invited me to stay with her in Bristol. There was a definite spark between us, and by now I fancied her like mad, though she was sixteen years older than me and thought it quite amusing.

'I'm old enough to be your mother,' she laughed, when I made my feelings known.

'Yes,' I replied. 'But I never felt like this about my mother!'

It was rampant lust on my part and I fell for Kate hook, line and sinker.

During our courtship I worked on *The Woman He Loved* starring Anthony Andrews and Jane Seymour as Edward and Mrs Simpson.

The TV film was made by the BBC and Universal and was a massive deal for me at the time, because Jane Seymour was one of the highest paid British actresses in the US. I had to meet her at the Dorchester to make the cast of her head that would be used to transform her into Mrs Simpson. I arrived at 7 a.m. at the front entrance, pushing a wheelbarrow full of buckets and plaster and telling the stony-faced bellhop I was here to meet Jane Seymour. He thought I was a nutter and didn't want to let me in, and he was not best pleased when my story turned out to be true and he was forced to see me and my wheelbarrow to a lift!

Ms Seymour was grace and elegance personified as she sat in her bathroom, letting me do my stuff with the plaster cast. I was very nervous as I had to get all her beautiful hair under a bald cap; accidentally encasing loose strands in plaster and having to chop bits off would have been career-limiting, to say the least.

Some of the filming for *The Woman He Loved* was done in Bristol and I took Kate on set. We were getting on brilliantly, and when I was paid I took her to Venice for a wonderfully romantic holiday, and then I proposed. It all sounds foolishly rushed in hindsight, but what can I say? I was absolutely infatuated, and I let my heart rule my head, which is not normally the way I am. To my delight Kate said yes straight away, and eight months later we tied the knot at a church in Bristol, and bought ourselves a house in the suburbs. My best man was an architect friend of mine from Gipsy Hill, and, to show you how imprudent the whole thing was, just before the ceremony he hissed in the vestry: 'It's not too late, Dave. We could do a runner, piss off back to London and forget the whole thing.'

I was in too deep and would never have done that, but if I'm truthful I was bloody tempted. I fancied the pants off Kate, but what the hell was I doing getting married?

Immediately before the wedding Kate had suffered a nasty health scare, and I had to stay with the vicar for a short time in the preceding weeks because I didn't live in the parish where the banns were being read, or something like that. The karma seemed off-kilter and I didn't have a good feeling in my bones, but I kept telling myself it would work out. Kate made my pulse race like billy-o; what more could I ask for?

Once we'd actually tied the knot I felt loads better. The die was cast, we had our future ahead of us and I felt a surge of relief and optimism. In fact, we were both on cloud nine at the reception on a boat in Bristol docks called *MV Locheil*, and we were still deliriously happy when we flew off on our honeymoon to Boston, where we hired the biggest and most ostentatious car we could find: a black Pontiac Bonneville. Our plan was to drive to New York and stay at the Waldorf Astoria, but there was a heatwave on and, after sweltering in the car and getting lost driving around Boston with no map, I saw a sign for ferries to Nova Scotia.

'Shall we head up north instead?' I said, on a whim.

'Why not?' Kate said, and we ended up sleeping under the stars on what was effectively a floating casino. Thankfully, the very long journey was worth it. We stumbled upon the wonderful Whitman Inn in Nova Scotia, and the scenery and landscape was wild, unspoilt and just incredible. It was right next door to the Kejimkujik National Park and it felt like you could hear the earth breathe. I absolutely loved it, and I made good friends with the hotel owners, Bruce and Nancy Gurnham, who told me later: 'We saw the big, black Pontiac come in and thought it was some bad old boys in a pimpmobile.'

Back in Bristol, Kate and I quickly discovered that the 1930s house we'd bought had dry rot, which required £30,000 worth of work to put right. We had no recourse; our surveys had been faked and we found out our lawyer was in jail for fraud. The house had been offloaded on us basically, and we had to borrow the money to pay for the repair work. It was rotten luck, quite literally.

When the builders were in sorting out the dry rot Kate and I lived in a caravan in Weston-Super-Mare. By now I was working on some Harry Enfield videos and had to commute to London, which just wasn't sustainable, and then I started doing shifts in Manchester again, because I had no choice but to go where the work was. One of the shows I did around this time was Granada TV's *Cluedo*, making up the screen siren Stephanie Beacham as Mrs Peacock. Stephanie and I got on really well together, and one day she asked me why I didn't go to Hollywood to ply my trade.

'I'm married and I've got commitments here,' I said through gritted teeth, as the answer I really wanted to give was: 'I wish I bloody could, Stephanie! I'd be there like a shot!'

The truth of it was that work was not flowing in as regularly as I would have liked, and Kate was in the same boat. Changes within Granada and the way programmes were commissioned and franchised meant there was less work to go around a growing pool of freelancers. It was another pressure on us, and before long we were running out of money because of the repair bills and the shortage of work. Kate and I knew we were going to have to sell our house of horrors for less than we paid for it, which would clean us out financially. I still had my flat in Gipsy Hill, though it had been on the market for ages. We couldn't bank on selling it and we didn't want to live in it either; it was a dump and also needed a lot of money spending on it.

One night Kate and I were watching *Local Hero* on TV, which featured the beautiful, windswept North East coast, and I had a bright idea.

'We could move somewhere like that,' I said, getting out some atlases. 'If we get a buyer for the flat and go far enough north, somewhere a bit remote, we'll have enough to start again.'

Kate agreed to look into it; we had bugger-all to lose. I'd managed to buy myself a Harley Davidson since we got hitched, but that is about my only good memory of all my time in Bristol.

Thankfully, my flat in Gipsy Hill did sell at long last, and once the sale had gone through Kate and I drove for more than five hundred miles scouring the North East and the Highlands of Scotland for potential places to live. We had no luck and were about to give up and head back to Bristol when we went through the town of Huntly in Aberdeenshire, about thirty miles inland from the east coast of Scotland. There was a second-hand shop called Rafferty's for sale for £12K freehold, and the dwelling house upstairs was also for sale, for £35K. Kate had owned an antiques shop several years before we met, and we looked at each other with a shared light-bulb expression on our faces.

'What if we opened an antiques shop?' one of us said.

'And we could live above the shop!' the other one replied.

It seems completely crazy when I tell the story now, but we put in an offer and had agreed to buy the shop and the flat upstairs by 3 p.m. that same day. I guess that shows how desperate we were to change our circumstances. We just wanted a clean break and fresh start. The area was beautiful and the air was clean, and I felt another surge of relief and optimism when we moved in. This wasn't the end of our troubles though, oh no!

I had a hiatus from make-up for about a year and Kate gave up looking for costume design work to focus on the business. We sold my Harley Davidson as we needed the money, which I was gutted about, but agreed to. The shop did alright, but sadly Kate and I weren't getting on very well at all by now. Then I got offered a lucrative contract doing the make-up on *Harry* with Michael Elphick, which was shot on location in Darlington, but meant I'd be spending a lot of time away from home. Naively, I thought this could be a good thing. Kate and I wouldn't be in each other's hair as much, I could live on my expenses in Darlington and we would be able to spend my wages on more stock to boost the shop, which we badly needed to do.

Perhaps inevitably, things didn't pan out as well as I hoped. The work on *Harry* was great, but the shift pattern meant I only managed to get back to Huntly once a fortnight. Kate and I were arguing more and more, and before we knew it we were fighting like cat and dog every time we saw each other. I buried my head in the sand, thinking we'd just have to sort ourselves out when *Harry* was over.

However, one night, six weeks before my contract finished in Darlington, I arrived home to find the house and shop empty, and when I say empty, I don't just mean that Kate wasn't there. She had disappeared, stripping both places bare and leaving just a mattress for me to sleep on. The shop's van was missing too. I'd made a very good friend in Huntly called Dr Dave Easton, the local GP, and it turned out he had helped Kate load the van before I got home, mistakenly thinking she was going to an antiques fair. Dr Dave went on to be a great support to me in the aftermath of Kate leaving and is still one of my best mates.

Kate had simply had enough and, looking back, I'm not surprised. It was an absolute shocker for me at the time, though. I was devastated, but more in a defeated, miserable way than because my heart had been broken. Kate and I should never really have got married. I was in lust with her more than I was in love with her, and I should have known better.

Kate and I spoke only once more, and that was to agree to an uncontested divorce. It was the best thing for both of us and I don't hold any of it against her.

We eventually came to an agreement about splitting our assets fairly, such as they were. Kate basically kept the possessions and I had the property, and in time the business was officially wound up so we didn't owe each other anything. Once it was all sorted I was very relieved that the marriage was over.

'I'd have divorced me, I were that bad,' I lamented to Dr Dave when I'd stopped bollocking him for loading my life into the van for Kate.

I eventually swapped my wedding ring for a couple of antique candlesticks, and when I told my tale of woe to the antique dealer she memorably commented: 'Aye, you'll have more fun out of them. They're a nice pair.'

I dusted myself down very quickly, which I guess says it all about the state the marriage had been in. A local businessman eventually took over the lease on the shop and I stayed living upstairs, as I had nowhere else to go. That was that. I was on my own, and I was not unhappy. In fact, it was a blessed relief that all the arguing had stopped, and I could please myself in the flat and take whatever work came along, wherever it may be.

Not long afterwards I started work on the TV film *The Negotiator*, starring Brian Cox. It was shot in Glasgow and turned out to be a brilliant job and a great laugh. I also made good friends with the costume designer on the set, a lovely lady called Delphine Roche-Gordon, who played an important role in what happened next in my career.

Things were looking up, and at the end of 1994 I took myself back to Nova Scotia for a holiday with the hotelier friends I made there, Bruce and Nancy. There was no room for me at their Whitman Inn and so I borrowed a tent and camped out in minus fifteen degrees. My glasses froze over and Nancy had to dig me out, but what was most memorable about the trip was the fabulous food. I offered to help in the kitchen because the hotel was so busy, putting on a New Year's Eve party, and we made turkey with Jell-o and marshmallows, fillet steak with water chestnuts and some amazing home-made corned beef. I was in my element cooking dishes that were new to me and, even though it was hard work, I found it relaxing and quite therapeutic to be busy in the kitchen.

When I got back from Nova Scotia I worked on the second series of *Harry*, and not long after that, thanks to a recommendation from Delphine Roche-Gordon, I was offered the job as head of make-up on a Catherine Cookson drama being shot in the North East. It was called *The Gambling Man*, and on the day I started work the first crew member I met was a big, blond-haired Geordie, whose name was Simon King.

12

Si's

Flambéed Bananas in Southern Comfort, Northumberland Lobster and Gloucester Old Spot with Chinese Crackling

'What have you got on today, Julian?' I asked the landlord of the Egypt Cottage pub. It was next door to Tyne Tees TV, and was one of two pubs frequented at lunchtime by the staff.

'Chicken curry, naan and poppadoms, Si,' came the reply.

'I'll have one of them then, Ju,' I said, rubbing my hands together. 'And another pint, please.'

'I'll 'ave the same, please,' came a voice behind me at the bar.

I looked over my shoulder and saw a round-faced, bald-headed guy with a neatly trimmed beard, whom I'd never met before.

'Hello! It's usually just me on the curry and beer, mate,' I smiled. 'The rest of the crew are on salads and mineral water.'

He laughed, we shook hands and he introduced himself as Dave Myers, the new head of make-up, prosthetics and hair on the set of *The Gambling Man*. At first glance he wasn't your average make-up designer, as the vast majority I'd worked with were female. I had a good vibe about him, though, and he seemed like a guy who would be gentle in his approach, which I like.

'I only had my interview this morning,' he explained. 'Talk about the new boy! Don's brought me over as he thought it would be a good way to meet everyone.'

That was Don Bell, the producer, and I explained to Dave that I was the second assistant director. Dave and I both knew that our roles meant we'd be spending a lot of time together, as I had to ensure all the actors were in the right place at the right time and I'd be depending on Dave to have them made up and ready to go on set exactly when required.

'Welcome aboard, mate,' I said. 'It's a great set to be on. You'll fit right in, I'm sure.'

Despite the fact we both liked a curry and a pint we didn't exactly look like two blokes destined to become the best of friends. Dave seemed like quite a serious, unassuming fella, and his first memory of me is that I was 'large, hairy and loud'.

I'd broken off from a game of pool to order my lunch, and once the curry arrived I sat down next to Dave. We were both well used to being thrown together with new colleagues, and I cut to the chase.

'I don't know about you, mate, but my ethos is to get the job done and get back to the pub as quickly as possible. Know what I mean?'

'I certainly do,' Dave grinned, taking a large sup of his pint. 'I think we're going to get on.'

Dave told me he was originally from Cumbria but had a flat in Aberdeenshire and was renting digs nearby.

'So how are you getting around? Don't suppose you've got a bike, dude?'

That was it: the conversation fired into another gear completely. We talked about our love of motorbikes in between mouthfuls of curry and beer, and the ice was well and truly broken.

As I predicted, Dave slotted in really well. He was a breath of fresh air, actually, as most make-up artists wound me up no end.

'They've got one job to do!' I'd ranted in the past. 'Get the actors made up on time! How hard can that be?'

I'd had make-up artists over-run so many times, faffing around with wigs and false moustaches and pots of rouge at the eleventh hour, making actors late on set. As I was responsible for all the timings, my job was on the line if the actors weren't in their spot, on the dot, because then the whole production schedule would fall behind, which costs money.

Dave was different, though. From day one there was a really welcoming atmosphere in his make-up truck; it was mint. There would be nice tunes playing, he'd brew really good coffee and he made the actors feel so comfortable some of them didn't want to leave. Greats like Robson Green, Ian Cullen and Bernard Hill would emerge not just made up, but content and raring to go, and always bang on time.

In time I'd look forward to hearing Dave's cry of, 'Kingie, kettle's on!' from the door of his make-up truck, which was parked up at the docklands or at Ryton Grove mansion, where a lot of the filming took place. Whatever pressure he was under, Dave turned out the actors immaculately every single time, on cue.

'Pub?' I said, when filming was over on Dave's first day.

'Aye,' he said, and we went over to the Egypt Cottage for several celebratory pints.

It was during the course of one of our after-work drinking sessions that Dave started to tell me about the problems he'd had in recent times.

'D'you know what one of the worst things was, Kingie?'

'No, mate. I can't imagine what you've been through.'

'It was having to sell my Harley when we moved up to Scotland. That really killed me.'

'I'm really gutted for you, dude.'

Dave just shrugged. 'Best to look forward. Now, what was it you were saying about the bikes you're doing up . . . ?'

As I had done for years, I still had my little sideline going, restoring motorbikes and selling them on. It was a purely financial exercise because, even though the pay was decent on the Cooksons, I still needed all the money I could get to keep the family afloat. I was doing up a couple of classic Japanese bikes at the time, and I told Dave I'd earmark one for him – a snip at £1,000 – if he was interested. He told me he had to save up, but as soon as he could afford it he'd let me know.

'I've been planning to treat myself,' he said. 'It'll be like getting back to normal, having a bike again.'

I admired his honesty, and I think we felt connected as mates quite quickly. Even though our temperaments and family circumstances were so different we had loads in common. It wasn't just the bikes and the fact we both loved our food, or even the way we rubbed along so well together on set. It was deeper than that, and Dave agrees with me. Right from the start we had an understanding and appreciation of what drove one another, and of the deep-rooted, basic instinct to survive that each of us had in spades.

I invited Dave over for a meal one weekend, so he could meet Jane and the boys. That was how Jane and I socialised when the kids were small. People came to the house, we cooked for them, and if they wanted to have a few beers and stay over, they were very welcome. One of the lads would usually end up being turfed out of their bunk bed and put in our room to make way for a guest, but the boys always seemed to sleep through, no matter how much noise we made. Jane and I much preferred to be at home rather than going out and getting babysitters, and we really enjoyed cooking for friends.

'What do you want to cook?' Jane would say when we had people round, because on those occasions she was the one who would work out the logistics and get everything prepped, ready for me to do the cooking when I got home from work.

Having a degree in Home Economics, Jane has always been an excellent cook and she had lots of great ideas, as well as a very useful *Good Housekeeping* cookery manual that she liked to refer to. She made fabulous family food like spag bol, sausage casserole and fish pies on a daily basis, but the dinner party stuff would be my domain.

'Whatever we do, if we cook it with enthusiasm and love, it'll be lush,' I always said.

I didn't like sticking to recipes; I'd much rather be a bit creative and inventive with food. The only time I used the *Good Housekeeping* book was if I did any baking, as the quantities have to be right, but otherwise I liked to experiment, adding spices and seasoning according to how the food tasted. I'd frequently visit the Brighton Oriental Food Stores in the West End of Newcastle to stock up on interesting ingredients. I'd been going there since I was about twelve with my mam or our Gin, who is another great cook and was really into Asian cookery even when I was a kid.

Dave didn't hesitate in accepting the invitation to the 'sleepover', as he called it, and he even stayed for Sunday lunch the next day, slotting into the family as if he'd been coming round for years.

'Mate, if I had a wife who looked like that I wouldn't go out either,' he joked when he left. 'She looks like a rock chick. All this and a Sunday roast – get in!'

The boys were three and five years old by now and Jane and I wanted to take them to France. Up until this point we'd only ever been on short camping or caravanning trips in the UK, but this time we hired a red Ford Sierra and drove to the Gironde for our first family holiday abroad. It was an extremely long drive from Newcastle down to the Atlantic coast of France, but Jane and I didn't care. We had our boys and we were going to camp, play on the beach, teach the lads to swim with waterwings on in the sea and have barbecues for a whole week.

We had the wonderful time we'd expected, and one of the highlights for me was regularly rinsing the local market for all kinds of lovely food, including prawns and soft cheeses, big salamis and of course some crispy French bread and fresh salad. On the last day of the holiday I couldn't resist going a bit mad in the local supermarket, and I blew more money than we could afford.

'How much have we got left?' Jane said.

'Er, only about fifty quid's worth of francs,' I replied, searching my wallet.

This was literally our petrol money to get back to Newcastle; we didn't have another bean because I wasn't due to be paid until we got home.

'Is that all? Well, if you hadn't done that big food shop, Si, we'd have had a lot more . . .'

'Sorry. You can't go home without taking a few nice salamis, though, can ya?'

'There's only one thing for it, Si. We'll have to avoid all the motorway tolls and drive slowly on the A roads. Then we might just get home on the tank of fuel we already have, and the fifty quid cash.'

What followed was a comical road trip during which every time Jane spotted a toll sign up ahead she'd bellow 'péage!' hysterically, as if we were about to enter the gates of hell. Then I'd take the next available detour, with Jane doing a magnificent job navigating. Incredibly, we made it all the way back to Blaydon on two tanks of petrol, running out just six miles from home and limping into a local garage.

'Can you let me have five pounds' worth of petrol and I'll come back and pay you tomorrow, mate?' I asked the cashier. 'I only live down the road.'

The fella behind the till obliged, and that's how we got home.

'See, I told you we'd be alreet, Janey!' I said triumphantly, but I don't think Jane considered it much of a victory, having worried all the way back about getting her precious little boys safely home.

When I returned to work, we were filming *The Gambling Man* at the docks one day when I spotted Dave sitting on some steps with Delphine. It was wet and slimy underfoot but sand paths had been laid down to stop people slipping over, so I bounded over to Dave to say hello without thinking. Unfortunately, I didn't realise the path I was on hadn't been sanded and my legs just went from under me. I was pushing twenty stone at the time, and when I put my hands down to break my fall I landed on them and felt something snap. I went pale, and Delphine and Dave rushed to help me.

'Stay still, Kingie,' Dave said, looking very worried.

'You might need to get to hospital,' Delphine added.

As soon as they started being kind like that, I began wailing in pain. It turned out I'd actually broken both my thumbs, and it was absolutely excruciating.

Dave was great, and once I was patched up he kept an eye on

me at work every day, making sure I was coping with the splints and bandages on my hands.

'I broke my thumbs once,' he said, trying to make me feel better.

'It's a bugger, isn't it?' I said. 'How did you manage, mucker? I can't imagine you'd be able to do make-up.'

'Oh, I was only six. I did it trying to launch myself in a plane I'd built, off a six-foot high wall in our backyard, but I launched myself instead.'

That made me laugh, which was a common occurrence when Dave was around. Other people were telling me to take a bit of time off, but Dave was cut from the same cloth as me and understood that I needed to carry on working despite the accident.

A few months on and Dave had got the £1,000 together to buy the Japanese bike from me. When he gave me the cash we shook hands on the deal – yes, I was out of plaster! – and he told me he was going to take Cheryl, a girl he was seeing, for a ride around the Scottish Highlands.

'So you're getting over your divorce alright, mate?' I smiled.

'Fabulously, Kingie, fabulously.'

Dave phoned me a few days later.

'Kingie, mate, the bike just ate itself.'

'What are you on about, dude?'

'The bike you sold me. It's a complete basket-case! It's fallen to bits, Cheryl's gone off in a cab and I'm stuck in the middle of bloody nowhere with this pile of crap. I want me money back!'

'Well, it's like this, Dave. I've kind of spent it, on shoes for the bairns, and the leccy bill . . . I could give you half back, for now?'

'Are you jokin'? You sound like a bleedin' Lindisfarne record!'

The exchange was surprisingly affable in the circumstances, and the upshot was that I borrowed a minibus and drove to Scotland to pick the knackered bike up and refund Dave £500, as that was all I had left of his cash. His two assistants from the make-up department, Nadia El-Saffar and Gillian Garner, heard the tale of woe and decided to come along for the ride, and a mate of mine called John also joined us.

Dave said we could all kip at his flat in Huntly, and once we'd sorted the bike out we ended up staying for what turned out to be a week of totally unplanned madness. I can't remember all of it. Dave's ex-wife had made a demijohn of peach schnapps that had obviously been kicking around his flat for a while, and I mistook it for pop and poured myself half a pint. After that it was all a bit of a blur, but I know I attempted to light my own farts, as there's a photograph of me caught in the act, sitting on Dave's sofa with my legs in the air.

Dave and I did a bit of cooking together for the first time that week, knocking up some ham and poached eggs for breakfast and flambéing bananas in Southern Comfort at one point.

'I'll do it . . .' he'd say.

'You're alright, mate, I'm happy to cook . . .'

In the end we'd just crack on together, and it was very easy, and very enjoyable.

We were well entrenched as mates by now. The bike drama was soon forgotten, and the pair of us went on to work on several more Cooksons together, including *The Moth*, *The Rag Nymph* and *The Wingless Bird*, with Dave always on make-up or hair and make-up, and me as a first or second assistant director, or location manager.

On *The Moth*, starring Jack Davenport, I was location manager, and it fell to me to find a large country house that we could use to recreate a dramatic scene in which the whole place is set on fire. After a lot of research and work on the ground, I managed to convince the owners of Eshott Hall in Northumberland to allow us to use their country mansion. Naturally, the deal was that we would make good any smoke damage and so on that would inevitably occur, and the owners, Ho and Margaret Sanderson, would be paid a fee in return for allowing us to take over their home for three weeks, and stunt up the fire.

'I can't believe I've pulled this off,' I said to the assistant location manager, Nicole Kavanagh, when we went to shake hands on the deal.

'Aye, you've done well, Si,' she said.

'I know. I've sweated on this one. It's no mean feat talking someone into letting you set off fires all over their house. And Margaret is worried sick about her wisteria . . .'

Nicole was a good friend and she knew how hard I'd grafted to get this signed up.

'What d'you want me to do?' she said as we reached the gravel drive.

'Just watch and learn, Nic. Let me do the talking. I can't have anything at all going wrong at this stage in the proceedings.'

'OK, Si, whatever you say.'

At that point Ho Sanderson arrived to greet us.

'Good morning!' I said in my best English gentleman's voice. 'How are you?'

'Terribly well, thank you.'

'Can I introduce you to my assistant, Nicole?'

'Good morning! Very pleased to meet you, Nicole.'

To my complete and utter horror, Nicole then chirped up with the immortal line: 'Hi Ho!' My heart sank, and to make matters worse she proceeded to collapse in a fit of giggles right in front of a noticeably less amused Ho Sanderson. Thankfully he still did the deal, but to this day I have not let Nic forget that story. We did both laugh about it afterwards, though, and I certainly forgave her; Nic is still a great mate today.

Dave soon became a regular visitor at our house. Alex and James, who were both at primary school by now, began to call him 'Uncle Dave', and in time Dave got to know not just Jane and the boys very well, but my mam and Jane's mam too, and other members of the extended family.

At Christmas in 1996 we had a big family get-together, with Dave bringing fresh seafood from Scotland for the starters, my mam cooking the turkey and Jane's mam making her trademark showstopper, a fantastic Snow Queen meringue. It was a hoot, and Dave and I found ourselves working around each other effortlessly in the kitchen again, raving about the fabulous fish and seafood you could get in Scotland and planning a fishing trip in the New Year.

'We'll catch some fish, build a fire and barbecue it,' we said. 'It'll be lush!'

That's exactly what we did, not just once but whenever we could snatch a couple of days off work together. Dave had got himself a new motorbike – not from me! – and we'd tear off around the Highlands, with me on whichever was the best of the bunch of bikes I had on the go at the time. We'd typically catch a couple of trout and cook ourselves up some supper, sometimes building ourselves a fire on the side of the river, sometimes going back to Dave's flat in Huntly.

Jane and the boys came along occasionally, in the school holidays, and we'd camp. I'd saved up for a big luxury tent for the family but Dave only had a little two-man job, which started leaking like a bastard when it began to chuck it down with rain one time. We were in the middle of nowhere in the Highlands, and I was laughing my head off when Dave got soaked wet through.

'It's not funny, Kingie, miserable git!' he huffed before packing up the tent and taking off on his bike.

'Alright, mate?' he said when he phoned later, sounding much brighter.

'Yes, Dave, all fine here. How are ya, mucker? What's that noise?'

'What, the bubbles? Oh, it's just the jacuzzi, Kingie. It's a lovely spa hotel I've found. How's the camping going?'

Dave started renting a flat at St Peter's Basin in Newcastle by the quayside, and for a short time he had a friend called Glen Howarth lodging with him, who was a script supervisor he'd made good mates with on one of the Cooksons, *The Tide of Life*.

'One of the directors is jealous,' Dave chuckled. 'He keeps saying: "I bet you two are cuddled up like spoons every night". Just as if!'

'What d'you mean, "just as if"? You're single, she's single. Don't you fancy her?'

'Course I do! She's spectacularly stunning and great fun, but she's also completely out of my league. I've got no chance, Kingie. I entice her out of her room at night with fine wine and good grub, but the closest I've got is to give her French manicures.'

Dave went on to tell me that Glen was an ex-model and ex-bunny girl who was divorced, had a flat in Hampstead and was sixteen years older than him. I knew her through work, and even though I would have loved to have seen them get together I had to admit Dave had a point: the two of them didn't make an obvious couple. Anyhow, great mates they were, and it was through Glen that Dave got his first break in films, as she gave him an introduction that led to him working on a movie called *Dad Savage*, with

Patrick Stewart, and then on to *I Want You* with a rising young star called Rachel Weisz. The work took him all around the country and he gave up the flat in Newcastle, though Huntly remained his bolthole.

'Are you alright, mate?' I'd ask frequently. Even though Dave had had a couple of girlfriends by now I worried about him being on his own, because it's not the way I would have wanted to live.

'I've got lovely friends, a motorbike, a fishing rod, and I can cook. I'm a pig in shit, Kingie!'

'Well, when you put it like that . . .'

Meanwhile, I was still on the Cooksons. I was an experienced location manager by now and I was grateful for the work every day. I was still putting in ridiculously long hours but I had to look on the bright side. I had more stability than I had ever had in my career, fairly regular money coming into the house and I'd managed to keep working in the North East, which was a big achievement. Also, as the boys got bigger and stayed up later it meant I was getting to see more of them than just lumps under the duvet.

One night Jane had arranged to go on a much-deserved night out with her friends, and I was in charge of Alex and James and was looking forward to cooking for them, as I always did whenever I had the chance.

'Dad, can you do us a wrap?' was a familiar cry at breakfast-time, because they adored the sausage-and-egg tortilla wraps I made.

I loved to see them enjoying the food I'd made, and on this occasion I'd got hold of eight live Northumberland lobsters from a mate of mine who had a fishing boat. It was perfect timing, as Jane was funny about seafood and always refused to cook it, but I was really looking forward to serving up a treat.

The lobsters were nippy buggers and I put them in the bath while I popped out to borrow a Baby Burco boiler from my brother Will, as I needed something that big to cook them in all at the same time. While I was out Jane came home to get ready for her night out. The shower was over the bath with the curtain pulled across, and Jane switched it on at the wall and waited for the water to be nice and hot before she stepped through the steam and into the bath without looking down.

'Argh! What the bloody hell?!!' was all I heard when I came in the front door moments later. How she hadn't noticed eight live lobsters had beaten her to the bathroom was unbelievable, but very funny indeed.

'Siiiiii! Can you come and take these bloody things out of here?'

I did, trying not to laugh as I apologised, and then the boys and I put on some tunes and had a lobster-race on the kitchen floor before we prepared our feast. It was a top evening, and the food was absolutely mouth-watering.

Dave was lobster-mad too, and during one of our Scottish adventures he managed to procure some fabulous specimens from the west coast, which we decided to take to a bikers' campsite that had a big bring-your-own BBQ. We couldn't wait to cook them, but as soon as we arrived we looked at each other in horror, knowing exactly what the other was thinking. All the other blokes had packs of economy burgers and plastic-looking buns, and it seemed to be a free-for-all with the food.

'I'm not sharing,' Dave said defensively, clutching the lobsters tight to his chest.

'Glad you said it first. Nor am I, mucker!'

We scuttled off into the woods like a couple of truanting schoolboys, built our own fire and cooked the lobsters to perfection.

'Shall we have a bit of salad?' Dave said, rummaging in his rucksack. 'Oooh, I've got a nice head of garlic here.'

'Oh aye. Look, I've got us some lovely butter, mate, and some belting tomatoes. Oh, while I remember, you know what I've got back home, that I'll cook next time you come?'

'What, Si?'

'Truffle!'

Whenever one of us got hold of something special we always wanted to share it, particularly with one another, as we both knew how much the other would appreciate it. We'd then get excited as we discussed all the lovely things we could make with it.

It had been like this with the lobsters, and by the time we'd cooked them on the fire with butter and garlic we were salivating. We enjoyed them immensely, and while we savoured every mouthful we babbled on about our respective bikes and pored over maps, planning where to ride and camp and fish the next day.

'Wouldn't it be great if we could live like this all the time,' Dave mused.

'Aye, wouldn't it just, mate. Wouldn't it just . . .'

'I'm serious. How great would life be if we could just ride bikes, cook food and talk bollocks?'

'Lush. It would be lush, mate. Dream on, eh!'

Dave invited me, Jane and the boys up to Huntly for New Year at the end of 1997, along with his glamorous former flatmate Glen, and Betsan Morris Evans, who had directed the Patrick Stewart film *Dad Savage* that Dave had worked on, and was also a mate of Glen's.

Betsan brought her husband and two young sons, and her family and mine checked in to a spectacular B & B called Springbank, while Glen stayed in Dave's spare room.

'There's nothing nefarious going on,' Dave said to me when I found out Glen had arrived several days before us.

'Why not, mate?'

'I've told you already. She's way, way out of my league.'

I think we all secretly wanted Dave and Glen to get together. Dave had recently split from the latest girlfriend he had, a bubbly, twenty-something Scot called Jenny, because he'd been working away a lot. He'd done a month filming a documentary in Costa Rica, and he told me that Jenny complained he never called.

'I was in the bloody rainforest, Kingie!' he laughed.

He'd also worked on a horror film with Jason Scott Lee, called *Tale of the Mummy*, which was filmed in Luxemburg in September 1997 and meant Dave spending his fortieth birthday out there alone.

'Didn't that bother you?' I asked. 'I'd hate that.'

'Nah. It was a mad, busy day. We were filming mummies going on the rampage in the toilets of a gay club. Everyone was knackered that night and I ended up wandering round a fairground with the wardrobe guy, Tiny Nicholls.'

'Did you tell him it was your birthday?'

'Nah. He's in his seventies. After the day we'd had I don't think he was up for any more excitement! I just had an early night and phoned Glen, actually, to tell her it was her fault I was in this situation.'

Dave was genuinely not bothered; he is an extremely self-sufficient, independent person, never short of mates or girlfriends, but when I heard that story I thought how great it would be if he could find what I had with Jane.

A few days before New Year's Eve all the friends and kids who were gathered in Huntly went for a fantastic Italian meal at Springbank, laid on by the owner Luigi who was a friend of

Dave's. It was a fabulous night; one of those evenings where the food is perfect and the atmosphere is buzzing along brilliantly, and everything feels right in the world.

I didn't know it until the next day, but Dave's night got even better, after we all said goodnight to him and Glen. The first I knew of it was when Betsan started crying with happiness the next morning, after she'd gone up to Dave's flat and discovered Glen's bed hadn't been slept in.

'I thought all me chickens had come home to roost,' Dave says now, recalling that night. 'I went to kiss Glen goodnight and kissed her on the lips. It was just unbelievable. We were already best mates, and after lots of teeth cleaning it all happened. I was like a dog with two doo-dahs, loved up to oblivion!'

I can vouch for that as an accurate description, and I can still picture Dave and Glen cuddled up together the next day, sitting in a big winged armchair in the flat, looking deliriously happy and completely and utterly loved up. Glen was over the moon and, rather frustratingly, she'd said to Dave: 'You took your time.'

'Arrgh! Why didn't I . . .' Dave started.

'Don't go there, mate!' I interrupted. 'Time to look forward, not back. Now just go and have a bloody ball!'

We were all on a massive high on New Year's Eve itself. I did a treasure hunt for the four boys, hiding sticks all around the streets of Huntly and then letting the lads beat the living daylights out of a piñata stuffed with sweets. It was a hoot, and then Dave and I set about making dinner for everyone, up at Dr Dave's country house. Someone had given Dave a leg of Gloucester Old Spot pork and we cooked it with five-spice powder to make Chinese crackling and did jasmine rice and a Thai green curry. It was awesome, and then we did our flambéed bananas, which had become a bit of a trademark dish of ours. The pair of us mucked about doing Keith Floyd impressions, slugging wine as we lashed Southern Comfort in the pan, caramelised a load of brown sugar and served the delicious bowls of loveliness up with big blobs of fresh cream.

'You two should be on the telly,' Betsan laughed.

'I was just thinking the same thing!' Glen said.

It was the best New Year *ever*. There was magic in the air, and 1998 looked set to be an absolute cracker.

13

Dave's

Chicken Zinger Burgers, Pizza Topped with Scampi and Veal Kidneys

Hallelujah! It was New Year's Day 1998 and I was on planet love. I'd never experienced such intense feelings before and I was absolutely besotted with Glen. We'd been close friends for a couple of years by the time we got together, and so there wasn't a gradual getting to know each other stage; we plunged headlong into a very deep and very passionate love affair. After the holiday I went down to stay at Glen's flat in Hampstead for a week because we didn't want to be apart, and I was so besotted I never wanted to ever be away from her again. There was no doubt in my mind: Glen was the woman I wanted to spend the rest of my life with. When we were together we laughed and had the most amazing time. It was like there was a glow around us, and everything felt just right, and wonderful. I still had to pinch myself that such a glamorous woman wanted to be with a bald and slightly paunchy northern git like me, but she did, and she made me feel special, and cherished. I couldn't get over it. Glen was blonde, slender and incredibly sophisticated, looking not unlike Joanna Lumley in *Absolutely Fabulous*.

'Was she drunk on New Year's Eve?' someone had joked, to which I could confidently reply, 'No, she was stone cold sober,' because Glen was off the pop that night, as unfortunately she was recovering from a stomach ulcer.

Glen had a school reunion to attend, and she took me with her, proudly introducing me to her friends.

'Jesus, Glenys, if you're an advert for HRT, sign me up!' one of her old classmates commented. I wasn't surprised to hear the compliment; Glen was glowing and looked a lot younger than her years. The age difference between us wasn't apparent at all. We were both divorced and neither of us had any kids, and there was nothing at all standing in our way.

When she took me up to Blackpool soon afterwards to meet her father, who was in his nineties, I decided to propose. Looking back, everything seemed to have happened ridiculously fast, but it didn't seem that way at the time. It felt like we'd been together for years, and I wanted us to be together for the rest of our lives.

We were staying in a hotel, and I nipped out and bought a ring and then got down on one knee. In hindsight I was pushing my luck, popping the question so soon, but everything felt so right. Glen hesitated for a split second and my heart nearly stopped, but then she said yes. It was a magical moment, one I'll never forget. I asked her dad for his permission, which he granted, and then me and Glen giggled like a couple of teenagers as we started to talk about when and where we would get married.

We went back to Hampstead and the next night we popped out to Waitrose on the Finchley Road to get a few bits, like you do. Everything was normal and Glen seemed her usual self, but as soon as we got back to her flat something very strange happened to her face. Glen's skin turned yellow, just as if a switch had been flicked. She commented that her stomach had been a bit sore and we both assumed this might have something to do with the ulcer she was still recovering from.

'I'm sure I'll be alright,' she said bravely, but she looked terrible. Her complexion was neon yellow now and she clearly wasn't right at all. We ended up at the doctors, and on 23 January, Glen's birthday, she was admitted to the Royal Free Hospital. From that point on everything went into free-fall, and it was bloody terrifying. There were scans and tests and nailbiting waits for results, and in the midst of a lot of panic and confusion I can remember hearing the words 'tumour' and 'stomach' and 'cancer'.

'She'll be alright, won't she, doctor?' I asked. 'We're getting married soon.'

I couldn't believe Glen was lying in a hospital bed within days of me proposing to her, or that I was having this conversation with a doctor. It was incomprehensible.

The doctor looked very grave as he explained to me that Glen was going to have a Wipple procedure, which is a major surgical operation. He said the tumour they had found in Glen's stomach had its own blood supply, and the surgery would remove part of the digestive system to bypass it. After that Glen would have chemotherapy to shrink the tumour, but only once she was strong enough to take it.

I'm not sure how much of what was happening Glen understood, because she was in so much pain by now she was heavily drugged up. She was very brave, though, going into theatre, and I told her I loved her and I would be waiting for her after the operation. I had every confidence it would be a success. It was unthinkable that there would be any other outcome, and thank

God, when Glen emerged several hours later, everything seemed to have gone well.

I slept on a camp-bed next to Glen's hospital bed while she was recovering from the surgery. She was tired and weak and still drugged up but I kept focusing on the positive. She'd jumped the first hurdle and it would only be a matter of time before the chemo would start. Then Glen would be on the home straight. That's what I was thinking, every waking hour.

Three days after the operation Glen's scar started to leak and she swelled up so much she looked nine months pregnant. The doctors explained she had an infection that needed draining, and my heart sank as I was told she was going to be moved to the intensive care unit, and that I would have to wait a while before I could see her.

'Have you ever been in an IT unit before?' a nurse asked when I was finally allowed in.

'No,' I said.

'Be warned: you may be shocked. She's in an induced coma.'

I *was* shocked. Glen, my fabulous, vibrant wife-to-be, was lying there with her mouth open, on a ventilator and rigged up to all kinds of tubes and drips and beeping machines. I couldn't credit what I was seeing, but even then, just as I had done with my mam and my dad, I thought Glen would go on forever.

I slept at the hospital nearly every night, living on Chicken Zinger burgers from the local KFC. Glen's family were amazing, and she had this huge infrastructure of friends and colleagues who all turned up with flowers and scented candles.

Si came down to support me, for which I was very grateful. He started crying when he saw Glen, because he's an emotional so-and-so like that, and he was with me when I plucked up the courage to ask the consultant what Glen's prognosis was.

'There's a fifteen per cent chance of her living,' the consultant said flatly.

This was the first time I had considered she might die, though I still didn't really believe it would happen. Si and I went back to Glen's flat that night and balled our eyes out together, telling each other she'd pull through. Of course she'd pull through; she couldn't not.

After three weeks Glen came out of the coma and seemed to be doing alright, though she was nowhere near strong enough for the chemo she needed.

'I'm not afraid of dying,' she whispered, which was very upsetting. Nobody had discussed the survival percentages with Glen and she never asked, thank God, but she obviously knew how sick she was.

After several more weeks of camping out at the hospital with Glen I was allowed to take her home, with instructions that if her temperature rose I was to bring her straight back in. This gave me a lot of hope. Fifteen per cent or not, they wouldn't let her out of hospital if she really was dying, would they?

I tried my best to give Glen some sort of normality back at her flat. One night we watched *Brassed Off* with Pete Postlethwaite, which was a depressingly poor choice in hindsight, and I'd try and tempt her with good, delicate food like baked cod and fresh salads, but she had very little appetite.

After a week Glen's temperature shot up and she was rushed back to hospital. She was placed straight in intensive care again, and then it was like a cheesy fade in a film. It's the only way I can describe it. Glen's system was shutting down and she was slipping further and further away, fading before my eyes.

Someone suggested we could have a 'deathbed marriage', which I saw as being wholly insensitive.

'What would I want one of them for?' I said, still clinging desperately to the hope she'd pull through.

There was a female doctor on duty that weekend, and her ears pricked up.

'You have been told all this care is palliative, haven't you?' she barked.

'What?' I stuttered.

There were several nurses around the bed and they all looked at their feet. That's when the penny finally dropped. Glen was not going to beat her cancer. It was no longer a matter of *if* she would survive, but of how long she had left.

I phoned Si in a hell of a state but his phone went straight to voicemail. When he eventually called me back and I told him the news, I heard him gasp and cry down the phone.

'You know I'd be straight back down to London if I could, Dave,' he said. 'But I'm in hospital myself at the minute, as it happens.'

'Oh, I see. Bloody hell, mate, what's up?'

'Don't worry, mucker. Nothing serious. I just had an argument with a horsebox.'

Though Si made light of it on the phone, he had actually had a very nasty accident on the set of *Colour Blind*, another Catherine Cookson. I got the full story later. He had arrived on location at a country house and discovered a horsebox blocking the area where he had arranged to park several vehicles. As he started re-organising all the vehicles he accidentally stepped in a hole in the ground, and his legs went from under him.

'Sparrow's ankles,' I said, as he told the story, as it was a phrase I'd heard him use several times before to describe his ankles.

'Aye, Dave, the curse of the King sparrow's ankles struck again. As me ankles went over I fell onto the rusty mudguard of this twin-wheel-based horsebox. I got me elbow caught between the two wheels, and then I followed through and fell onto the tarmac, and my arm kind of all exploded. When I tried to get meself up it was like me arm was made of jelly. And it hurt. A lot.'

'So you broke your arm, not your sparrow's ankles?'

'Aye. I did. Spectacularly so.'

Si had been rushed to the nearest medical centre, which was Hexham sheep hospital, where they found he had a spiral fracture all the way from his elbow to his shoulder. He had fifteen breaks in total and he'd been pinned back together with a truck-load of metal and was now on heavy-duty painkillers, waiting to have a large plaster cast put on. You really couldn't make it up.

Glen was drifting in and out of consciousness on bigger doses of morphine by now, and I had to face the truth. I was going to lose her, and it was going to happen quite soon.

She clung on for a few more weeks, getting weaker by the hour, and one night I sat beside her bed with the hospital chaplain, who was a really kind man.

'How will I know she's dead?' I asked.

There was a nurse in the room who turned and gave me a gentle smile. 'You'll know,' she said.

The next night, on 9 May, I was sitting beside Glen when I felt a kind of veil waft across her, and I knew. The nurses left me on my own with her for a while, which I found a very weird experience. Glen was there, but she wasn't. I eventually made some phone calls, letting people know what had happened, and I couldn't quite compute that I was telling them Glen was dead when she was still lying beside me.

The funeral was horrific. I just wanted the day to end, and I retreated to Huntly as quickly as possible afterwards, to lock my door and lick my wounds.

I'd been due to start work on the film *Wing Commander* with Saffron Burrows, which would have been one of the biggest things I'd ever done, but I'd pulled out when Glen got ill. I didn't feel able to take on anything else yet, and for a while I just existed in my little bolthole in Huntly, trying to get my head round what the hell had just happened. I'd been three months on a camp-bed watching Glen die, and now the *Brookside* omnibus had become the highlight of my week. It was terrible. I'd imagined a lifetime of happiness with Glen, and it had been snatched away in the blink of an eye. It was bloody cruel, that's what it was. She didn't deserve it.

Si was in regular contact, checking I was alright, and he suggested we should have a holiday together when the boys were off school in the summer. I readily agreed. We all needed a break, but unfortunately before we set off Si had another break – the kind he really didn't want. His sling snapped and his arm shattered all over again, landing him back in plaster for several more months.

We went ahead with the holiday nevertheless, and I'm very glad we did. Si and Jane brought the lads up to Scotland and we had a really good time, camping and having barbecues and just chilling. We made home-made pizza with scampi on top and Si did some fabulous belly pork. The pizza wasn't brilliant, to be fair, as the scampi went a bit mushy, but Si's boys did what we always did with each other when something didn't go quite right, and just took the mickey.

'Oi! You're as bad as your dad!' I said, pretending to be offended. 'I've worked me fingers to the bone making these pizzas and all you can do is mock and call them mushy!'

'Sorry, Uncle Dave,' they choroused, polite as ever.

One day James, who was seven at the time, asked me where I got my barbecue set.

'It was Glen's actually.'

'Cheers, Glen,' James said, looking up to the sky.

Another day Si and I had a rare argument, about how to make couscous. Si wanted to do it with milk and I insisted it was made with either stock or water. We both got very animated, convinced we were right, and Alex and James stood looking at us, perplexed to see two grown men arguing about couscous. In the end, James stepped forward.

'They're both equally good, but in their own way,' he said calmly, which shut us up.

In the evenings Si and I would sit around chewing the cud and dreaming of another life, one in which we could do stuff like this more often and not have to slave away in our day jobs. Between drinking bottles of beer and eating steaks and seafood we'd throw around various ideas, as we had done for a while now. Farming lobster was one of our more hare-brained schemes. Going into antiques together was another, and we seriously discussed opening a business delivering sushi to offices at lunchtime. We both love sushi and this idea was our favourite; the only trouble was we later found out a proper sushi chef course cost £5,000 as you had to do it in LA, so it wasn't a goer as we couldn't afford that kind of money.

Si was now working as location manager on the drama series *Badger*, starring Jerome Flynn, and I went back to work in September, taking jobs on another couple of films nobody has ever heard of, that were being shot in Luxembourg. The first was *The Point Men* and the second was *Fortress 2*, both starring Christopher Lambert.

I was driving a white Vauxhall Frontera by now, which Si called my 'kebab man's car' and I drove it to Luxembourg so I could get around while I was there. On my days off I liked to go to Metz as it was an easy drive into France. I'd treat myself to foie gras or veal kidneys in a lovely little restaurant, and I'd sit admiring the Chagall stained-glass windows of the cathedral. Sometimes I'd take other people with me; once it was Willie Garson, who went on to do *Sex and the City,* and another time it was the movie star Andrew McCarthy. I'd always make sure I had some time on my own in the cathedral because I'd go into the crypt and light a candle for Mam, Dad and Glen. I wanted to show I hadn't forgotten any of them and it always made me count my blessings, and feel lucky to be here. However, I felt lethargic and terribly run down the whole time I was in Luxembourg. I didn't think much of it at the time, putting it down to the fact I'd had such a rough year and was just getting back into work. I'd return to my hotel and have the odd beer in the evening, but that only made me feel worse. I'd started to feel like there was a cord pulling inside my head, which was really weird.

One particular day I felt really wretched when I was in the cathedral, so much so that I had a sense of impending doom that I simply couldn't ignore. It was so powerful I did something I've never done before or since: I looked up to the sky. 'I need help from somewhere,' I said in my head. 'Please, whatever's going to happen to me, please sort it out.'

It probably sounds ridiculously dramatic and it's really not my style, but it honestly felt like a die had been cast that day. I chilled instantly, because I knew I'd set something in motion.

Two days later I was at work, making up the beautiful American actress Pam Grier for *Fortress 2,* when something very odd happened. It was as if the make-up I was applying was sliding off her face. Then I couldn't focus and had black dots floating in front of my eyes.

'I need to see a doctor,' I said to the sound recordist.

'Can you drive?' he asked.

'No,' I said. 'Absolutely not. I can't even remember how I got to work today. I need a driver; I think my computer's completely crashed.'

I was taken to a nearby hospital run by German nuns, and they were very hard and no-nonsense.

'It's probably a trapped nerve in your neck,' one of them said, but then a doctor started talking about viral meningitis and ordering a CT scan, for which I was very grateful. This was more than a trapped nerve; I could sense it.

When the scan picture eventually appeared, which felt like an age later, I caught a brief glimpse of it and was shocked to my core. There was a massive shadow, the size of a King Edward potato, in the left-hand side of my brain. I'd been looking at pictures like this for three months with Glen, and I was instantly filled with terror. To make matters worse, the cold nurses started being really kind to me. That's when I knew I was in trouble, but nobody was telling me exactly what was wrong, not yet.

I had a headache from Mars and I was put in a double room with a Belgian farmer who snored like a bastard. The nurses gave me two balls of cotton wool for my ears and told me to rest, but I couldn't sleep. Panic and depression filled me; I was convinced I had a giant brain tumour that was incurable, and that I was going to die, just like Glen.

The next day I was taken to see a consultant, terrified of what he was going to tell me.

'It's a brain tumour, isn't it?' I blurted out.

'No, actually. It's not.'

'Then why have I got a potato-sized lump in my head?'

He explained it was an extremely large but relatively harmless cyst, known as an arachnoid cyst. It was so big my brain had grown around it, and he supposed it had been there for a long time, possibly since I was a child. Now it had reached the size where it was putting pressure on my brain, hence the black spots in front of my eyes and Pam Grier's make-up sliding off her face.

The treatment the consultant suggested was called a 'craniotomy', which means they basically take your lid off to relieve the pressure caused by the cyst. He explained there were risks involved, as the pressure is released very quickly when your skull is cut open, which can lead to 'complications'.

As soon as I heard that I decided I wanted to go home, get a second opinion and be treated in the UK. If the Luxembourg consultant was right the cyst had been kicking around for donkey's years and I didn't need an emergency operation, so waiting a few more days wasn't going to make any difference.

The following morning one of the unit drivers from the film-set drove me back to Huntly in my kebab man's car, where Dr Dave got me admitted to the Aberdeen Royal Infirmary. I felt like a condemned man despite the diagnosis being much less scary than I'd first feared, and I was desperately hoping the second opinion would give me a better alternative to being opened up like a pressure cooker; I'd seen what happened to Mam's mushy peas when the seal was broken, and I didn't want my brains splattered on the ceiling.

There *was* a better option, thank God. I was seen by a wonderful Irish neurosurgeon called George Kaar who suggested inserting a shunt into my head, to relieve the pressure slowly, plus drains to remove the fluid gradually from the cyst. I'd still need to have a disc-shaped section of my skull sawn out and then put back in, but it seemed like a much less risky operation than letting all the pressure escape at its own speed. I agreed to go for it.

It was explained to me that I would have a general anaesthetic but they'd need to bring me round to talk to me halfway through, to make sure things were working, and I would have to sit very still throughout the operation, with my head in a clamp. I couldn't be given any pain relief either, except for some mild paracetamol, as anything stronger might interfere with my brain.

'Your brain will be open to the world, so don't move,' I was instructed.

'I'll do my best.'

The anaesthetic knocked me out for what felt like a very short time, and when I woke up I felt euphoric.

'Where are you?' a voice asked.

'In Spain!'

'You're kidding?'

'Course I am! I'm in the Aberdeen Royal Infirmary, my name is David Myers and I feel great!'

Dr Dave was there when the surgery was over. It appeared to have been a success. I had to lie completely flat afterwards, and then my bed was gradually raised over the next twenty-four hours, just one inch at a time, so that the pressure in my head was released slowly.

I must have looked quite a sight with my head all wrapped in bandages, but I felt really good, better than I had in a long time. I'd suffered from headaches and migraines for years but I'd just put up with them, as you do. Now I felt incredibly clear-headed, like a weight had been lifted. The shunts and drains fitted to take the fluid off the cyst were left inside, which took a bit of getting used to, but they never gave me any trouble. They are still there to this day, and if you touch the surface of my skin you can feel them running down the side of my head and neck before they travel down into my body just above my sternum.

I went home after just five days, and it was Christmas Eve. Dr

Dave and his wife Jane brought me lovely food and invited me round for Christmas, but their middle daughter had a new set of drums so I didn't stay long. It wasn't fair on anyone really – who wants a poorly friend spoiling their family Christmas? I was happy just to be back in my flat, alone but alive. I felt so much better than I had done for a long, long time. Apart from the fact I went completely deaf on Boxing Day, which freaked me out, I could generally feel myself getting better every day, and my energy levels soared.

On New Year's Eve I inevitably thought of Glen. It was desperate compared to the previous year, and what had happened within the space of twelve months was absolutely unbelievable.

'You couldn't have written this crap in *Brookside*,' I said to Si when we spoke on the phone.

Thankfully, after a very tricky six months or so, he was finally out of plaster, and as we wished each other happy New Year we both agreed that we deserved better luck in 1999. We were quietly optimistic; it could hardly get any worse, could it?

Unbelievably, after more than thirty years of suffering from alopecia and having spent the last twenty years shaving my head, my hair started to grow back normally, albeit with a receding hairline. Looking back, the most problematic patch of hair had always been directly above where my cyst was. To this day no doctor will admit to me that my alopecia was caused by the cyst, but I'm absolutely convinced it was. In time my hair grew back thick and long, and while all my forty-something mates were complaining of middle-aged baldness, I ended up with a better head of hair than I'd had all my life. It was bloody fantastic, and I loved not having to shave my head any more.

As soon as I was well enough Si phoned me up to organise a get-together, as he thought it would do me good. I ended up going down to Newcastle, and one day we passed the local Harley Davidson dealer, Just Harleys, on our travels. Si and I both looked at each other.

'Shall we?' we giggled mischievously.

We asked if we could go for a test drive, and to our surprise we were immediately given two gleaming Harleys.

We were both smitten by the bikes, and even though we really couldn't afford them, we ended up buying one each on hire purchase. I got a Heritage Springer Softail and Si had a Springer Softail that had a bit of a chopper vibe.

'Jane's gonna kill me!' Si said, but actually she was brilliant about it. She'd just lined herself up a new job as a carer after years of staying home with the kids, and she felt pleased that she was bringing in some money, and that Si had got a treat like this after all the hard work he'd put in over the years.

Soon after that me and Si went off on a fishing trip on the new bikes, heading north to Inverness then via Ullapool to Loch Assynt, and on to Cape Wrath – the north-western-most tip of Britain – and up towards to Loch Drumbeg. It was an epic trip. Si had no windscreen on his bike and so I deliberately rode through cowpats when I was in front, hoping he'd catch one in the kisser. On the open road his Harley vibrated so much the lenses were shaken out of his glasses. He only had his sunglasses as back-up, and so we couldn't ride anywhere in the dark.

One day we caught so much trout we ended up swapping some for shepherd's pie in a local hostelry, which was lush. The next morning I woke up to a snorting sound and looked out of the window of our B & B to see a right kerfuffle going on.

'Kingie! A Highland cow's trying to mount me Harley!' I cried.

'Eee you're right, man! I think it's the fringed leather saddle-bags that have confused it!'

We ran outside in our underpants and had quite a task un-coupling the randy beast from the £13K bulk of chrome, steel and new leather. All three of us must have been a sight for sore eyes.

It rained a lot on our trip, and when we eventually got back to Si's house, many hundreds of miles later, we stank of leather and wet fish.

'Bathroom!' Jane ordered when she saw, and smelt, her drip-ping wet husband.

That night Jane went up to bed early, leaving me and Si to have one too many drinks.

'Oh God, I was meant to get the dog clipped!' Si said when the family pet appeared in the living room.

Jane was due to start her new job the next morning, and in an effort to be a supportive husband Si decided he wanted to give Meg the haircut she needed. Meg was a Lakeland terrier and I was sure this was a job for a professional groomer, but Si insisted I should get my clippers from my Frontera, which I'd parked on his drive while we were away. I had about £25K's worth of hair and make-up gear stored in it, and in my inebriated state I thought it was rude not to assist Si.

Between the two of us we gave poor Meg a flat top and shaved her arse bare with a beard trimmer before she went completely berserk and wouldn't let us anywhere near her.

'Oh well, let's get ourselves to kip,' Si shrugged. 'We'll finish the job in the morning.'

At that point we heard a commotion in the drive and both ran outside to investigate. To our dismay we discovered that my car, and my £25K's worth of make-up and supplies, had just been nicked. I'd built up a fantastic collection of cosmetics, false mous-taches, sideboards and hairpieces, and I was more gutted about losing those than my car. I called the police in a flap, asking them to come quick, as we must have only just missed the thieves.

Two officers in stab jackets turned up ten minutes later to find Si and I slightly the worse for wear, dressed in pyjama bottoms and T-shirts, and me about to come out with a line they really didn't expect to hear.

'I've had all me make-up nicked, officer!' I wailed.

The policemen were lost for words, and at that precise moment the half-shaven dog walked in, flummoxing them even more.

'I can explain, officer . . .' Si started.

A stony-faced Jane then appeared, just to add to our woes.

'I don't want to know!' she said, eying Meg reproachfully before turning on her heel, leaving us to deal with the mess.

Thankfully, my make-up was found dumped on a driveway the next day, though I never did get my kebab man's car back. As for Si and Jane, they patched things up, of course. Jane was incredibly tolerant of Si's mad moments, and they never fell out for long. In fact, it wasn't too long after this that they had some amazing news to announce: Jane was expecting another baby. It was surprising but wonderful news, and I was thrilled to bits for them.

14

Si's

Tinned Tuna Penne, Aberdeen Angus Steaks and Morecambe Bay Cockles

The turn of the century was particularly significant for me and Jane, as our third son arrived on 17 April 2000. We called him Dylan because he literally arrived on a wave after Jane's waters broke dramatically, and his name means 'son of the wave'.

'He's a bald surfer!' I said to Jane as I wiped away my tears. It was incredible to have three sons. Alex and James were now coming up for ten and eight, and we were all besotted with the new addition to the family.

We had a great caravan holiday when Dylan was just three months old, going up to Arran with all the boys plus Dave and a girl he was seeing called Lindy, who got on really well with Jane. I remember we all went out for a pub meal one night, and James was offered the children's menu.

'No, thank you,' he told the waitress politely. 'I'd like the asparagus off the main menu for starters, with some hollandaise sauce, if you have it?'

We'd brought the boys up to appreciate good food. I can remember Dave commenting that it was always such a pleasure to eat out with Alex and James, and I felt really proud. That exchange exemplifies the holiday, actually. There was a lovely, warm feeling in the air, we were all comfortable in each other's company and Dave was now such a close mate he was like one of the family. Jane and I asked Dave to be Dylan's godfather when the time came, and of course he was as pleased as punch. I think we all felt we were in a good place in the new millennium.

There seemed to be good karma in the air back at work, too, or perhaps my guardian angel was looking out for me once again. I took a phone call from a bloke called Keith Hatcher one day, and he told me he was the location manager for the upcoming Harry Potter films, which would be shot partly in the North East.

'I'd very much like to talk to you,' he said. 'Can we meet?'

'Certainly,' I said, my ears pricking up and a smile spreading across my face. I knew the Harry Potter books were incredibly successful, and I knew the films were not just eagerly anticipated, but expected to be Hollywood blockbusters. I'd wanted to work in feature films for a long time. In the past I'd done a bit of location scouting for a few big films, including *Saving Private Ryan*, *King Arthur* and *Batman Returns,* but I'd never been hired as crew before. To work on a Harry Potter film was the crème de la crème; I was incredibly excited even to be in the frame.

Keith came up from London and explained that he'd heard I had a great reputation and was very well connected in the North East. He then asked if I would consider working as an assistant location manager on the first film, *Harry Potter and the Philosopher's Stone.*

'Yes, obviously,' I said, stunned and flattered.

I couldn't quite believe what I was hearing. It was remarkable, and I felt like an incredibly lucky human being. I'd worked bloody hard for this break, mind you, but I still felt blessed and very grateful. Inevitably, I was terrified once I'd signed on the dotted line. The glitterati of the film industry were involved in this production. It read like a *Who's Who*; there was Roy Button, head of Warner Bros. Europe; the executive producer was Duncan Henderson, who'd done *Dead Poets Society* among many other smash hits, and the producer and assistant director was Mark Radcliffe, who'd made mega movies like *Home Alone* and *Mrs Doubtfire*.

I had an immediate sense that I was plying my trade on a massive scale. On my first day on set I had five walkie-talkies hanging off my belt as soon as I arrived, and I remember taking a deep breath and giving myself a talking to.

'It's just the same as working on the Cooksons; it's just a different environment, and bigger.'

I'd said the same when I started on the Cooksons, telling myself it was just like *Byker Grove*. That mentality worked, and I hoped it would again. The crew on *Harry Potter* was bigger than I could have imagined, though, and there was a feeling of mayhem in the air every day. I'd catch the occasional glimpse of Richard Harris or Dame Maggie Smith and just think, 'This is mental!'

Alnwick Castle in Northumberland was used as the location for Hogwarts back then, but before filming began I realised we had a problem, as it was close to RAF Boulmer and there was a lot of low-flying aircraft using the air space above it.

'How do I put a no-fly zone over Alnwick Castle, and within a five-mile radius of the grounds?' I asked an old contact of mine, Squadron Leader Henry Pottle, who was based at RAF Boulmer.

Henry had helped me out on various jobs in the past and was particularly brilliant at providing weather reports that were uncannily spot-on.

'Oh,' he said, sounding uncharacteristically hesitant. 'Mmm. That's MOD territory. I'm afraid you're going to have to approach the Home Office.'

Phoning someone I didn't know in the Home Office with this request did not sound like it was going to work out, but I gave it a go, blurting out my request quickly in the vain hope it wouldn't sound so absurd if I said it fast.

'I know it's near an RAF base, but can I have a no-fly zone above Alnwick Castle? We're making a Harry Potter film, see, and we can't film with the low-flying aircraft above . . .'

'Ridiculous!' the cut-glass voice replied on the other end of the phone.

'No! Please let me explain more. Can I come and see you? It's really, really important.'

In the end I was reluctantly granted permission to meet with the appropriate powers that be at the MOD and Home Office, and unbelievably my ambitious request was rubber-stamped.

'Thanks for your help,' I said to Henry afterwards.

'You're welcome, but I didn't really do anything!' he replied, though to this day I'm convinced he must have had a word behind the scenes to help me out.

Another 'you couldn't make it up' request soon had to be made, this time to Newcastle City Council, as I needed to find a safe location to store the animals that would appear in Professor McGonagall's classroom. I was much more comfortable with this one, as I was on home turf.

'Hello! I need permission to keep a zoo in a warehouse in the city,' I said breezily, as if it was the type of request I put in to the council every day.

'What kind of a zoo?'

'Well, quite a varied kind.'

'What sort of animals are we talking about?'

'Let me see . . . horses, snakes, reptiles, bats, moles, cats, dogs, butterflies . . . oh, and a baboon.'

After much form-filling and explanation – during which I omitted to mention that the baboon was very bad-tempered and dangerous – we got permission. The next challenge was transporting the huge red-bummed baboon safely to Durham Cathedral, as one of the rooms off the cloisters there was used as Professor McGonagall's classroom.

'Chris to Si,' I heard on my walkie-talkie. 'Can we lock the cloisters down now, mate, we're gonna bring the baboon in.'

It was the assistant director, Chris Carreras, and as I said 'yes' I was thinking: 'This has got to go to number one on the list of things you don't expect to hear on a walkie-talkie.' The fact Durham Cathedral is a UNESCO World Heritage Site and the baboon was a real badass just added to the absurdity of the situation.

On set I'd occasionally nod and say hello to Daniel Radcliffe and Emma Watson if they happened to walk past me. My boys enjoyed hearing glamorous-sounding stuff like that, but the reality was I was just one of four hundred crew members and, however feted they were, actors like Daniel and Emma were just normal, polite kids, doing jobs that are extraordinary to most people. Nevertheless, there was a tremendous amount of kudos attached to working on the Potters, and it was a buzz to be able to say I was a part of it.

After *Harry Potter and the Philosopher's Stone* the locations team completely changed and I was the only one kept on for the second film, *Harry Potter and the Chamber of Secrets*. Not only that, I was promoted to location manager, which was a great vote of confidence and put another feather in my cap. I was less nervous

Right: Newly born in the arms of a true professional, 1966.

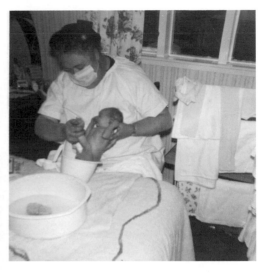

Left: Me and one tired-looking Mam. I miss her every day.

Above: Dad in the back in the hat on the *Benjamin Tay*, one of his favourite ships. Mam used to love when he would bring back spices from his travels.

Left: Here I am in 1969, aged 3, doing the water collection at the caravan near Bamburgh – our family's spiritual home.

Right: Me with Auntie Hilda and Uncle George, who were my sanctuary when Dad was ill. I miss them to this day.

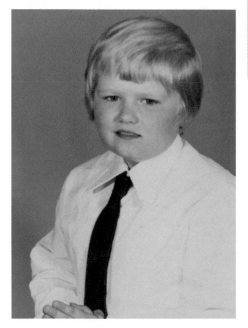

Left: My First Holy Communion portrait from St Joseph's Church, Birtley, County Durham. Mam was so proud.

Right: 1972, aged 6, and in Central London with Dad. I got fleas from that bloody parrot!

Left: A slimmer me and a new haircut to start Big School, aged 12.

Left: 1986, pouting *and* playing the drums. I knew I'd go far!

Right: One of the many bikes I fixed to supplement the family coffers, 1989.

THIS IS MY XS 750 CANNY IS'NT IT!?

Right: Jane and me at the birth of our son, Als, on 27 September 1989. Two happy but terrified 22 year olds with a baby!

Below: Alex playing in the family swimming pool at Derwentwater Caravan Park, 1990.

Right: Striking a 1990s pose on a chopper and living the dream.

Left: In 1993 I turned up in Scotland at Dave's flat, with two make-up artists who worked with us on the Catherine Cookson set. We ended up staying for a week. Mad party. See page 151 for the full details!

Left: James and me in the Gironde, 1994. Still our very favourite place in the world.

Right: Our three boys. Where does the time go?

Right: Dylan's favourite seat, 2003.

Above: What a proud day. So happy I could talk about my best mate
at his wedding, 2011.

Above: 'So you think so do ya?!'
Travelling and eating our way around
the world – can it get any better?

Above: 2013, just when we thought there
was nothing left to do – here I am doing
the tango on tour.

second time around and I loved the buzz on the set from day one. To be on my second film filled me with hope about the future. In terms of prestige I'd taken another big step up the career ladder, and I didn't want this to stop. The Cooksons had finished their run by now, with *A Dinner of Herbs* being the last one. They had been fabulous productions to work on while they lasted, keeping me going for the best part of six years, but now it was time to push on with films. That's what I wanted above all else.

One evening I invited eight of my colleagues and bosses for dinner.

'What time are they coming?' Jane asked a few days before. As usual she wanted to be well prepared, and she knew that the dinner was important to me in terms of networking, and was happy to support me as much as she could.

'Half past eight.'

'Great. What time are you in from work?'

'Seven, hopefully.'

'OK, I'll prep the food and decorate the table and get the kids ready for bed. What did you have in mind for food?'

I'd really thought about this, and Jane didn't flinch when I rattled off my list, as she was well used to the way I cooked for a special occasion.

'Oysters and prawns to start. Then chicken breast stuffed with pine nuts, rocket, basil and sun-dried tomatoes, and wrapped in streaky bacon. I'll mix the cooking juices with Madeira wine and lemon zest and reduce it down to a glaze and serve that over the top. New potatoes and a lovely big salad to go with it.'

'Sounds great, Si!' she said, and it was; the food went down very well and we all had a thoroughly good evening.

It was generally quite tough on Jane when I was on the Potters because I was working longer hours than ever and she now had Dylan to care for too, but she understood what I had to do, and she appreciated I was doing my best for the family. She was bloody brilliant, in fact

'You're like a tigress around your children,' I'd often say, which is how she'd been from the minute she became a mam. Jane would do anything for the boys. Nothing was ever too much trouble, and I felt very lucky to have such a supportive partner. I was thirty-four years old, and I was doing more than alright.

Dave was doing well too.

'We've made it into the movies!' we'd laugh.

'Yeh. When are we going to be masters of our own destinies, though? When are we gonna make our fortunes?'

We were still kicking around ideas, but everything we came up with was too risky or just didn't work. After the lobster and sushi ideas were dismissed we started thinking about using our experience in the TV industry to sell a programme on extreme fishing. It would mean the two of us being on the other side of the camera, which quite appealed, but the format we devised just wasn't strong enough. Still, we consoled ourselves with the fact that at least our day jobs weren't boring.

I can remember Dave laughing his head off after he came back from filming *The Piano Player* in South Africa with Dennis Hopper, who was playing a crazed crook. Dave told me Dennis Hopper arrived with a fabulous haircut befitting of a Hollywood star but immediately ordered Dave to shave all of his hair off, because he thought it would suit his character to wear a bad toupee.

'I was crapping myself, Kingie! I tried to run all this past the producers first, but Dennis insisted he wanted to surprise them. I couldn't argue with Dennis Hopper, could I?'

The bosses were gobsmacked and then things got worse for

Dave, as during filming Dennis took it upon himself to throw the toupee in a campfire, as a way of depicting his character's liberation.

'As he chucked it I realised we were filming out of sequence, and we only had the one toupee. "Catch the flamin' toupee!" I screamed!'

Still, to this day Dave says Dennis Hopper was one of the best actors he's ever worked with. Roger Moore is another favourite, after they worked together on a film called *The Enemy* and Roger cracked a new joke every morning, setting everyone in a good mood for the day.

Rubbing shoulders with stars was all in a day's work for both of us and we appreciated that we worked in an exciting industry, and were lucky to do so. It was just incredibly frustrating for Dave and I that we didn't have better pay and job security after all these years of hard graft.

I'd finished the two Potter films and for the time being I was doing some commercials for Coke and Nissan, but what I was really banking on was getting more big movie work. Alex, James and Dyl had gone to the première of the first Potter film in the cinema at Alnwick Castle and had been very proud to see my name on the credits. I desperately wanted to bag another blockbuster and keep doing my kids proud, but it was 2001 now, and I knew that after the terrible tragedy that was 9/11 American film budgets would be cut. Hollywood wouldn't want to film in the North East because it was more expensive than staying on home turf. If I wanted to carry on working in films I would either have to move away, which I wasn't prepared to do, or I'd have to take several steps backwards and work on low-budget projects, as that was going to be all that was available to me in Newcastle. My work dried up very quickly, and not just the film work but absolutely everything. Production budgets were being slashed left, right and centre. When I'd finished the commercials I was working on, I had no choice but to go back to *Byker Grove*. It had always been my lifebelt when I had no other work, but eventually they didn't want me either, which was really bloody petrifying.

'What am I going to tell Janey?' I panicked to Dave down the phone. 'I'm unemployed!'

'Mate, something will come up,' Dave said. 'It always does. You're a doer. You'll make it happen.'

In hindsight I think Dave had become quite philosophical since losing Glen and having his brain operation. He knew that what mattered more than anything was that me, Jane and the boys had our health, and we had each other. A shortage of money was serious, but it was something that could be sorted. In his mind I'd managed to earn a crust for all these years, I still had fire in my belly and I would turn things around.

'It'll just take time,' Dave said. 'But you'll get there.'

He was right, of course, but time was not a luxury I could afford right now, because I didn't have any slack in the system at all. Jane and I had no savings and a big mortgage to pay every month, and in a frighteningly short space of time I was putting everything on credit cards, maxing them all out. We didn't have two pennies to rub together. We lived as frugally as we possibly could, and I can remember buying big catering packs of pasta to feed the family.

'What pasta are we having tonight?' the lads would ask and I'd rifle through the cupboards and knock up whatever I could with the ingredients we had.

Tinned tuna penne was often on the menu, and I'd chuck in a tin of sweetcorn and a bit of garlic and onion, or whatever else I could find to add flavour.

'This is lush!' the lads always said, whatever concoctions I gave them, and I thanked my lucky stars that Mam had taught me how to cook on a low budget.

Unfortunately, whatever cut-backs Jane and I made, we still didn't have enough money to go round. The next step was to take a six-month sabbatical on the mortgage, which we did very reluctantly, as it felt like such a desperate measure. We'd been in the house for about seven years by now; losing it was unthinkable.

I can remember Dave phoning me one day when he was on his way down from Scotland to visit us.

'D'you want me to bring you anything, Kingie?' he asked.

'Meat!' I said.

He turned up later with the biggest Aberdeen Angus steaks I'd ever seen, and the kids went wild. Even now they still talk about the time Uncle Dave arrived with 'protein'; it was the highlight of what turned out to be a very grim eight months.

After the mortgage sabbatical ended the banks started to foreclose on me. That was one of the worst days of my life, and not long after that I knew I had to sell the house, because otherwise it was only a matter of time before Brettenby Gardens would be repossessed.

The boys were great and so was Jane. They all took it in their stride remarkably well, but I really did feel I'd let them all down. It hurt like hell packing up and leaving the family home we'd worked so hard for and loved so much, but we had no choice. I was £20,000 in debt even after the house sale, and after staying with our Ginny for a while we eventually moved into a smaller house on an estate. I hated it with a passion, but funnily enough the kids quite liked it.

'It's brilliant!' Dylan told Dave, which put a tear in my eye. 'It's better than your house!' the cheeky little devil added.

Around the same time Dave decided it was finally time to leave Huntly and start again somewhere.

'I've been thinking I might go back to Barrow,' he told me. 'It's the easy option I suppose, but why not?'

Dave had been away from his home town for more than twenty years but he'd gone back periodically to visit his mam's sister, Auntie Marion, and he always said how easy it was to slot back in, and how he enjoyed talking the same language as the ladies on the till in Tesco. I could never imagine leaving my roots in the North East; Newcastle is in my blood. Dave isn't a sentimental git like me and he wouldn't say the same, but the attachment was clearly there.

Dave went and had a look around, and he visited Roa Island, which was one of the places where he used to fish with his dad as a young boy. There was a house for sale on Piel Street, and the place is so small it was one of only twenty-odd houses on the island. Dave put in an offer as soon as he saw it.

'Keep your fingers crossed, Kingie,' he said. 'I really fancy it.'

It would be a base more than a full-time home, as Dave's work was taking him all around the world. His latest job was in Toronto, working as Christopher Lambert's personal assistant on the film *Absolon*. The two of them got on very well and Dave was pleased to have the work, but the truth was he was feeling quite jaded at this point in his career, having worked in make-up for more than two decades. He'd also done so many films by now he could hardly remember their names.

While Dave was becoming increasingly disenchanted, I was getting more desperate. As my debts stacked up I was racking my brains every waking minute to come up with a plan that would pull me and my family out of trouble. A phrase Dave had used years before had stuck in my head, and I thought about it more than once.

'How great would life be if we could just ride bikes, cook food and talk bollocks?'

I began to kick project ideas around in my head involving me and Dave, on our motorbikes, exploring pastures new. We'd talked once about how we'd love to go on some epic bike rides that would enable us learn a bit of history, eat great food and soak up some culture along the way. What if we could make a TV programme out of it? This seemed to have far more scope than our extreme fishing idea. It could be a story of friendship; two mates on their bikes, on the road, on a journey of discovery.

We'd talked before about how it would be a leap of faith for anybody to put me and Dave on the other side of the camera, but what did we have to lose? Glen and Betsan had both said we should be on the telly when they saw us cooking together on that memorable New Year's Eve, and why couldn't we be?

Before approaching Dave with my idea I ran it past a friend in the industry, another assistant director called Lisa Jones. I just wanted to test the water and I didn't even mention Dave's name to Lisa, but as soon as she got the concept she said: 'Dave Myers. It has to be Dave Myers, right?'

That gave me the push I needed. It was 2002 by now. Emails were still relatively new to me, but I bashed out the bones of my idea on a computer, got hold of an email address for Dave, who was staying at the Grand Hotel in Toronto, and sent it to him.

For my part it really was a case of desperate reinvention, and I was praying like mad that Dave would like the basic idea and agree to take it further. He ran it past some colleagues before he came back to me with the characteristically blunt response: 'Nobody thinks it's crap, Kingie.'

'Get in!' I thought, because I knew that once Dave bit there would be an explosion of ideas, and we'd be off. I wasn't wrong. Dave started spending all his free time in Toronto on it, and I worked my nuts off researching where we could go and what we could put into a programme or a series.

When Dave was back in the UK we put our heads together to write a polished treatment to pitch to potential backers. Between us we decided that it could be a good idea to travel the pilgrim routes and learn about what the pilgrims ate. Not only were we genuinely interested in this, but we figured it gave the initial road trip idea some structure and focus.

We called our pitch: *Motorbikes, Food and the Search for Nirvana*. Once it was ready we came up with a list of six producers and programme makers to send it to, with whom either one or both of us had worked in the past, including the drama director John Stroud and the Cooksons' producer Ray Marshall. We'd put many months of work into the idea already, and so once the treatment was sent off it was a very tense waiting game indeed.

It took an age waiting for some of the replies. Ray Marshall eventually told us he was looking for a quiz show to commission at that time and four of the others just didn't bite for one reason or another.

Eventually John Stroud invited us to the Bush Bar and Grill in Shepherd's Bush, which gave us a much-needed boost. By now more than a year had passed since I'd had the initial idea, and this was our last gasp.

'That'll be a treat!' Dave said, knowing it was a good restaurant and eagerly anticipating the food.

'Get in!' I said, imagining the menu.

Yes, we were preoccupied by our stomachs even when our futures were riding on this meeting! Of course, on the day itself, in the summer of 2003, we were very much focused on the job in hand. John was a very highly respected, award-winning comedy director who'd worked on shows like *Spitting Image* and *Harry Enfield and Chums*, and he wanted us to meet Vikram Jayanti, his old public school friend who was an Oscar-winning documentary filmmaker, responsible for the Muhammad Ali blockbuster *When We Were Kings*.

The meeting went extremely well. I can remember John making a frame out of his forefingers and thumbs and looking through the gap, as if he was filming us. He said he could see we had potential, and that with his comedy experience and Vikram's documentary prowess he could envisage bringing our core idea to life, as a kind of documentary-cum-travelogue, peppered with interesting food, facts and northern humour. The pilgrim route element might be dropped, but we didn't object, if that's what it took.

John ran his own production company, Big Bear Films, while Vikram owned VIXPIX Films, and between them they stumped up £1,200 for us to make a pilot, with which they would attempt to flog our programme idea to the BBC. We were delighted, and also quite tickled by the fact two northern boys like us were to have an Oscar-winning director working on our very first efforts in front of a camera.

By now Dave had moved into the house on Roa Island, and he'd also taken an advanced mountain-flying course in a microlight. It was something he'd always fancied having a go at, and we decided to film the pilot in Morecambe Bay and at Dave's house, using the microlight and a couple of knackered old Suzuki GS 1000 bikes we picked up.

John Stroud spent the weekend with us, and on the first night we cooked a meal and got him very drunk on good malt whisky. He had what we jokingly called a 'Stroud-over' all the next day as we planned the short film, which may account for the nonsense he let us get away with!

The results are totally laughable when we look back today. I start off saying: 'Cockles don't grow in Tesco you knooow! They grow in the sea! Oh, here's Dave!'

Then Dave swoops over in the microlight saying: 'Eee, I've got loads of cockles!'

In fact, he'd got stuck in the sand and we had to dig him out before we started looking for cockles. There wasn't a single bugger to be found that day, and so we had to cod things up, using a bag full of pebbles instead. We got dive-bombed by seagulls and then we did a bit of cooking in Dave's quirky old kitchen, using what I insultingly called his 'DHSS cooker'. We also referred to the Jane Grigson fish book, as we wanted to make the point we weren't chefs, or even trained cooks, just a couple of blokes who liked our food and were interested in its origins and how to make it taste good. All the while we really did talk a load of twaddle. Honest to God, it was like Bonnie Langford on *Junior Showtime*; we were doing everything we could to entertain and hopefully make ourselves shine. The great thing was that it all came very naturally to us. Neither of us was bothered about being filmed and there was no question of us feeling nervous or embarrassed about talking on camera. We were simply being ourselves and doing what we loved doing best; mucking around, having a laugh and cooking together.

It had taken another six months from our initial meeting with John and Vikram to get as far as filming the pilot, and by now Dave was working on *Prime Suspect* with Helen Mirren, which was shot in London. It was a prestigious job, but the downside was that he was staying in terrible accommodation in Watford – and it was getting him down.

As for me, the North East continued to be the last place the big studios were sending their money, and it was still impossible for me to get the kind of work I wanted. I'd started picking up jobs on commercials and low-profile dramas, but I was perpetually terrified of being unemployed. In short, Dave and I were both living in hope of our big break, and all the time our pilot was in production it was on our minds every single day.

After the microlight, Dave saved up his *Prime Suspect* money and bought himself an ocean-going catamaran, which seemed like a good idea as the Irish Sea was minutes from his door. He then treated the pair of us to a week-long 'day skipper' course, optimistically thinking that if things went to plan we could use the catamaran in a future show. We were so keen to make our idea work we were open to using any props we could that might help make a programme more interesting, just as we had with the microlight. At that stage we saw our bikes as being more functional than anything else; they were our preferred method of getting from A to B, and it was a bonus they looked good on camera.

The skipper course proved to be a hoot, and a welcome breath of fresh air, literally. We joined four other budding sailors on a yacht in the English Channel and Dave and I offered to do all the cooking if the others did the washing up. We knocked up a tasty spag bol and various curries and they all went down a storm. The skipper was delighted; he said he'd never eaten so well at sea before. In the evenings we went ashore, had a few drinks, took the mickey out of all the toffs at Cowes and generally had a bloody good time. It was the sort of semi-impromptu adventure we wanted to do on telly, and we loved it.

Our pilot was eventually submitted to BBC2 in early February 2004, and it sat there for many, many months. For some of that time I was working as location manager on a TV film called *Lawless* with Trevor Eve, which I didn't enjoy much, and Dave was working on *Spooks*, which was a very cool gig, just not what he wanted to do any more.

We finally got our lucky break after Roly Keating had taken over from Jane Root as controller of BBC2. Roly had gone to Oxford, and John and Vikram knew him through the old boys' network. On the back of our pilot he commissioned one show, which was his first ever commission for BBC2. We'd almost given up hope; it was bloody fantastic news, and we were of course completely cock-a-hoop.

'Get in!' I said, feeling incredibly excited. 'Can you believe it, mucker?'

'No, Kingie. It's mind-blowing. Me and you are actually making a telly programme together!'

Vikram suggested we do the show on Portugal, because of its great landscapes and rich food history, and the fact people typically knew little about it beyond the golf and holiday resorts of the Algarve.

'Great idea,' Dave and I said straight away. We were so chuffed I think we'd have agreed to fly to Jupiter if it gave us the break we'd been waiting so long for. Unbelievably, it was nearly three years since I'd sent the initial email to Dave suggesting we get together and write a treatment, and our patience had been rewarded at long last.

We had got a joint agent by now and Dave and I had also emailed each other a version of the original treatment, which we both signed as a way of trademarking and copyrighting our idea. The basic concept hadn't changed, although we'd moved away from the pilgrim route idea, as it was potentially too limiting.

Now we had the commission in the bag there were emails and plans flying around all over the place, and one email had 'Hairy Bikers' as its subject line. Nobody can remember who wrote it and as far as we know it wasn't even meant to be a suggested name for us, but it was an affable description and, despite the fact we weren't nearly as hairy then as we are now, it stuck.

The producers loved it and thought it was ideal, but funnily enough Dave and I weren't sold at first.

'What d'you think?' I said to Dave, admitting that I wasn't sure about the hairy bit because we both had quite short hair and short beards, as we needed to look respectable in our day jobs.

'I was more bothered about the biker bit,' Dave said. 'I mean, we love bikes, obviously, but are the bikes the focus we're aiming for?'

'Well, not exactly, they're just one element,' I said. 'But then again, we're brand new to this process. I think we should listen to what the experienced people are telling us.'

'I agree, but it's funny to think I went through so many years with alopecia and now I'm a Hairy Biker. You couldn't make it up really, could you?'

So that was it: the Hairy Bikers were christened and now all we had to do was go and deliver an hour of telly that would put us on the map and get us another commission.

Before we went to Portugal, Dave and I went to eat out in Stockwell, in an authentic restaurant in the Portuguese area, and then we got a load of cookbooks and tested out some recipes in Dave's house, working on them for several days. After that we invited some of his neighbours round for a feast, laying on seven dishes we thought might work well, but to be honest the results were average.

'You know what the problem is?' I said.

'I think we've been slaves to tradition,' Dave replied. 'Perhaps what we ought to do is take the core recipes and improve them.'

'Exactly! But I don't think we can do that until we've tasted the real thing and sussed out the local produce.'

'I think you're dead right, Kingie.'

We flew to Porto on 30 September 2004 for the initial recce. Once that was done, the plan was to return to the UK and pick up a couple of Triumphs from M & S Cycles in Newcastle, then ride them down to Portugal, via the ferry of course, before we started filming.

'At least the bikes'll be good if you're getting them from Marks,' Mam said, which had me in hysterics.

'It's not that M & S, Mam!'

'Oh! I thought there was only one M & S. Well, I hope they're good quality, Simon. I want you and Dave to be safe, do you hear me?'

'Yes, Mam. I promise we'll take care of each other, we always do, you know.'

Mam had got to know Dave very well over the years and she treated him like one of the family and always asked after his welfare and sent her love to him. Her comments reminded me how lucky I was to be embarking on this adventure with my best mate. Whatever happened, we had each other, and we had each others' best interests at heart.

It was still a little bit nerve-racking, never having made a full-length TV programme we were required to star in like this before, and knowing that we were going to be incredibly hands-on in terms of the production. Dave and I were not just going to turn up and do our stuff when the cameras were rolling, oh no! The Portugal show would be exactly like making the Morecambe Bay pilot but would take seven weeks, including the recce. Dave and I would do everything from the research and talking locals into appearing on camera to buying all the ingredients and cookery equipment, planning the filming schedules and organising the bike routes, crew and accommodation.

About the only thing we didn't have to do ourselves was book our hotel for the first night on the recce. Somebody at one of the production companies had done that for us, and neither Dave nor I will ever forget it. We eventually found the place at 2 a.m., after our airline managed to lose Dave's luggage in the bowels of Porto airport for a couple of hours.

'Please God, don't tell me that's it?' I said to Dave.

'I don't believe it,' he replied. 'It looks like an absolute fleapit!'

It appeared to be the cheapest, seediest B & B in the whole of Portugal. When we got inside there was worse news to come. Dave and I were sharing a room, and it only had one small double bed in it. We looked at each other in horror. The room wasn't even clean; the carpet was so sticky you wouldn't have wanted to stand on it in your bare feet.

'Do I have to sleep in there with you, dude?' I said to Dave, feeling my temper rising.

'Do I have to sleep in there with you, mate?' he said to me, looking thoroughly affronted.

'Sod it,' I said. 'I'm too tired to argue about it tonight. I just need to get myself to kip.'

'You're right, Kingie. There's nowt we can do now. We'll sort it out in the morning. There's obviously been some kind of mistake; we'll get over it.'

My head was banging when I got into bed, and pretty soon there was another banging noise too, like a dull thumping sound. Dave seemed to be asleep; either that or he was ignoring it. I imagined it must be some kind of ceiling fan that had gone on in the room below, and it was doing my head in.

'Will you stop that!' Dave suddenly blurted out, half asleep.

'What d'you mean, stop that?'

It suddenly dawned on me what Dave was thinking, and then he shouted: 'Are you knocking one out, Kingie?'

'No, I'm effing not, mate! Look, it's not me, honest!' I showed him both my hands. 'Look, I'll put them behind my head if you don't believe me.'

I did, and we both listened as the thump, thump, thump carried on. I don't even think we laughed at the time, because it was just such a grim and desperate situation.

Dave soon fell asleep again, and as I lay there doing my best to nod off as well, I heard him muttering and moaning, like he was having a bad dream. All of a sudden, he started thrashing about, quite violently, actually.

'Bloody hell, he must be fighting bleedin' Mordor,' I thought. Then it got worse, with Dave crying out and bouncing up and down, and I started to panic.

'Jesus, he's having a fit!' I thought.

Bearing in mind that his brain surgery wasn't too far behind us, I decided I had to do something in case he had a proper fit or swallowed his tongue. In my tired, aching head I thought the best thing for it was to restrain him, and so I leaped up and sat on him.

Dave woke up in a blind panic. It turned out he'd been dreaming about seeing dead people, and for a horrible moment, when he saw me on his stomach, he thought one of them had come alive and was trying to crush him to death.

'Argh! Stop! Please don't kill me!'

'It's alright, mate,' I said as he screamed in shock. 'Calm down.'

'Kingie!' he spluttered eventually. 'What are you doing?'

He could hardly get his breath, but now I realised that it was because I was nearly flattening him with my twenty-stone weight. You couldn't have made it up. There I was, in my underpants, straddling him with my bits next to his belly. And in a bloody double bed, too.

'Get off me!' he wheezed. 'Get off! What the effing hell is going on? One minute I thought you were in a masturbating frenzy, and now this. I think this is all going horribly wrong, Kingie.'

15

Dave's

Caldo Verde, Barbecued Zebra Burgers and Goat's Penis Hot Pot

After surviving the night in the B & B, Si and I spent a week driving around Portugal in a boiling hot Fiat Punto that had no air conditioning and stank of Portuguese fags and aftershave. We only had ourselves to blame for the latter; Si had bought a bottle of Old Spice and applied it liberally, and to this day the smell of it transports me immediately back to Portugal.

There had been some debate in London about the format of the programme, and whether we were going to present a hotchpotch of stories from all over Portugal or follow a more structured narrative. In the end it was decided that the journey itself would be our narrative, and we'd film a slightly chaotic collection of vignettes and hang them on a linear trip, so to speak. Si described the journey we would make as being like a washing line on which we would pin stories along the way, and it's a description and formula that stuck, and one we still use today.

It was also agreed that because we weren't trained chefs there should be an added dimension to any cookery we did. Our mission would be to chat to locals and sniff out good tales that would enable us to learn about Portuguese culture and food, try a new recipe and feed ourselves along the way. When you boiled it down it was really just the pair of us cooking our supper and having a laugh as we always had done, except that we'd be disseminating interesting information about our travels too. That was the aim, anyhow.

'This is it then, mucker,' Si said as we set off, armed with Lonely Planet maps, some research we'd done in the UK and our mutual hopes and dreams of making a television programme that would change our lives. We had our friendship too, of course, though back then I'm not sure we realised just how important this was. We took it as read that we'd be there for each other and support one another, perhaps not reckoning on how much we'd help each other through what was essentially a very alien experience to both of us.

'I can't really believe we've got this far, can you, Kingie?'

'No, mate. It's insane really. What if we mess up?'

'We won't. We can't, Kingie. There's no way that's going to happen. Now drive on! We've got a programme to make for the BBC!'

Unfortunately it didn't seem like a good omen when we stopped off for our first meal in Portugal and Si ordered the chitterlings, which are pigs' intestines. Prepared and cooked properly they can be very tasty, and both Si and I have always been up for trying what others might consider to be brave choices from the menu. However, the chitterlings that landed on Si's plate had not been cleaned out.

'I can't eat this shit!' he said.

'Si!' I hissed. 'Don't swear! Keep your voice down!'

'I'm not swearing, mate. I mean it literally is a plate of shit. Look!'

Once I'd had a proper look I could see he was right; the dish was completely inedible, and it stank.

'Do you want a bit of my baccala instead, Kingie?' I said, offering him some salted cod.

'What's it like?'

'Mildly alright.'

Thankfully, things soon started to look up when we got to work and managed to track down a 'playboy baker' we'd found out about through our research. Apparently Senhor Joao was something of a local celebrity in Chaves and was a man who made the ladies swoon with his fine pastry skills, not to mention his dashing good looks. When we clocked him he certainly appeared to live up to his reputation: he was all gold chains, tanned skin and heady aftershave. Most importantly Senhor Joao made the most wonderful loaves with ham and chorizo inside plus mouth-watering veal pastries, and he agreed to appear in our show.

'It will be my pleasure!' he beamed, flashing his white teeth.

'Is it OK if we just have a good look around the bakery so we can decide where to put the camera, when we come back with the crew?'

'Of course!'

'And will you be able to tell us all about the history of the bakery, and show us how to cook veal pastries, on camera?'

'Of course!'

Senhor Joao happily agreed to all our requests and we set a date when we'd return with the film crew. Si and I were thrilled to have lined up such a catch. This was exactly the sort of interesting, traditional cookery item we were after, and we were on a roll, if you'll pardon the pun!

We drove hundreds and hundreds of miles during the rest of

the recce, taking in places like Bragança, Boticas, Porto, Aveiro and Santarém as we researched other possible tales. On our travels we lined up an impressive list of items to film, including pieces on web-footed poodles, the 'wine of the dead', a lobotomy museum, and the very interesting ways local dishes like trout de Bragança and caldo verde are created. It was simultaneously exhilarating, incredibly interesting, exciting and a little bit daunting.

'John and Vikram are gonna love this!' I said to Si when we encountered the web-footed poodles in the Algarve.

'Aye, they will, and what can possibly go wrong, eh, Dave? What's that they say about never working with animals . . . ?'

'Look, they've been doing this since Roman times. Surely the dogs know what they're doing, don't they?'

The Portuguese water dogs have indeed been used for centuries to herd fish into nets after wading into the water with their webbed feet. We figured it would make brilliant telly to see them in action, and then use the fish we caught to prepare a local dish.

'You're right, Dave,' Si said. 'It'll be a laugh fishing with the dogs, and imagine how fresh the fish will be? What will we do with it?'

The pair of us were off, throwing out recipe ideas like there was no tomorrow and rifling through Portuguese recipe books to pick something out that was suitably local, and had an interesting bit of history attached to it. This was typical of the way we worked. One idea led to another, or some might say we made it up as we went along!

'Hey, I could get the crew to bring my motorised inflatable dinghy over from Barrow, to use for the filming.'

'Belting idea, Dave. We'll have to get some of those waterproof pants the fisherman have got on too, so we can do some wading. Bloody hell, we'll look a picture.'

'Exactly! It'll be a hoot.'

We had a week back in the UK after the recce before returning to Portugal with the crew, and when we set off Si and I were desperately hoping that all our hard work would come to fruition as planned. We were as keen as mustard to get going, and after picking up the bikes from M & S Cycles in Newcastle we rode all the way to Plymouth to catch the ferry to Santander. We met the crew on the boat, and when it was time to attach radio mics, Si and I obviously looked like a pair of novices because the sound man looked at us cautiously and asked: 'Er, you two are used to this, aren't you?'

'No!' we chimed in unison.

Si and I were well used to seeing mics on the actors and presenters we worked with, but of course being on the other side of the camera was very new to us. We weren't fazed, though. We were finally living the dream we'd been working towards for so long, and we were determined to learn fast.

Needless to say, not everything went to plan. When we turned up to film at Senhor Joao's bakery, for example, the place was shut; there literally wasn't a sausage to be filmed. John Stroud was with us as he was directing, and he reluctantly agreed we should wait in a local cafe to see if the glamorous baker would show up.

'It's a Monday,' John commented. 'Are you sure he's not shut on a Monday?'

Si and I looked at each other and shook our heads, as this was certainly not something the baker had mentioned to us. An hour went by, with a full crew idling in the cafe, and then the heavens opened. We had lunch and another hour had passed by the time

John said: 'That's it! We can't sit here any longer. We've got to film *something*!'

Si and I had been thinking the same thing and had sussed out there was a local ham factory down the road, so we went and knocked on their door.

'Hello!' I said. 'We're making a television programme for the BBC, about food in Portugal. Please can we film your ham?'

Though it must have been the most unexpected request the factory owner had ever had on a rainy Monday afternoon, he welcomed us in with open arms, and we're so glad he did. The place was magic, like a shrine to the best hams we'd ever seen in our lives.

'Bloody hell, Kingie. The ham factory's saved our bacon!'

'Very good, Dave, very good. I was sweating like a pig in that cafe, I can tell you!'

Happily, we filmed at the bakery the next day and John Stroud was delighted with the footage. Senhor Joao was a joy to behold making his breads and pastries. He made them with great passion, which is something we've come to really admire and appreciate on our travels. There is nothing like good, honest authentic cooking, and food that is made with love.

Fortuitously, the 'wine of the dead' filming went much more smoothly. We learned it was wine buried by locals when the French invaded in 1809, as they didn't want the indignity of seeing the French make off with their precious hooch. When they dug it up years later it tasted fantastic; Si and I had to sample it, just to verify the story, of course!

On another day we made caldo verde, which is a traditional Portuguese cabbage soup, but to make the cookery as interesting as possible we'd arranged to make it with the help of local sailors on the deck of a hundred-year-old port boat. It was great fun, particularly when their cabbage-shredding machine churned the stuff out like confetti. I thought it was going to bury us all! Si and I added some extra rich red spicy chorizo to the caldo verde just to give it a twist, which was exactly the sort of thing we did when we were cooking at home, just to be experimental and see what it would taste like. It worked, and that's how the recipe we still use today was created.

We also did a monster fish stew called caldeirada that we decided would be fitting to prepare on a beach, and we sampled pork alantejo, a stew made from pork and clams that the Spanish inquisition invented to catch out Jews and Muslims. The cookery was really leading the programme, and in researching and sourcing local foods and recipes we unearthed all kinds of interesting tales, just as we'd hoped, plus we found ourselves in situations we really hadn't bargained for, and often just went along with on the fly.

For example, we'd decided to make the local speciality trout de Bragança, as we figured this would provide a great excuse for us to attempt to tickle our own trout out of the water, and then cook it fresh on the riverbank. On the recce the water was two foot deep and absolutely infested with trout, so we thought it would be easy to make a lovely little fishing piece. However, when we arrived back for filming, the two-foot river had turned into a twelve-foot waterfall, which completely scuppered our plans.

'It's a maelstrom!' I said. 'Bloody hell, we're gonna have to come up with a new idea here, Kingie!'

Between the pair of us we quickly dreamed up an alternative scenario, despatching the crew to buy some trout from the local market while us two clowns stripped down to our underpants and biker jackets; there's a fetching photo of us taken like this.

Next I told this spoof story, pretending my dad had taught me to massage the trout and then flick them into the net, and then Si and I were filmed grinning triumphantly, with the fish-market trout in our nets. They still had the price tags on and were not even local trout, so there was no attempt to deceive; it was simply the best bit of fun telly we could come up with in the eye of the maelstrom.

We also had a right hoot when we filmed with the web-footed poodles, though Si's concerns about working with animals did hold water, so to speak. It was a cold October day in Faro and the dogs clearly didn't fancy wading into the muddy lagoon. As planned Si and I had my trusty rubber dinghy to hand, hoping to be able to motor out into the water in it and watch the poodles at work.

'I have a very good idea,' the helpful owner said after the dogs repeatedly refused to enter the water. 'You give me the dinghy and I take the dogs out in that.'

We agreed, as John Stroud was looking at his watch again and worrying about production schedules. Besides, instead of getting boring waterproof waders, Si and I had acquired float tubes, which are a kind of rubber ring that you sit in, complete with a harness and backrest, and flippers. This meant we'd be able to float out after the dogs, so what could go wrong?

Unfortunately, the owner of the dogs then did something we really didn't anticipate – he simply chucked the poodles over the side and straight into the cold lagoon with no warning whatsoever.

'Bloody hell! I feel terrible!' I said. 'Look at the poor dogs!'

'They're alright,' Si said. 'It's not as if they're not used to the water, but it could have been done with a bit more decorum!'

I reminded him of those words when the two of us waded in

after the dogs, trying to look like we knew what we were doing but rapidly finding ourselves out of control in our float tubes.

'Couldn't we have done this with a bit more decorum!' I joked, attempting to lighten the atmosphere, though I was actually feeling a bit anxious as we were drifting at quite a pace now.

'Bleedin' hell, Dave, we're being blown towards North Africa!' Si suddenly shouted. 'Stroudie! Help us!'

'Don't worry!' John shouted from the banks of the lagoon, where he was now reclaiming the rubber dinghy from the dogs' owner. 'I'll come out and tow you two back!'

John chugged out in the dinghy, and me and Si grabbed hold of the rail on the back – without decorum, I hasten to add – and then a horrible realisation hit us all. With two chunky blokes plus John versus a tiny motor there was no contest really, and now we were all heading for Morocco!

'Dave, I'll have to leave you behind!' John said as he prised my fingers off the grab-rail. 'Don't worry, we'll be back soon.'

Then the dinghy pulled away, leaving me bobbing helplessly in the water and yelling 'bastards!' at the top of my voice. Si just cracked up laughing.

I soon laughed about it too, of course, once Stroudie had rescued me and I was back on dry land, and it's one of those memories Si and I still chuckle about together even now.

That was our last day of filming, and after that Si and I rode the Triumphs from Faro back to Newcastle. This is a good example of the kind of mad things we did back then, going the extra mile when we really should have known when to stop. Nowadays, after working non-stop for seven weeks and riding the length of a country, we'd get the bikes picked up in a van at the end of a trip and fly home, for safety's sake more than anything.

It was hammering down when we left Faro, and when we finally got home, several hundred miles later, Si was diagnosed with pleurisy.

'I hope this has all been worth it, mucker!' he wheezed.

'I'm sure it has. Besides, whatever happens next, we've had a blast.'

'You're right, Dave. It's in the lap of the gods now. We've given it our all, and we'll just have to keep everything crossed.'

Our edited show, named *The Hairy Bikers' Cookbook*, was finally delivered to the BBC on Christmas Eve, for transmission on 6 January 2005. After returning from Portugal I worked on a new series of *Spooks* while Si worked on some commercials as soon as he was well enough. It was a bit odd being back in our old jobs, not knowing what would happen next. We did a couple of radio interviews to promote our show, and the first one was with Richard Bacon, who told us he thought our day jobs sounded more interesting than the programme. We've laughed about that with him since, but at the time we were as nervous as hell.

On the night the show was screened John Stroud very kindly threw a party in his house and invited all the crews, as well as Jo Clinton-Davies who was head of commissioning at the BBC so had ultimately been the person to give our series the green light. Si and I had obviously seen the edited programme and both knew in our hearts it was very good, because whatever ideas we had had, Stroudie had made everything a million times better. Nevertheless, the two of us were bricking it when the announcer said: 'Coming next on BBC2, *The Hairy Bikers' Cookbook*.' Si and I looked at each other with a mixture of pride and terror on our faces as our quirky theme music, which was by the London band Lemon Jelly, started and we saw the credits roll.

We watched in a sort of stunned daze, because it seemed so surreal to see ourselves on telly. The moment it finished everyone at the party was on their feet saying, 'Congratulations!' and Si and I embraced and jumped up and down like idiots. Then both our mobile phones pinged into life, with each of us getting about seventy texts that also screamed: 'Congratulations!'

Once the euphoria of the evening was over, our minds were firmly focused on what really mattered: the reaction from the public, and the verdict of the TV critics.

'Bloody hell, what if no one's watched it after all this?' I said, only half-joking.

'Nah, we'll have plenty of viewers,' Si replied. 'It's just a question of exactly how many.'

We both knew that our futures depended on this number, and we were hoping for a million, as this was what the bosses had been aiming for.

'Good news, boys,' John Stroud said.

'Go on.'

'You got more than a million.'

'How many more?'

'More than *two* million – 2.7 million!'

We simply couldn't believe it; it was mind-blowingly brilliant. Apparently we'd 'inherited' about a million viewers from the darts that had been on before us, and the audience stuck with us for the full hour. This was beyond magnificent and, shortly afterwards, we got more amazing news, the best we could have hoped for: Roly Keating had commissioned a whole series. A whole bloody series! It was like all our Christmases had come at once.

'Congratulations! You've got a million quid to spend on beer, food and petrol,' was how John Stroud broke the news to us. Of course, the million quid was the budget for the series and not our pay packet, but it was still the news from heaven.

I was working with Anna Chancellor – 'Duckface' in *Four Weddings and a Funeral* – on the set of *Spooks* when I got the call. I started grinning from ear to ear, so much so that she asked me what on earth was going on, so I told her. Anna seemed pretty gobsmacked that her hair and make-up man was going to present his own show on BBC2. 'Congratulations!' she said, before asking who on earth was going to do her hair now!

Word eventually spread around the set and everyone was genuinely pleased. I wanted to leave straight away but my bosses asked me to work a month's notice, which I agreed to do; I didn't feel I could leave them in the lurch. When I finally left, the crew clubbed together and bought me a gift token for a fishing tackle shop as a leaving present, which I was very touched by.

Si was location manager on a Müller Light commercial when he got the news. When John phoned him he didn't hold back and went absolutely berserk on the phone shouting: 'Get in! Yeeeesssss!' The only part of the conversation Si remembers now is when John said: 'More people win the lottery than get the chance to do this.' That said it all about how big this news was.

Now we found ourselves in the unbelievable and incredibly enviable position of getting together to decide where in the world we wanted to go to make our series.

'Can you believe this, mucker?' Si guffawed as we got out another load of Lonely Planet guides and maps and spread them on the desk at Vikram's office near Tottenham Court Road. 'This doesn't happen to working-class lads like us! We're going round the planet even though we're skint!'

Si hadn't been out of Europe before and now we had the world at our feet. It was mind-blowing; we were actually about to go and completely live our dream, eating and riding our way around the world together. It would be just like our trips around the Scottish Highlands but on a global scale, and the icing on the cake was that we'd be making our living from it.

Our good friends and Si's family were delighted for us, although I think it was hard for everybody to get their head around. It really was like we'd won the lottery, or at least the creative lottery, and people were scratching their heads and trying to work out what it all meant. Si's mam was quite emotional and was saying, 'I'm made up for the pair of you. Make sure you stay safe now!' and Jane was typically stoical and supportive, despite the fact she'd be home alone even more than usual, looking after the three boys. I thought about my mam and dad, and how they'd have loved all this. If they were looking down I knew what they'd have been saying: 'Why did you leave it so bloody long, you daft pair!'

Between me, Si, John and Vikram, we settled on Namibia, the Isle of Man, Ireland, Transylvania, Vietnam, Turkey and Mexico as feasible and interesting destinations for our debut series, and Si and I were off on our adventures by the spring of 2005.

There was to be a seven-week turnaround for each show, as we'd done with Portugal. We could write a whole book on each country we visited if we had that luxury, as there are so many stories that really stand out in our memories.

In Namibia, we decided to use a microlight again and so I had to take my African flying licence, for which Si and I set aside three days. Alarmingly, we arrived at the airfield at the crack of dawn to discover the light aircraft I was expected to fly was a complete mess, with none of the instruments working and a guy called Snake-eyes filling the petrol tank from a dirty old jerry can.

'Crack on, Dave!' Si said, although in hindsight I realise he wasn't in his right mind; we'd tried Jägermeister for the first time the night before and he had a colossal hangover.

'Sod it,' I thought, 'we're here now.' I took off down the runway and performed two 'touch and go's around the airport, which is where you just take off, fly to about five hundred feet and land.

'That's fine!' the examiner called. 'You passed! I'll stamp your licence. If you want any more petrol just ask Snake-eyes.'

'OK,' I said, stunned. 'Er, by the way, why is he called Snake-eyes?'

'He had one of his eyes taken out by a snake.'

'OK.'

The next day I took Si out for a flight at dawn, and it was one of the most amazing experiences of my life. As soon as a shard of light appeared the whole African plain lit up. There was a dried-up river bed that all the animals used like a motorway, and we watched in awe as herds of giraffes, zebras and elephants walked along it. Then we flew over a township and had some of the locals take pot-shots at us before we headed back, navigating our way using the mountains. When we landed it was like a piano being dropped off a cliff; the maximum weight per person in the plane was sixteen stone, and Si and I were nineteen and seventeen stone respectively.

After that we went and had a big African cooked breakfast at a wonderful cafe and slept for a few hours before going to the pub in the early evening. Then we repeated the whole experience early the next day, planning more of the same the following morning. However, before we left the airfield I was asked if I'd take out some extremely high-ranking Swedish officials at dawn the next day, as they were important visitors who were helping to build a dam for the local people.

'My experience of bush-flying amounts to about an hour and a half,' I said. 'I don't think I can do it.'

'Yes, you can!' came the reply from the airport manager. 'Think of the local people and their dam! How can you not help? See you at 5.30 a.m. tomorrow, Mr Myers!'

How could I not help indeed? The next morning Si manned the coffee machine on the ground while I took a string of government officials into the sky.

'Cappuccino?' Si smiled like an unkempt trolley dolly while I took the bigwigs up one at a time, flying my bollocks off. Honest to God, we were like the world's worst low-budget airline. At one swap-over I even heard Si say to a transport ministry official: 'Any chance of a cheap Volvo?'

We picked up our motorbikes in Windhoek, at a BMW garage, and were offered 650s but we asked for 1200s so we could look good as we rode across the Namibian desert. This was a massive mistake, as neither of us had ridden off-road or on sand before, and we soon found out you had to go at 80kph or you just fell off. This required enormous concentration and energy on such big bikes, and we fell off regularly anyhow, which was physically and psychologically crippling. At one point Si just shot off his bike, did a cartwheel and blotted out the sun, leaving a mushroom cloud of sand in his wake. Every time he came off I did too, and vice versa.

'Bloody hell, Si, we're like lemmings jumping off a cliff,' I said.

'You're not wrong. What were we thinking of, Dave? This is madness!'

The river beds were our nemesis. The only way to get through was to ride faster than your right mind told you to and get the bike on a plane, just like a speedboat on water. In theory this keeps the front wheel up and the rear wheel tractoring through the soft ground, but it was incredibly difficult to do, and when you fell off it was like being hit in the chest with a three-ton bag of flour.

We were black, blue and sweating like pigs in leather blankets by the end of it. We did more than a thousand kilometres across the desert by the time we finished, travelling to the very north of Namibia.

Along the way we'd watched elephants by moonlight, slow-roasted lamb in an earth oven, picked up some desert survival techniques from our amazing fixer and tracker, Paul van der Ploeg, and taken part in a traditional spitting competition in which you had to spit dried animal droppings. Not only that, we'd met the wonderful women from the Herero tribe, who wear Victorian dresses with bustles, we'd lit elephant poo to repel mosquitoes, stomached mopane worms in the German colony of Swakopmund, eaten huge ostrich eggs with toast soldiers and cooked delicacies like barbecued zebra burgers and salt-baked crayfish. The wide variety of food available was incredible and choosing what we cooked was an absolute joy. We would walk into a local market and be like a pair of excited schoolboys let loose in a sweet shop. One minute we'd be ogling over the delicacies and incredible array of produce on offer and the next we'd be tossing around ideas about what we could do with the food.

'Look at this crocodile meat!' Si said one day. 'It looks amazing! Imagine what we can do with that. I reckon that would be good for doing something like a satay. It looks like it could barbecue really well.'

'Crocodile satay? That sounds good. Let's have a look at it. Ooh yes, it looks like chicken or pork so that could work. How does it come?'

'I don't know, Dave. I'll ask.'

'Alright, Kingie, but make it snappy, will ya!'

'For cryin' out loud, Dave, can't you do any better than that . . .'

It was great fun experimenting with food, and we both enjoyed the creative process of coming up with our own recipes. For example, the first time we made zebra burgers they were a bit dry, so we tried them again with some minced fatty bacon and they turned out much better, which was really satisfying.

There were more funny moments than anything. My mates back on Roa Island knew I was a massive fan of Delia Smith and before the trip they wrote to her asking for a signed photograph. Delia sent me a wonderful picture in a Wedgwood crystal frame that said 'To Dave, best wishes, Delia', and I put it up in our Bedouin tent.

'You fancy her, don't you?' Si accused cheekily.

'Of course I do. Who can resist a bit of Delia?'

This became a running joke, in fact, and a few years hence I took the framed picture onto *Saturday Kitchen* and said: 'The spirit of Delia is upon us, Kingie. Our dish is bound to go right now, because you never get a duff Delia, do you?'

Another time I took it a bit further. 'I had a dream last night that Delia came to me naked with a bowl of garlic mash,' I declared on telly.

I was just having a laugh, and to my great amusement the *Guardian* newspaper ran a story afterwards saying: 'TV Chef Fantasises over Naked Delia.'

I'm happy to say I've met Delia many times since those early days. She's a great sport and we've become pals but I still hold her on a pedestal. I mean, it's Delia, isn't it? I was cutting out her recipes from magazines and newspapers and following her tips twenty years before I ever met her.

When we had our week at home before the next trip it was

difficult to describe to anybody what we'd just been through. Even Si was lost for words with his family, and in the end he found himself saying to Jane: 'I simply cannot do it justice. You'll see it all on the telly.' I could identify with that; we'd been in another world where absolutely everything was different and marvellous to behold. You had to be there, you really did.

The Isle of Man was our next destination, chosen because Si and I had always wanted to go to the TT Races together but never managed it because of work. Now we had the chance to make it our work to go there, which was lush, and another one of those things I dearly wished my parents had been around to witness, having taken me there as a small boy.

Si and I had the not-very-bright idea of taking a couple of tricked-out Monkey bikes across the Irish sea on my catamaran from Roa Island, and we were going to make a crab soufflé and sea bass on the way, as we thought it was appropriate to cook seafood and fish while at sea and they are both favourites of ours.

The bikes wouldn't fit on the boat without us sawing the cabin to bits, though, and then my mate Chunky, who is the lifeboat man on Roa Island, warned us: 'It's blowing up a bastard!'

In typical style we set off regardless. Most of our crew was already in the Isle of Man but we had a cameraman and soundman with us who started freaking out and shouting, 'Get me off!' when the wind really did start to blow up, and we found ourselves in the eye of the choppy storm. After a disastrous attempt at making the crab soufflés, which turned out like beer mats as they got knocked sideways and collapsed every time we hit a wave, we admitted defeat and docked in Fleetwood, where we bought fish and chips for tea. We salvaged things eventually by cooking local lamb and scallops on the beach on the Isle of Man, chosen because they are two significant native foods. The scallops are exquisitely sweet and marble-sized and known as 'queenies', and the Loaghtan lamb is a unique prehistoric breed that cannot be beaten for flavour or texture.

'Listen to this, Kingie!' I'd said as I read about the breed. 'The Loaghtan lamb is a strange and grumpy beast which wanders aimlessly around the island. It's a bit like you with a hangover then!'

'Cheers, mate!' Si said. 'If you carry on insulting me, you might not get to taste my scallops.' In the event Si cooked tequila flambéed queenie scallops, which were honestly one of the best things I've ever tasted.

We had a great time taking part in the free-for-all Mad Sunday ride, which is open to all-comers. The Monkey bikes weren't fast by anybody's standards but were bloody good fun and we reached the dizzy speed of 65mph on a downhill bit, keeping to the left so faster riders could pass.

'You do realise this could be interesting, having us pair tootling along while superbikes rage past at 180mph,' Si had pointed out to John Stroud.

'Good. I like interesting,' Stroudie smiled. 'Besides, you're the ones who picked the Monkey bikes.'

'Yes, but that was because they were the only things we could get on the catamaran. To think we could have had racing bikes . . .'

We liked 'interesting' too, if the truth be told, and just being in the midst of this historical spectacle and being immersed in the smell and noise of thousands of bikes was a wonderful experience, even if I was on something that had loud pipes and a tartan seat, and looked like a Bay City Rollers memorial bike.

Ireland was our next destination, and I think it's fair to say that it was very drink-fuelled. After filming one evening, we stopped off at Flukies Cosy Bar in Belcarra, County Mayo. We only wanted a loo break and a swift pint, but there was such a great atmosphere there that we thought it would make a fabulous place to film.

'Don't suppose you do ceilidh?' Si asked. 'Only we wanted to do a bit of filming in a really great Irish pub, complete with ceilidh dancing.'

'No problem,' came the reply. 'We'll have that arranged for ya in two shakes of a lamb's tail.'

True enough, ceilidh dancing was laid on for us the next night, and the place was absolutely rammed.

The atmosphere was just amazing, and the place was rocking. When it was time to start filming, Si took the mic and addressed the room.

'I'd like to welcome everybody!' he began. 'Thank you for joining us . . .' As he spoke I ran up behind him and pulled his baggy pants down. It just seemed like a funny thing to do at the time, perhaps due to the merry atmosphere in the pub, but I would never have done it had I realised what would happen next.

'I've gone commando, dude!' Si gasped.

To my complete astonishment, when I looked down there was Si in all his naked glory, clutching his gingernuts in front of a room full of staunch Irish Catholics who didn't know where to look.

'I'm sorry, mate,' I said.

Si just laughed as he pulled his pants up, and I thanked my lucky stars we were such good mates, as he forgave me in an instant – or perhaps this generosity was just down to the amount of Guinness he'd consumed!

We both have very fond memories of Ireland. We made it our

mission to go in search of top tips for the best Irish stew, only to be told by one poker-faced fella: 'It's Coco Pops.' We also swapped the bikes for a horse and cart supplied by a bloke called Tom.

'What's the horse called?'

'Jerry,' he said.

'You're joking? You're Tom and Jerry?'

'We are indeed.'

We gave the horse a taste of the Irish whiskey syllabub we made, which actually made him, and us, laugh. We had a ball, and it made great telly.

Si and I were in high spirits throughout the Irish trip, and some news from London gave us a further boost: a couple of big publishers were interested in bringing out books to accompany the series. It was incredibly exciting, but we told ourselves not to count our chickens just yet. We had no knowledge of the publishing industry at all and didn't even know what style of books they were thinking of. Still, we had another pint of Guinness to celebrate. It would have been rude not to.

Transylvania was the next country on our list, and while we were there we got the most incredible news about the book deal. Unbelievably, Penguin wanted to publish two books to accompany the series.

'Can you believe it, mucker?' Si whooped. 'You and me, we're going to be published authors!'

'No, I can't, Kingie. When I think of all the cookbooks I've used over the years. Mam's *Radiation* cookbook, Delia, Jane Grigson. Blimey, people are going to be following *our* recipes, Si!'

'They might even cut them out and stick them in a scrapbook,' Si teased, because he'd taken the mickey out of me when he found out I did that, the cheeky beggar! We still weren't exactly sure what the format would be at this stage, though we imagined the books would be part cookbook and part travelogue, to reflect the shows. We were more than happy to be guided on this; after all we were two northern blokes who liked our food and our travels, and literary experts we were not.

The rough plan in Transylvania was to visit the local food markets in Bucharest, check out Dracula's birthplace at Corvin Castle, have an outdoor mud-bath, make some spicy Romanian sausages and track down a bloke called Elvis, who was king of the gypsies.

We also wanted to go to the Museum for Victims of Communist Oppression in Sighetu Marmaţiei. We knew it would be a terribly sad and sinister reminder of the past, but we felt no programme on Romania would be complete without it. We needed a hotel for the night, but as we drove into Sighetu, the first one we came across was shut.

'What's that down there?' Si said, pointing to a sign that said 'Pension'.

'Not sure. Think we'll carry on.'

'No, let's go and check it out.'

'Oh God, alright then, but I don't think it'll be any good . . .'

How wrong I was. As we walked into the small reception area we discovered Pension Casa Iurca was a wonderful folksy-style hotel, in a Hammer House of Horror sort of way. Everything went dark as me and Si stepped inside, because we blotted out the light that had been shining through the front door. There was a striking but incredibly austere-looking woman on reception who checked us in very coldly and said she'd show us to our rooms. We followed her up a spiral staircase, and I was looking up at her legs thinking: 'Phwooar!'

Nudging Si, I whispered: 'I fancy her!'

'What? She's dead scary!' he replied.

'Nah! You have to be a bit distant when you're checking in a couple of big hairy bruisers like us.'

I found out her name was Liliana Orzac and, as luck would have it, it turned out she had a degree in tourism, had worked at the memorial museum for three years after the Revolution and was happy to help us film there when we returned with the crew a few weeks later.

The museum was an even more desperately sad place than we'd imagined. Pictures of thousands of Romanians killed under Ceausescu's murderous rule lined the walls, and me and Si were choked with emotion, but Liliana, or Lil as I started to call her, really helped us through the day. She'd lived through Ceausescu's regime and dealing with such horrors was unfortunately second nature; she was incredibly composed and had a common-sense attitude I really admired. I gave her a lift on my motorbike and she gathered a few props that we needed for filming, and also provided us with loads of useful advice and information.

'I still fancy her,' I said to Si.

'Give over,' he replied.

When our work was done and we were about to leave, Lil gave me a goodbye peck on the cheek and a bottle of home-made plum hooch called pálinka, and we swapped email addresses. I liked her a lot and felt I'd made a friend, and I was looking forward to keeping in touch after we'd left for our next destination: Vietnam.

On the flight to Ho Chi Minh City, better known as Saigon, Si and I got upgraded to 'Thai Silk Orchid Class' and arrived smelling like a whore's pants, thanks to all the free posh toiletries we were given. Then Si went for a pee and got chased by a snake.

The food was an eye-opener in Vietnam. One night we visited a Hanoi beer hall. Si and I sank a couple of pints and started feeling peckish, but the menu was all in Vietnamese and so we just pointed at a random selection of dishes, hoping we'd made a good choice. A fish with Cantonese rice was magnificent, and then some grilled meat arrived with a side dish of skinny-looking black pudding.

'Eurgh! This duck is tough,' Si said.

'Nah, it's not duck, Kingie. It's got four trotters. It must be a really scabby suckling-pig.'

'No, Dave. I know my pork. It's not pig, it has to be duck.'

The crew was with us and we were filming, and I got a bit stuck between my teeth and started digging away with a toothpick. As I freed the meat I glanced up to see the director holding up a piece of paper out of shot. It read DOG.

'Oh bugger,' I said, feeling my heart sink. 'I've got a lump of dog between my teeth, Si. I don't bloody believe it.'

We would never have willingly eaten dog; it was something we'd discussed and had both categorically agreed was bad and unnecessary. When we burped afterwards it smelt of damp dog and was truly awful. We'd made a big mistake and it was one we never wish to repeat, or have repeated on us . . .

We willingly sampled coconut grubs and crispy scorpions on another evening, though, as we were in a traditional Vietnamese cafe and wanted to try what the locals eat.

'You like them?' the waiter smiled.

'Yes, thank you,' we smiled, as they were both not bad.

'Then I bring you more!'

We had spotted deer penis on the menu, and we felt obliged to ask about it, more out of curiosity than because we wanted to eat it.

'Deer penis is too big for two,' he said without any hint of humour or embarrassment. 'You try the goat's penis hot pot, it is on special offer.'

'Oh!' we gasped. 'What's the special offer?'

'You get the testicles for free!' he smiled. 'OK?'

'OK,' we nodded, immediately wondering what on earth we'd done that for.

'Can you imagine asking for a willy hot pot in the pub in Barrow or Newcastle?' I said.

'D'you know what, I can't, mucker.'

When the hot pot arrived it was what can only be described as a huge cock and bollocks in a broth.

'Looks like I've got a bit of bollock,' I said as I was served a large ladle-full.

Si started laughing and then looked down in horror at his bowl.

'I've got the pointy end!' he gasped.

Having come this far we did actually have a taste, just so we could say we had.

'What d'you reckon?' Si asked, wincing and wiping his mouth.

'Tastes like a load of old balls to me.'

It was an interesting cultural experience to say the least, but as I commented later: 'I can't imagine a goat's penis giving anyone pleasure except a lady goat.'

In Hoi An we were doing some filming on the ancient Chinese bridge that spans a tributary of the river. Our plan was to set up stall and do a bit of cooking to feed the ladies who worked on the sampans, which are the flat-bottomed wooden boats. I was on my own doing my 'Alan Whicker' bit and talking about the country's colonial past when Si accidentally fell off a kerb. I didn't clock any of this because I was busy filming, but a Swedish woman saw what happened and dashed to his aid.

'Hello, I'm a Swedish osteopath', she told Si.

'Hello, I'm in pain,' he responded in a withered voice.

'I am sure you are,' she said, gently examining the damage. 'You have broken your ankle!'

'Sparrow's ankles,' Si wailed, and he was promptly rushed to the nearest hospital. He'd already gone by the time I found out what had happened, and I was left there scratching my head and thinking you really couldn't make this up. I was preparing to make lemongrass noodles and crispy beef in the street and I tried to rescue things by codding up a fake double act, with me pretending to be Si. What else could I do?

Four hours later I heard a 'tick tick tick', which was the sound of a very large man – namely Si – on toothpick-sized crutches.

'I salute you!' he cried as he sat beside me, which really should have sounded an alarm bell.

Sadly it didn't, and I was about to start cooking the beef when I suddenly noticed that Si's fingers were lying in the hot fat.

'Si? What are you doing, mate? Are you away with the fairies or what?'

That's when I discovered he had been seen by two separate doctors in neighbouring hospitals, and that he'd been given two massive doses of morphine, which were clearly still in his system.

The crew got hold of a wheelchair for Si, which unfortunately seemed to create more problems than it solved.

When it was time to film a cookery element we wedged Si and his chair under the table beside me as I prepared to make deep-fried spring rolls.

'Now then, Kingie, no touching the hot fat!'

'Shut your face, Dave. I'm fine now. Tell me what I can do to help. I hate sitting here feeling useless.'

'Here, chop a few vegetables. But BE CAREFUL!'

'Right you are, Dave.'

It was raining when we set up and so the crew had rigged up umbrellas to protect our street kitchen from the elements. Unfortunately the rain got heavier and heavier, and very soon I was cooking in monsoon-like conditions. Then the inevitable happened, and rain started splattering into the hot oil.

'Help!' I cried, jumping away from the wok and doing a little expletive-accompanied jig as the dancing fat splashed my face and arms. 'It's all over me! Help!'

I was wearing a plastic Chinese hat that started to melt, and then large flames jumped from the pan.

'Someone put the fire out!' I cried. 'Quick! Put the fire out!'

'What's happening?' I heard Si scream, and that's when I realised he was still sitting right next to the pan, trapped there in his wheelchair.

'I'm on fire! Help! I can't move! I can't get the brakes off this bleedin' chair! Who put the brakes on without telling me? Me hat! What's happening to me hat? It's melting!'

God love him, I did feel sorry for him, and I had an awful flashback to my mother, stranded in the flower bed in the park in Barrow. The locals just gave us confused looks, like we were slightly freakish street performers.

We ended the Vietnam episode with Si and me travelling in a modified carriage-cum-rickshaw that had a kind of dog-cart for Si to sit in at the back, while I was up front. Si was very squashed and was all legs-akimbo, and as we rode down the street everybody stopped and stared at us, and even buses slowed down to have a good gander.

'How do we get to China?' I asked Si as we trundled along, and that was how we ended the Vietnamese episode.

I emailed Lil from an Internet business booth during our stay in Vietnam, to tell her what I'd been up to, and I phoned her on her birthday in December too. There was nothing romantic going on but I really liked her, and so I invited her to England for a visit.

'Don't worry, I won't try anything on,' I said, because I could tell she was nervous.

'I'll think about it, Dave,' she said.

Lil was the mother of two children aged nine and fifteen, and was understandably cautious about visiting a big hairy biker from Barrow-in-Furness whom she barely knew. I'd had girlfriends since Glen but, to be honest, I was wary of what might happen too; I'd had my share of complications and heartache.

Still, I crossed my fingers and hoped she'd make the trip. I think I even told her a little fib, saying I had loads of air miles that were about to expire and needed to be used up quick! Well, you can't blame a guy for trying.

While I waited for her reply I was off with Si on our next adventure, to Turkey, and it was a very good trip. We explored a weird museum of hair, built a thirty-five pound doner kebab, visited the bizarre cats of Van and sampled bananas dipped in hallucinogenic honey. In Gaziantep, close to the Syrian border in the south, we memorably learned how to make baklava, which is a finely layered pastry filled with syrup, made in a fascinating process.

'This is one for you, mucker,' Si said, because of the two of us I am the one who particularly enjoys working with pastry, and we were meeting a master baklava-maker called Imam Cagdas who was renowned for making the traditional pastries with an incredible forty layers of silk-thin pastry, rather than the customary fifteen.

'It is indeed!' I said, rubbing my hands together. 'It's funny how we've both got our "things", isn't it?'

Over time, Si and I have both naturally leaned towards specific jobs in the kitchen.

When it comes to pastry, I like the fact it requires precision, rather like some of the prosthetic work I did as a make-up artist, or the fine art work I did at university. I love the craft of it, and the finicky measuring and fine-cutting involved. I'm the same with pasta; I'll happily sit for hours making intricate ravioli, which is not Si's idea of fun at all. He would much rather stick his big hands in a messy bowl of dough and knead the bread; I'm sure there must be a link between the way he cooks and the powerful, industrious miners in his ancestry.

As well as being the pastry man, I always put my hand up first to gut and fillet fish, no doubt because I grew up by the sea and this was something I did at my father's knee. Si, on the other hand, is the natural butcher of the pair of us, very much at home boning a joint of meat or tenderising a steak. Sorting out crustaceans is his bag too; he's never happier than when he's cracking shells, and he also tends to be the one who mans the pan or the fire while I'm bustling around and remembering the quantities.

'Recipe slave!' he says sometimes to wind me up, because I do like to stick to the quantities and instructions, while Si is much more inclined to break the rules and experiment.

Anyhow, my eyes were on stalks as we entered the incredible pastry room belonging to Imam Cagdas, but moments later I was squinting and sweating. The windows were covered with polystyrene tiles to keep the humidity and heat in the room, and flour was thick in the air.

It was a hellish environment, but nevertheless we both marvelled at the twelve sweating men who were working like demons to hand-roll the pastry into the finest sheets you could imagine. Each layer was placed on a tray and brushed with melted butter before another sheet was added, until Imam's father appeared to add the finishing touch by pouring on the syrup. He was the only person allowed to perform this prestigious job. The finished pastry was absolutely divine.

Our abiding memory of Turkey, however, is of crossing a checkpoint at the Iranian border. The area had only recently been de-militarised due to the on-going guerilla war with the PKK, the Kurd nationalist organisation known for its skills in kidnap, ambushes and assaults on the Turkish army. The PKK were still camped in the hills and security was very tight, so we knew we had to keep our wits about us.

Si was quite a bit ahead of me when the checkpoint came into view, but he didn't slow down and simply rode on, looking as if he didn't have a care in the world. I imagined this was his chosen tactic for hopefully sailing through the checkpoint without a hitch; just act like a tourist, don't be afraid and don't draw attention to yourself.

It wasn't a bad plan, but the only trouble was, Si appeared to have forgotten that both our bikes had BBC cameras in the panniers, and so we weren't exactly tourists, were we? I could see that the crossing was crawling with bored conscripts and I knew that if they thought we were journalists we could be in for a rough interrogation, so I started to panic.

'Si, come back!' I was silently screaming, but it was too late. By now he was already at the checkpoint, and I started sweating profusely inside my leathers, desperately hoping the soldiers would wave him through without stopping him.

They didn't, and the next thing I knew Kingie had a Kalashnikov AK-47 pointing at his head.

I was bricking it and I hung back, wondering what the hell to do. Should I speed up and go and support Si or would that make things worse? I started panicking that my best mate might be shot before my eyes. 'Please don't hurt him!' I thought. 'We're supposed to be having kebabs later!'

'Where are you from and where are your papers?' the soldier asked Si, while still pointing the gun at his head.

'England, and here are my papers.'

'Where are you going?'

'To Van, to eat kebabs.'

'Kebabs?'

'Yes. We've been told they have great kebabs in Van. And apparently there's a monster in the lake there too. It's called the Lake Van Monster.'

'Really?'

The soldier started laughing, at which point Si seized the opportunity to say: 'Excuse me, I don't want to be rude, but would you mind pointing your gun away from me?'

The soldier obliged and then unexpectedly said: 'Nice bike you have there. Can you do a wheelie on it?'

Having not been party to the conversation, you can imagine my surprise and relief when I saw the gun being lowered and Si pulling away from the smiling soldier to perform a rather spectacular wheelie on his bike. A few other conscripts gathered around and they all started laughing and clapping, so Si carried on, pulling several more impressive wheelies for their entertainment.

'Oh, there's my friend!' Si exclaimed loudly, indicating for me to join him. I dutifully did, marvelling at how his Geordie charm had worked wonders, even in this situation.

'Hello! I'm his friend!' I said, giving my best impression of being the drippy mate bringing up the rear, and just another daft tourist.

Thankfully the soldiers then waved the pair of us through, wishing us a safe trip, but I don't think my nerves recovered for quite some time.

'And you say I'm the one who's as mad as a box of frogs, Kingie,' I said afterwards. 'Were you not panicking about the cameras in your panniers?'

'Cameras? In my panniers? I thought you had them all, Dave . . .'

Happily, our efforts to cross the border were not in vain, because when we learned how to cook the giant doner kebab near Van it was magical. The process was a fascinating work of art using sheep's tail fat, and once we'd been taught how to do it by a master craftsman, Si and I bought a kebab machine to make our own. Now all we needed was a good location and some locals to share the feast with, as even me and Si could not polish off a thirty-five pound kebab.

'Can we use your terrace?' we asked some locals whose home was overlooking the Syrian plains, which made a wonderful backdrop for our filming.

'Yes,' they readily agreed. 'That is not a problem, as long as you stop when there is a call to prayer.'

'Yes, of course.'

What followed was one of the best barbecues we'd ever had, and that's saying something as we didn't even have a drop of alcohol to wash it down with. The food was fabulous, but what really blew us away was the incredibly warm and welcoming hospitality of the people. We left our hosts the kebab machine as a thank-you gift for giving us such a memorable night.

By the time we got to Mexico, our final destination, it was January 2006 and our Namibia show was due to be broadcast back home any day. We were very nervous about how it would go down, but fortunately we had plenty of Latin American distractions to keep us from fretting too much.

There was nothing we didn't like about Mexico. We loved the

friendly people, the roads were fabulous, especially as we were on blingy Harleys this time, and the markets were a treasure trove where we were blown away to find you could get about three hundred types of chilli at one stand.

Neither of us had much experience of cooking Mexican food, and so when we first arrived we booked ourselves into a fast-track cooking school, called Seasons of the Sun. This was a great move, because not only were we taught how to cook Mexican food, but we were taken to the market and shown which chillies were used for which recipes, which was extremely useful.

The most memorable day of the trip was when we got dressed in ponchos and cowboy hats to perform a really bad rendition of 'La Bamba' in the main bandstand in Oaxaca, while also having a chilli cook-off. We looked like a couple of heavies in a spaghetti Western and were joking about and in a really good mood before we started filming, but then we got some news from home that really pissed on the chips.

Vikram had read our first national newspaper TV review, and from the look on his face it wasn't good.

'What does it say?' we asked him, sweating under our ponchos.

'Shall we save it until after filming?'

'NOOO! Just tell us. Put us out of our misery!'

The reviewer had described our Namibia show as 'the biggest TV car crash since *Eldorado*'.

We couldn't believe our ears, and we felt like we'd been kicked in the stomach. All we wanted to do was hide under our sombreros and lick our wounds, but now we had to go and strut our stuff in what was the equivalent of Trafalgar Square, packed with a huge crowd of excited people expecting to be entertained.

While we grinned and performed, Si and I were both having very dark thoughts about the future. What if we'd travelled around the world, pulling out all the stops and barely seeing our loved ones for months on end just for this? What if it meant we'd blown our chances and would never be commissioned for another show again?

These were frightening thoughts, but thankfully we didn't have to suffer too long, as another review came in soon afterwards, and this one was totally different. The *Guardian*'s Nancy Banks-Smith, God love her, had written a review that could not have been more glowing.

'*The Hairy Bikers' Cookbook* is not so much a breath of fresh air as who left the bleeding door open,' she wrote. Her review included quotes from the show, like my remark that 'the beauty of barbecuing zebra is that you get nice stripes over it' and Si saying, ''ere we are at Bamburgh' when we stood on the vast Kalahari Desert sand dunes. She really got us, and we were dead chuffed.

Our first book was to be published a few months later. It was hard work putting it together, cracking on with it whenever we had time between filming. We wanted it to be a bit like an album, with pictures and stories cataloguing our travels, and including sections about the bikes and the road trips as well as the food and culture. Just writing the recipes was incredibly time-consuming, because of course we wanted them all to work perfectly and so we'd test them and test them again until we got the best result.

'How's the onion doing, Kingie?' I'd say, pen poised to write down the timings.

'Another minute, I reckon, we want them translucent.'

'Ready now?'

'No, bugger! They're overdone.'

'Right, let's start again . . .'

That was how it went as we painstakingly worked out the exact quantities and cooking times for each stage of every recipe. We did it very willingly, however. This was another golden opportunity we had been given, and we were very happy to have it.

For the first time in many years we both felt we had some financial security behind us. It was the first breath we felt we could take since the *Bikers* began, and we were very grateful for it.

'I'm getting myself a new car,' I told Si. 'What about you?'

'Well, mucker. You know I told Jane about twenty years ago that we'd get married as soon as we could afford it? We're finally doing it.'

16

Si's

Violet Martinis, Sea Bass with Chorizo Crust and Ultimate Fish Pie

Jane and I tied the knot on 3 March 2006 at Newcastle Civic Centre, surrounded by close family and friends and of course our three boys. Alex was now sixteen, James thirteen and Dylan was coming up for six. Before the wedding me and the boys all got booted and suited and had a proper gentlemen's dinner at the Jesmond Dene House Hotel in Newcastle, along with my brother Will, Dave and a few other close mates, including Simon Harrison, my old bandmate, who had introduced me to Jane. It was lush. The food was amazing, made by my mate Terry Laybourne, who's a fabulous Michelin-starred chef, but the best thing of all was that I was surrounded by the people I loved who had been with me through thick and thin, and had seen my boys growing up.

I had my beard trimmed down really small for the occasion, and Dave memorably told me I looked 'like a big girl with a Brazilian'. Cheers for that, mate. Anyway, the most important thing was that Jane looked happy and beautiful on our wedding day, and she dazzled again when we held a big party with one hundred and fifty guests the following weekend at a restaurant called Secco, which did us proud. I can remember feeling a real sense of achievement as I looked around the room that night. I'd kept my promise to Jane at long last, and we'd got married in a very special way.

John and Vikram came to the party, and by now we'd heard on the QT that the BBC was going to commission another series, which of course helped the celebrations go with even more of a swing. Afterwards Jane and I had a wonderful week in Venice, just the two of us, and while we were away Dave was making arrangements for Lil to visit him in Barrow; she'd finally agreed to make the trip, after Dave had given her several invitations.

'There's nothing nefarious going on,' he told me, which rang a distant bell.

'I think I've heard that line before,' I replied, remembering when he got together with Glen.

'We're penpals,' he insisted. 'She's coming for a holiday.'

Lil took her first ever flight, into Manchester Airport, and Dave kicked things off by treating her to a night at his local in Barrow, where she saw old men play dominoes. Things got better, thank God. He took her for a Chinese and Lil ate her first ever prawn, and then he brought her over to Newcastle, where we all met up and had a fine old time drinking Violet Martinis. After that Dave showed Lil the sights in London, took her to see *Mamma Mia!* and gave her a tour of the set of *Spooks*.

'So, what's happening, mate?' I asked.

'Told you. We're good mates. Anyhow, she's told me I can't fall in love with her as she has children.'

Somehow I didn't think we'd seen the last of Lil, but Dave was keeping his powder very dry indeed.

The Hairy Bikers' Cookbook was published in April 2006, and

Dave and I went on a three-week-long book-signing tour up and down the country. This was the first time either of us realised we had a 'following' as such, and we really enjoyed it when people came into the bookshops and wanted to meet us, and chat about our recipes and our travels.

'Hey, mate, it's a big buzz seeing our faces grinning off the shelves, isn't it?' I said to Dave when we got to the first bookstore.

There was no reply and I realised Dave was in a world of his own, gazing at the book with our photograph and names emblazoned on the front.

'Hello, earth to Mr Myers. Come in, Mr Myers.'

'Oooh, sorry, Kingie. I was lost in thought for a moment. It's really quite special this, isn't it? I mean, we've actually got a book out. It could be on people's shelves for decades, like my old Ken Hom and Keith Floyd books. The reality is only just sinking in. This is mega!'

'I know what you mean, mate. The theory is one thing, but seeing the book on the shelf is another matter entirely. How lucky are we? And now we get to chat to loads of nice people, and they call this work!'

Dave can obviously talk the hind legs off a donkey and I love a good natter and a josh with anybody, so the signings were something we were not fazed by at all; in fact we relished them.

The book tour was a huge success and our book went to number one, which was a great buzz, and when Jordan's autobiography knocked us down to second place for a couple of weeks we still celebrated.

'Who can complain at having two weeks underneath Jordan?' I said.

'You're right, Kingie. Not many men can say that!'

We were still waiting for the final confirmation that our third

TV series was being commissioned, and in the meantime Dave took himself back to the Isle of Man for the TT Races.

With money from the book in the bank by now, Dave had splashed out on a Benelli Tornado Italian superbike that he was going to ride at the Mad Sunday race we'd done together the previous year. This time he was going with Dr Dave. I wished I was going too but I couldn't because of family commitments, and so I told Dave to take plenty of photos, keep in touch and tell me all about it.

A few days later I took a phone call but didn't recognise the voice on the end of the phone.

'Who is it?' I asked. 'I can't hear you properly, mate.'

'It's nee,' came a muffled voice.

'Dave? Is that you, dude? Are you OK?'

'No, 'ot 'eally,' he managed, and then a grave-sounding Dr Dave came on the line.

'Sorry, Si, but Dave's been in a serious accident. He's going to be alright, but he's had a proper good hiding.'

It turned out Dave had had two kipper baps and a pot of tea – a detail superfluous to the story, but Dave can always tell you what he's eaten in any given circumstance – and then he got on his bike, joined the throngs of other riders and hit a bloody big scaffold truck head on in the middle of Devil's Elbow. There was nothing left of his bike and the smash looked so dramatic people were walking past taking photos of the wreckage. Dave needed to be helicoptered to Noble's Hospital, but he was too fat to be lifted in the door at the back of the rescue chopper and had to sit squashed in agony next to the pilot. The pain was so bad he couldn't see properly when he was carted into the emergency department, and he readily accepted the offer of morphine.

'Aye, it were like getting on a magic sledge to oblivion!' he said later. 'The relief was just incredible.'

Dave's chest and knees were black with bruises, he'd suffered internal bleeding and had to have pins inserted in his left wrist and shoulder. As for the bike, all Dr Dave salvaged from the several thousand pounds' worth of wreckage was the speedometer, as a keepsake.

While Dave was still in plaster we got the call to say our next series, to be named *The Hairy Bikers Ride Again*, was all systems go. The BBC had commissioned four hours' worth of programmes from India, Argentina, Belgium and Morocco.

'Fabulous!' Dave said, eyeing his plastered wrist and wondering if he was actually going to be able to ride a bike again, let alone traverse several different continents.

There was no question of taking time off. We just prayed he'd make a speedy recovery, and somehow we muddled through. We had started appearing on *Saturday Kitchen* with James Martin by this time, whom we admired as a chef and got on very well with; and we had a few other commitments in the diary too, like public speaking and appearing at food fairs, mostly at home and occasionally abroad. We loved all that, and so we just kept going. We both felt we had to make hay while the sun shone, and so that's what we did.

I was spending more time with Dave than I was with Jane and the boys by now, but again we just accepted that was how things needed to be at this juncture in our careers. It was tough being away from home so much, but on the positive side Dave was just like family and we enjoyed spending time together, so it was very doable.

'I don't suppose you could iron a couple of shirts for me?' Dave asked when we were staying in a hotel not long after his accident.

He's always been dead fussy about his clothes whereas I'd never used an iron in my life, but I did my best. Then he tried to have a shower, with his arms wrapped in plastic bags to protect his plaster and bandages.

'Kingie, mate, I hate to ask . . . I can wash me bits but I can't manage me pits, would you mind?'

He's also very fussy about hygiene and smelling nice, so I couldn't refuse the poor bugger, could I? Dave was stark bollock-naked, and when I started washing his armpits he began singing 'Je t'aime', to which I responded: 'Listen, mucker, if there's any movement down there whatsoever I'm off!'

We had to laugh and, as often seemed to be the case, when one of us had a problem, the other soon came out in sympathy. My latest medical complaint was quite embarrassing, because I developed a strangulated testicle, probably caused by too many hours on the bike. I had to go to hospital and suffer the indignity of a pretty young nurse trying to wrestle the giant thing into an elasticated sling that was way too small and catapulted back on me, with agonising results; so painful that I passed out, actually.

Dave and I didn't have any secrets. We had ridden so many miles on bikes together we'd been known to share tubes of haemorrhoids cream. One time, memorably, we went into a chemist's abroad to get some medication.

'What's Spanish for haemorrhoids?' I asked Dave.

'No idea, mate.'

The girl behind the counter didn't speak English and so I decided there was only one thing for it, and launched into a mime of me putting cream on my finger, bending over and rubbing it on my bum. The poor assistant looked at me blankly, and by this time I was getting a few strange looks, and so I did that typical

English thing of saying the word slowly and loudly, hoping to make myself understood.

'Haem – orr – hoids,' I said, again pointing to my backside.

'Ah!' she said. 'Haemorrhoids!'

Unbeknown to me the word sounds exactly the same in Spanish and I could have saved myself my little charade, but at least it had been entertaining, and Dave and I both fell about laughing.

Anyhow, I told Dave all about my latest problem before he next came to visit me and Jane at home.

'Don't laugh,' I said. 'I'll be wearing a pair of Jane's old elasticated maternity pants because they're the only things I'm comfy in.'

It's just as well I was so frank, because when he knocked on the door Dylan, who was six at the time, ran to greet him shouting: 'Uncle Dave! Have you seen the size of Dad's testicle? It's gigantic! It's as big as a mango!'

Despite our ailments, Dave and I did a day of cookery demonstrations at the Good Food Show at the NEC in Birmingham that summer, which was a big deal for us.

'Bloody hell, Kingie, this is quite a rise in a couple of years,' Dave said, looking at the crowds thronging the stage. 'I feel like an overnight pop sensation!'

The organisers had put us up at the Hilton and we were on stage after Gordon Ramsay, who was great with us and made us feel very welcome. Women had thrown panties at him and the stage was covered when it was our turn to go on, so we just chucked them all back out into the audience for a laugh.

It was very exciting being in a big venue and meeting loads of people who were interested in food, and particularly the food we were cooking. Dave and I were buzzing. We cooked the crispy beef and lemongrass noodles together that he had done in the street in Vietnam when I broke my ankle, talking twaddle while we did so.

We loved every minute. To us it wasn't vastly different from cooking on screen, because we were always unscripted and just being ourselves in front of the camera. We behaved the same whether we were making noodles in each other's kitchens, in a far-flung country or anywhere else for that matter. We had each other's back too, and if one of us dried up or stumbled with anything on stage we knew the other would step in.

Afterwards we got chatting to an ebullient home economist called Sammy-Jo Squire, who asked us who our 'home ec' was.

'Er, we haven't got one,' we said. 'What would we want one of them for?'

She looked at us agog.

'What about your cookbook? Who tested the recipes? Who styled the food?'

Now it was our turn to look agog. We had no idea about home economists, recipe-testing or food-styling, and Dave and I explained to an increasingly incredulous Sammy-Jo that we planned the recipes between us, did all the shopping and preparation ourselves, and then made the food look as presentable as possible for the photos.

'So let me get this right,' she said. 'If you're in a foreign country and you want a specific cut of meat for a recipe, you two have to source it?'

'Yes,' we said. 'It's not always easy, running around on the motorbikes doing the shopping. One time we really struggled to find a loin of lamb so we had to buy a whole lamb and . . .'

'Boys, I think I'd better take you two for a drink,' Sammy-Jo said, and we are both extremely glad she did.

Over a few G & Ts we learned that what we'd been doing

on the road wasn't the norm at all. Television cooks typically had a home economist on hand to help buy and plan the food, prepare and test recipes and assist with presentation. It wasn't a luxury: Sammy-Jo explained it was the most cost-effective and efficient way of doing things, and it ensured recipes were safe and accurate, and dishes always looked their best on telly or in a book.

All of this made perfect sense and seemed so obvious, but we were still learning all the time. It was only quite recently that we'd sussed out that clear glass mixing bowls worked better than ceramic ones on telly, so viewers could see the ingredients. We could have done with knowing that a couple of years earlier, but nobody enlightened us on such matters before we met Sammy-Jo.

It wasn't anybody's fault. We never set out to be TV cooks and the food element of our shows had evolved naturally, but clearly a home economist would be a great asset to us now.

'We obviously need to ask John and Vikram if Sammy-Jo can come with us on the third series,' I said. 'She's essential; potentially life-changing!'

'You're right, Kingie. It'll make such a difference to us. Apart from anything else, she'd be a massive help with the next book.'

'You're not wrong there, Dave. That would really take the pressure off. Thank God we did this show.'

For our second book the publishers wanted us to provide twenty-five recipes from each of the next four countries we were visiting, and me and Dave had been fretting about how we would achieve it, on top of making the series.

We relayed all of this information to John and Vikram and thankfully they agreed that Sammy-Jo could come and assist us for the week after the recce when we worked on the cookery, and so that is what she did. From that point on Sammy-Jo became not only an incredibly helpful addition to the team – she is one of the best home ecs in the country – but also a very good friend.

Though India ended up being the first show of *The Hairy Bikers Ride Again*, we actually filmed Argentina first, which was an incredibly special trip with so many amazing memories. Dave and I took tango lessons and danced in the main square at Buenos Aires; we lay on a beach at the Valdes Peninsula with thousands of penguins and elephant seals around us and we watched about two hundred whales swim up with their calves, which was mind-blowingly beautiful. We also caught a spectacular thirty-five sea bass within half an hour of starting to fish, and then we cooked some on the beach, filleted and covered with a delicious chorizo crust. The local chorizo was good quality and we wanted to come up with something a little bit different, to make the dish special and celebrate the fish. It worked like a dream, and to this day it's still one of our favourite dishes.

We'd picked up a child's drum kit in Buenos Aires, and we saw an opportunity to have some fun with it on the beach after we'd finished cooking that day.

'How about if I play the drums and you do a bit of singing, then, Dave?' I said after we'd kicked around a few ideas with the crew.

'A bit of "Don't Cry for Me Argentina?" Yes, I'm up for that, Kingie!'

'Nice one, Dave. It'll be a hoot.'

'It's a very good idea. For these things to be funny it always works best if you actually possess some level of skill, and just give it a twist.'

'Yes, Dave,' I said, thinking to myself, 'here he goes, getting all fastidious and technical'. 'Let's crack on, shall we? The great thing is I can actually play the drums, but the question is, can you pull off the singing?'

'Course I can! Try stopping me!'

We set everything up with the crew and Dave learned all the lyrics, and then I started playing the drums in the background while Dave burst into song with the cameras on him.

The camera work was timed perfectly, cutting to me when I beat the drum, revealing me sitting on a rock with this ridiculously small drum kit, wearing combats and a bandana.

He got louder and more passionate with every line until he was sounding practically operatic when he belted out: 'But nothing impressed me at all! I never expected it to!'

At that point he then changed gear completely and started getting all Sid Vicious, delivering the line 'Don't cry for me Argentina . . . !,' with wild, punk-style abandon.

That was my cue to do a Keith Moon, going mental on the drums and smashing them to smithereens in the process, which wasn't difficult because they were so small.

'You tosser!' Dave then jokingly accused me, giving a pompous quiver of the lip for added effect. 'That was my finest moment and you've ruined it!'

As we did all this, a child walked past, completely unscripted, and put his hands over his ears to block out the racket we were making. Then a lone dog howled and walked away, which was also caught perfectly on camera. The timing was superb, and to this day we still roar with laughter at memory of it.

It was my fortieth birthday while we were in Argentina and Dave treated me to a beautiful Breitling watch, which made me go all emotional. It was something he knew I really wanted, and it was a massive gesture. We'd come such a long way together and were definitely more like brothers than mates now.

Another birthday present was one I'd promised myself for a long time, if ever I had the good fortune to visit Argentina. I'd wanted to get a tattoo of Che Guevara ever since I was a teenager and heard the quote: 'The true revolutionary is guided by great feelings of love.' With hardly any persuasion Dave was up for it too, and we hatched a plot to get matching images on the top of our right arms. Dave sketched out the design and we spotted an ideal tattoo parlour in the town of Puerto Madryn, which was blasting out Led Zeppelin and looked right up our street. Three hours of pain later and we were not just brothers, but brothers with matching arms.

'I think you're having a mid-life crisis, Kingie,' Dave said.

'I think I am, mate. And it feels fooking fantastic!'

In hindsight, it would probably be more accurate to say that both Dave and I were feeling a sense of freedom and relief that we'd never had the luxury of experiencing before. It seemed like the right time to let off some of the considerable amount of steam that had built up over the years, and to celebrate the success we were having.

We shot the Belgium episode just before Christmas, and Lil flew out to Brussels to visit Dave. They were obviously getting on really well but it still looked like they couldn't be anything more than penpals; there were too many complications, though they enjoyed spending time together.

India was our next destination, where we hired a house in Chennai that came with an obligatory 'house boy' called Andrew, who was in his forties and had a family. We didn't really want a house boy, but it seemed we didn't have a choice. Fortunately, we quickly discovered that Andrew was a trained chef and so he helped us with the food instead. Sammy-Jo came out as planned, and it was fabulous, with Dave and I taking turns cooking, writing notes and picking up authentic tips from Andrew. Soaking up knowledge from the locals was something we tried to do as much as possible when we were travelling, and if ever there was a local cookery class available we would take it.

Unfortunately, after a couple of days, I started to feel and look dreadful. I was sweating and my skin was all clammy, and so I went to lie down, hoping it would pass. That didn't help at all, and then I found I couldn't breathe properly. Worse still, I developed a pain in my arm and went a bit blue, which frightened the life out of me. I was convinced I was having a heart attack, and I told Dave I needed to see a doctor pretty damn fast.

We had an excellent fixer working with us, and the next thing I knew he was saying there were no street maps of Chennai and arranging for his brother to come over on a motorbike, to show us the way to the hospital. Then Dave was putting me in the back of a tuk-tuk, and apparently I was off my head and asking: 'Where am I?'

'You're in India, Kingie. We're going to the hospital.'

'Oh,' I replied. 'Will me mam be there?'

To complete the circus Sammy-Jo was perched on the back of the fixer's brother's motorbike as we careered along dirt tracks and half-built roads. When we finally got to the hospital I was gasping for breath and clutching my chest dramatically. As I was wheeled inside I can clearly remember seeing a huge, illuminated image of Mother Theresa, and there were lots of kind faces and angelic voices all around me.

'Bloody hell, I've died,' I thought.

The image turned out to be an eight-foot-high portrait of Mother Theresa that was hanging in the foyer, but I didn't realise that until much later. Dave was also in a state by now, and he remembers feeling like everything was going into free-fall, as it did with Glen, and then with his brain op.

The karma wasn't good, and suddenly the nurses were asking me if I was a Christian and making sure I had my rosary beads with me, which I did, as always. Dave and Sammy-Jo were asked to step outside the room while I was given an ECG to check my heart, and I wondered if I'd ever see them again. Unbeknown to me, when they were in the corridor, Dave's phone rang.

'Hello? Is that M & S?'

'*Stella?* Is that you?'

'Oh, is that you, Dave? Oh! I've dialled the wrong number by mistake. I was trying to phone Marks. How's our Si?'

Dave's number was scribbled on a pad in Mam's kitchen in case she ever had trouble getting hold of me, but this was the one and only time she had ever called him.

'He's a bit busy, Stella,' Dave said, feeling spooked. 'I'll get him to call you.'

'Thanks, Dave. Ta-ta.'

Thankfully, my diagnosis was nowhere near as serious as we all feared. It was quickly established that I was suffering from extremely severe dehydration, which had buggered up the valves in my heart. I had high blood pressure, and it didn't help that I was taking nicotine tablets to help me stop smoking, or that I'd been knocking back double espressos when I should have been drinking plentiful supplies of water.

The doctors and nurses were extremely kind and attentive as they rigged me up to a rehydration drip. I hadn't been in receipt of that level of care away from home for a very long time, and Dave and I both really appreciated it. As soon as I had my colour back and was feeling stronger I told Dave and Sammy-Jo I was happy for them to leave me there for the night. They eventually left for a while, but returned later with a Tiffin box containing some dinner for me, which was really thoughtful of them. Mind you, Dave was dressed up to the nines and Sammy-Jo looked like the Queen Mum in all her finery, and it turned out they were planning to go and eat lobster and drink some fine wine to get over the ordeal.

'Bully for you!' I said sarcastically, though I didn't mean it. They deserved a bit of pampering.

'Aren't you staying?' a doctor asked in surprise when he clocked Dave and Sammy-Jo.

'Oh, gosh no,' Dave replied politely, doing his best English gent impression. 'We wouldn't dream of imposing. We know Mr King needs to rest.'

The doctor looked at him in horror.

'But you *must* stay,' he said. 'Your friend has had a terrible shock. He needs you here. At least one of you must stay.'

This was characteristic of the holistic care delivered by the hospital, but of course it scuppered Dave's plans completely. When the doctor left the room Dave sat cross-legged beside my bed with a grudging look on his face, saying: 'Give me the Tiffin box, bastard!'

Thankfully, I was back on my feet quickly and over the next few weeks we had some priceless experiences, like riding hundreds of miles in the freezing cold mountains to visit the Tata tea plantation, and experiencing the incredible sense of power and holiness at the Meenakshi Amman temple of Madurai, where the kids ran around screaming and laughing and ringing the bell. It was simply magical.

John Stroud produced our final show of the series, Morocco, and he was amazing and helped make it great fun. Dave and I cooked a tagine in the middle of the square in Djemaa El-Fna in Marrakech; we saw the start of the Lisbon Dakar Rally and I played drums with a Berber drum circle which made my fingers bleed but was a life's ambition fulfilled.

Another day, high up in the Atlas Mountains, we cooked a whole lamb that we wanted to share with a group of Berber villagers, but we were dismayed to discover that the women were not allowed to sit at the table and eat with the men.

'I've got an idea,' Dave said with a devilish glint in his eye. 'Leave this with me!'

He talked to the crew and went off and kitted himself out with a flamboyant belly-dancer's costume that included some fetching nipple-tassels, a glittery ball in his navel and a tray of candles that was Velcroed on top of the hat on his head.

We'd seen dancers like this in Marrakech and Dave reckoned he had all the moves sussed out; he even practised the high-pitched 'zaghroota' sounds that belly-dancers somehow make with their tongue on the roof of their mouth.

'You just announce me, Kingie. It'll be a right laugh!'

Once all the men were seated for the lamb feast I took the mic and, in my best MC voice, said: 'Ladies and gentlemen. Allow me to introduce your entertainment for the evening – the lovely Fatima!'

With that Dave appeared in all his belly-wobbling glory, caterwauling, and then he began to tour the tables, pouting his red lips and fluttering his false eyelashes as he went. At one point he was actually on the table-tops, giving what appeared to be a lap-dance to a few very bemused-looking gentlemen, and I suddenly realised the particular table he was on was butted up to a balcony with a forty-foot drop.

'Mind the edge, Fatima!' I called, and thank God he did, because I don't think the tray of candles balancing on his bonce would have offered much protection if Dave had taken a header.

After that we did one of our best and most spectacular rides ever across the Atlas Mountains, and that's saying something, as so far we'd averaged a thousand miles per country we visited. Dave had coped incredibly well, incidentally, as even now he still had a brace on his hand from his TT crash, but he didn't complain.

We had survived making another series, and *The Hairy Bikers Ride Again* was going to be broadcast as eight shows from April 2007, to coincide with the next book launch. We now not only had a taste for travel, we were addicted to it. Me and Dave were probably two of the most over-stimulated humans on the planet, and we didn't want any of this to stop.

The question, as ever, was, would the BBC want us to carry on? Ben Gale had just taken over as the new commissioning editor for factual shows, and so that threw added uncertainty into the mix.

We set a date to talk to our producer John Stroud about future plans, and in the meantime Dave had a break and went to Disneyland Paris, with Lil and her daughter Iza. Even though Lil had told Dave repeatedly, 'You can't fall in love with me!', of course he had. In fact, he'd fallen for Lil in such a big way that he wanted her to move to Barrow, and she was thinking about it. Lil's son, Serge, was now seventeen and about to go to university, so the decision hung on Iza, who was eleven. She would be able to start her secondary schooling in Cumbria if they got things organised before September, but Dave and Lil weren't sure she would buy it.

'We figured the best thing to do when you want a child to agree to a plan is to put it to her in Disneyland!' Dave said, only half-joking.

The Mickey Mouse magic worked wonders on Iza, who is by nature very spirited and outgoing. She said she liked Dave and she was happy to give the move a try, despite speaking very little English. What a gutsy girl.

Lil had only seen the sea once before she came to England, and now she had agreed to leave everything that was familiar to her and bring Iza to live on a tiny, windswept island in the Irish Sea, with Dave. I mean, it *had* to be love.

When Dave got home from France he had a couple of things on down south, and so he arranged to meet John Stroud in a pub in Ladbroke Grove. John was an incredibly active guy, always skiing with his family or playing five-a-side football. We admired his energy, but when Dave saw him that day he wasn't his usual self. John was dragging his foot, which Dave assumed was the result of one or other of his sporting activities, but as they sat there having lunch, one of John's arms went too, and he really didn't seem right. John subsequently went for tests and, unbelievably, it turned out he had suffered a stroke in the pub with Dave that afternoon. Very sadly, worse news soon followed. John was diagnosed with brain cancer. He was fifty-two years old and one of the most vibrant, lovely, talented blokes you could meet. It was a terrible shock. Dave and I prayed that John would get better and it didn't seem possible that he wouldn't; this was the dynamic man we'd travelled around the globe with just the year before. More importantly, John had a wife and two children who adored him, and needed him to get well.

As John underwent treatment, his friend and business partner at Big Bear Productions, Marcus Mortimer, took us on. Marcus had directed *The Two Ronnies* and was a great bloke whom we liked immediately.

'Come on, we'll go and meet Ben Gale!' he said cheerfully.

Marcus's positivity rubbed off on us, and when we sat in Ben Gale's office, Dave and I both felt optimistic. We were not new boys any more. Our TV shows had got cracking ratings, the vast majority of our reviews were fantastic and we now had not one but two bestselling books under our belt.

I'm sure there must have been some pleasant chit-chat, but practically the only words I can remember coming from Ben Gale's lips that day were these: 'Do you still have contacts in your day jobs?'

I felt sick to my stomach, and I know Dave felt exactly the same. I was forty years old and Dave was nearly fifty. The very last thing we wanted to do was go back to our day jobs.

I can't remember exactly how the conversation proceeded, but in the end, despite his extremely alarming question, Ben Gale did agree to commission a one-hour Christmas special. We snatched it with both hands. It was a massive relief to have come away with something, though when we started putting ideas together for the show Dave and I felt a bit like we did when we worked on the original Portugal pilot; it was make or break all over again. Vikram had moved on to other things by now too, so it really was like going back to square one and starting from scratch with completely new people.

Dave and I both worked incredibly hard on the Christmas show, coming up with all kinds of mad ideas and settling on an off-the-wall Geordie-cum-Cumbrian nativity theme. After weeks of graft I managed to find camels in Newcastle, three Northumbrian shepherds and I'd lined up my mam and my brother Will to play the three kings alongside me. Dave, meanwhile, was all geared up to play baby Jesus – that was going to be one of the comedy punchlines – and we were both drowning in tinsel and baubles and generally busting our arses to make it a belter of a show. It was at that point that we got the message from Ben Gale: 'Please don't mention Christmas. There isn't space in the

Christmas schedule for your show any more. It is going to have to go out as a winter special.'

The blow made us incredibly despondent, and I will never forget the disappointment I felt. Dave and I were sitting in a car park in Manchester during a downpour, and our parade had been well and truly rained on.

'Shall we just open a kebab shop instead?' Dave said.

'Perhaps we should, dude. Do you think we'd be able to live off it?'

Of course, it was just talk. We could sink or swim, and neither of us had any intention of letting our fledgeling telly careers go down the plughole without a fight. It was onwards and upwards, although unfortunately the other bad news was that we didn't have much time to pull a new winter show together; in fact the schedule meant we had just one weekend to come up with the content.

Lil moved over in September with Iza, so for the first time ever Dave had a family to provide for, just as I did. In fact, within a fortnight Lil's son Serge arrived too. He's a gifted mathematician and had been offered a computing scholarship at Aberdeen University, which he had been thinking about taking up the following year. However, with his mum and sister now in Barrow he put in a call on the off chance, to see if he could start earlier. 'Yes. You've missed Freshers' fortnight but you can start the course as quickly as you can get here,' came the surprising reply, and so Lil drove Serge to Scotland in Dave's car and fixed everything up within a few days.

'Bloody hell, Kingie. You came back from Romania with a straw hat and a bottle of vodka, and I got a family!' Dave joked. I was absolutely made up for him; he was over the moon.

It was Dave's fiftieth birthday shortly after Lil arrived and she wanted to throw a party for him at home. Unfortunately, Dave and I had agreed to do some after-dinner speaking at a charity event in London that same weekend. Neither of us particularly wanted to go, but having committed to it we wouldn't have dreamed of pulling out; it's not the way we are.

We did our bit and, after the dinner, Dave slipped away to make a phone call to Lil.

'Look in the bedside drawer,' he told her. 'There is a little red box in there.'

'Hurry up home,' she told him, and when he got back she was wearing the 1870s antique engagement ring he had picked out for her after she had booked her ticket to England.

I bought Dave a Breitling watch for his birthday, the same as the one he'd bought me for my fortieth, and he was thrilled to bits with it.

After his birthday celebrations, Dave and I cracked on with our 'don't mention Christmas' winter special. We'd thrown the kitchen sink at the new show, coming up with a tenuous narrative in which we both bigged up our home counties. The show ultimately included a hotchpotch of stories that somehow linked Ultimate Fish Pie from Fish Quay in North Shields, chestnuts roasted at the top of Blackpool Tower, Dave being handcuffed semi-naked to a lamppost in Newcastle, a feast cooked by the Thai community in Barrow and Dave looking like Mr Toad, speeding up the Tyne at seventy knots in a Formula One powerboat named the *Hairy Mary*.

My mam's cookbook had cropped up in conversation several times, so in addition to all this mayhem we decided it would be great if we could talk Mam into appearing on the show. By this time she had moved into sheltered accommodation, and we asked her if we could film her there, and talk about the little black family cookbook that she still had never let me have.

'Well, I suppose so, as long as youse are not going to start nagging me to give ya the book.'

'Well, why won't ya, Mam? I mean, me and me best mate are cooking on the telly. Surely I deserve to have it now?'

'No. I'm telling ya, Simon. You're not bloody getting it.'

It had become a bit of a joke, and when we did the filming Mam was fantastic, playing along really well.

'You're not bloody getting it!' she repeated for the cameras. 'And I'm taking it with me when I die! And don't think you can go digging me up because I'm getting cremated . . .'

In the final scene of the show, which was called *The Hairy Bikers Come Home Winter Special,* me and Dave were seen turning off the lights in Mam's sheltered accommodation as we said goodnight, which at the time seemed perfectly innocuous. The programme was broadcast in January 2008, and to our relief and delight 3.4 million viewers tuned in, which was our highest ever audience. Hilariously, though, thanks to that final scene, lots of viewers had questioned whether Dave and I were more than just best mates. Apparently, seeing us turning off the lights together at the end of the day had sparked all kinds of chat among gay men on the Internet, who wondered if Dave and I actually lived together in the sheltered accommodation. We were described as 'woofilicious' by some of our male admirers, which we thought was a hoot. Even funnier, not long afterwards a bloke who saw Lil and Dave arm-in-arm together whispered conspiratorially to Lil: 'Don't worry, love, I won't say anything to Si . . .'

Anyhow, whatever misconceptions the sheltered accommodation scene caused, the main thing was the hard work we'd put into the show had paid off and millions had tuned in, though this did not mean it was plain sailing from here on in.

By the start of 2008 we had no new shows in the pipeline. Dave went to Sammy-Jo's for dinner one night and discussed our predicament, which resulted in her kindly suggesting we talk to her contacts at BBC Birmingham, and perhaps come up with some ideas for the BBC Good Food channel. One of the things Dave and I had discussed many times was doing something with baking, because on our travels we rarely had the luxury of an oven. This was well before the nation had fallen in love with TV baking and, in hindsight, it was a brave move for us because baking is all about science and alchemy, whereas we were used to being off-the-cuff and experimental with food. Logical restraints had never put us off before, though, and after a bit of a brainstorm we proposed the idea of travelling around Britain searching out the best recipes for bread, cakes, pies and puddings, throwing in our usual mix of daftness and digging up some interesting yarns along the way. Very happily, Nick Patton, head of studio at BBC Birmingham, went with it and gave us four half-hour slots and a Christmas special. We felt like we'd won the creative lottery all over again and now had enough work to see us well into 2009, which was a bloody big relief.

'Have you thought of a title?' we were asked at one of the early meetings.

Before we could draw breath a girl across the office piped up, 'Hairy Bakers', and of course that was perfect, and it stuck.

Once again Dave and I went into over-drive, working out how to make the new series not just good, but our best ever. After the winter special we'd got into the swing of using our own props and calling on friends and family to help, and this time, among many other crazy things, we had Lil, who is a talented tailor, making yokel smocks for us to wear. I ended up singing in the middle of a crop circle while wearing mine, which in hindsight was totally bonkers.

'But this is meant to be a serious programme on making bread,' one of the producers had commented when we first floated this idea.

'Yes, but we like to do things a bit differently. Trust us. It'll be fun, and it'll work.'

There was a long and thoughtful silence but thankfully we did get our own way and, as the series went on, I think the programme makers started to really get me and Dave, because they allowed us a lot of creative freedom.

When we went to Henley Royal Regatta to make cookies for some of the boatmen, they provided us with straw boaters and blazers, set us up with our own stand and let us get away with being slightly, well, outrageous.

'Wraaaah! Wraaaah! Wraaaah!' Dave and I would guffaw at the incredibly posh gentlemen passing in their boats.

'Wraaaah!' a dapper gent would snort back from river, waving cheerfully as he did so. 'Wraaaah! Wraaaah!' we'd reply. We didn't exchange a word but somehow we communicated with these incredibly well-heeled blokes, and it was very funny indeed.

'Why do they all choose to dress like schoolboys?' Dave said, genuinely bemused. 'What's that all about?'

'Wraaaah!' I replied.

'Wraaaah!' he returned, raising his eyebrows and nodding.

'Wraaaah!' I smiled back.

We called the plum-in-cheek language 'Henley's Tourette's', and to our delight the producers included some of our mucking around in the show.

Dave and I were in our element making *The Hairy Bakers*. It took us all over the country, doing everything from making beer-and-cheese bread to baking a five-tier wedding cake, and presenting some lovely ladies from the Women's Institute with our own version of the classic Victoria sponge. We were learning about baking all the time, and it was very refreshing filming on our home soil after all the foreign travel we'd done. We had one foot in the entertainment camp and one foot in the factual programme camp, so it's hardly surprising the TV executives had needed to get their heads around what we were about, but we really felt like we'd proved we could occupy both territories, and do it well.

The final proof was in the pudding, of course, and we got more than four million viewers for the first episode, which was about two million more than the programme makers expected. You are only ever as good as your last viewing figures, and with this result we suddenly found ourselves being the flavour of the month. We didn't realise it at the time, but in fact *The Hairy Bakers* would mark a huge turning point in our careers.

17

Dave's

Stuffed Turkey Ballotine, Lemon Soufflé and Poulets de Bresse

'Bloody hell, James, we're like three sardines in a tin here!' Si said.

We had become good mates with James Martin after appearing on *Saturday Kitchen* many times, and he'd invited us to stay with him in France and make a guest appearance on his new show, *James Martin's Brittany*. He was towing his caravan around the region with his Porsche 4 x 4 and cooking with whatever fresh ingredients he could find each day. It sounded blissful, but we were disappointed when we arrived and found that happy camper James expected me and Si to share a fold-out double bed in the caravan.

'Bloody hell, not this again!' we both groaned as we hauled half of the thin foam mattress onto the floor to make a bed for Si, cringing as we reminisced about the time we shared a bed in that fleapit in Portugal.

James was very protective of his caravan and issued strict rules about 'do's and don't's'. Peeing was permitted, but if you wanted a number two you had to go elsewhere. This was irresistible to us, and so of course we made full use of his facilities, just to wind him up. Then I dressed up in a mankini one day and jumped in James's Porsche. Seeing his horrified reaction as my bare bum cheeks brushed his leather seats was hilarious, and Si and I laughed like a pair of naughty kids. This was the sort of caper we used to get up to so much more in the old days, when work pressure wasn't so intense, and it was something that came naturally to us, and that we didn't want to lose.

When work had been thin on the ground before *The Hairy Bakers* was in the offing, Si and I had talked about putting on some live stage shows, combining a bit of chat about our cookery and travels, and some mankini-style comedy madness. We both loved performing and coming face to face with people who enjoyed watching us on the telly, and of course it would be another source of income, to keep ourselves solvent between shows. By the time we were working on *Bakers* wc had decided to take the plunge and give this a go. *Bakers* was only going to be four half-hour shows and a Christmas special so it wasn't going to keep us afloat for long.

After some very fun planning and rehearsing Si and I hired out the 550-seater Forum Twenty-Eight theatre in Barrow in September 2008, to put on a kind of 'evening with' show, which involved Si and me chatting about our travels and adventures and included entertainment from a local tap-dancing troupe. To our delight we sold out for two nights, and so we decided to book loads more nights in decent-sized venues, while also improving the show all the time, which in retrospect it really needed!

In the early days we did this sketch that we called 'Big Chef, Little Chef', and the idea was that four chefs – caricatures of Jamie Oliver, Ainsley Harriot, Gordon Ramsay and Nigel Slater – would all be auditioning to sing in a choir. The joke of it was that during the audition they would keep coming out with their identifying catchphrases, so Nigel would say something terribly posh like 'Air her-ler there!' while Gordon would of course spit out an expletive.

'I know,' I said to Si, once we'd got the bones of the idea in mind. 'They could all be singing "Downtown" by Petula Clark.'

'I like it, Dave. And then we could have their heads under four silver domes, lined up on a trolley.'

'Aye, and when they get above themselves, we can put the lid back on!'

We tested this idea out on an audience at the Riverside in Hammersmith, complete with a section in which I dressed as a cowboy and rode an eighteen-foot-wide mechanical rodeo bull, and Si bashed himself over the head with a tin tray, while dressed as an Indian and giving an out-of-control rendition of 'Rawhide'.

We'd got to know Bob Mortimer by this time, and we asked him if he'd have a look and give us a bit of advice and direction.

'What d'you think?' I asked him, while rubbing cream into the bruises I'd sustained from falling repeatedly off the bull.

'I know the bull is an unmitigated disaster, but what about the rest of it?'

'You can't possibly put this in front of a paying audience,' Bob replied.

Bob helped us knock it into much better shape, and eventually, a good twelve months or so later, we took *The Hairy Bikers' Big Night Out* tour up and down the country for about four months, with great success.

We opened the show with a spoof of the Nina Simone classic, 'Ain't Got No, I Got Life'.

'I've got me hair, got me beard, got me man tits and I'm weird,'

Left: Our first attempt at cooking on camera. A pair of puddings in front of the lens, 2003.

Right: Filming our first pilot in 2004 in float tubes. It said in the brochure we would resemble swans – from the fish's point of view.

Left: Us and Vikram Jayanti filming the very first test film for the Bikers. Note on old scrappers – Suzuki GS 1000. Both self-destructed shortly after the filming, 2004.

Left: 'Right, let's give it a go. Honest, Kingie, I have a licence!' Namibia, 2005.

Right: 'Where the hell are we now?!' Namibia, 2005.

Left: 'Simon, watch my feet.' 'It is not the feet I'm looking at, pet.' Argentina, 2006.

Left: 'Aw, come on, give us a kiss. One day I will be on *Strictly*.'

Right: Hairy spice! 'Anyone seen wa camel?!' Morocco, 2006.

Below: What a pair of oddjobs! Belgium, 2006.

Above: Belgium, 2006, in search of the perfect chip. Wish it would have stopped raining.

Above: Never looked better – great faces for radio.

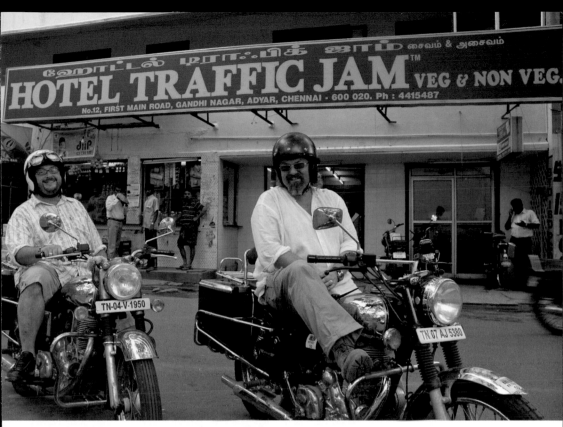

Above: 2006, born to be mild. We love India!

Above: Is it me or are we on a slope?

Above: Blissful enlightenment, man!

Above: One of the happiest days of Dave's life – pointing out the parts of the beast, with Si as a suitable model. Amazing how hard it is to get sharpie pen off. Oh dear!

The Hairy Bikers

Left: Dave's wedding, 2011.
'No, Dave, you kiss the bride – not Kingie!'

Right: Night out
in Tokyo. Kingie
gangster-style, 2013.

Below: Wok smuggling!

Left: Dave with a full head of hair in Edinburgh, 2015.

Above: Twenty years on and we are still best mates. Here's to the next twenty!

our lyrics went. 'Got my belly, got my bike, got my kitchen, got my scales, got my tools, got my tales, but most of all I've got YOU!'

At that point me and Si went wild, jumping up and down and having a big cuddle.

We included our favourite clips from our shows, like performing 'Don't Cry for Me Argentina' on the beach in Patagonia and me belly-dancing with my nipple-tassels in Morocco, and we also did a very funny sketch demonstrating cuts of beef, using Si on all fours as a live butcher's model, and a pen that turned out to be permanent marker. At the end of the show we took questions from the audience about everything from our favourite motorbikes to, spookily enough, the likelihood of one of us ever appearing on *Strictly Come Dancing*, and we signed books and posed for photos for anybody who asked. It was a thoroughly good laugh, and we loved it.

Around this time Si and I started making plans to move to a new agency that would suit our changing needs better, and we eventually joined James Grant Management, who proved to be a great support. Also, thanks to our connection with James Martin, we were introduced to Amanda Ross at Cactus TV, who was keen to work with us and produce a new daytime series. Amanda hired a guy called Dave Skinner to develop some ideas, and he suggested we could do a food tour of Britain, in which Si and I would visit different counties around the UK, learn about how classic dishes have evolved and meet the local food producers. It was something me and Si both really fancied doing and we were very enthusiastic about, right away. Eventually the idea was developed to include a cook-off element, which meant we would compete against a top-rated chef from each county we visited to produce a winning dish that would be judged by a local panel. This was a bit scary, but me and Si were both up for it. After all, nobody could laugh at us for not beating a Michelin-star chef, and at least we were prepared to have a go.

BBC2 Daytime ultimately commissioned thirty episodes of the *Food Tour of Britain,* which was a fabulous result for us. More good news followed after Cactus introduced us to Amanda Harris at Orion Publishing. Amanda had been impressed with *The Hairy Bakers* and believed in us enough to commission a cookbook to accompany the *Food Tour* series. We were dead chuffed. Things were most definitely going our way.

'All we've got to do now, Kingie, is, er, ride 15,000 miles around the country for five months.'

'Aye, and they're saying it's going to be one of the worse winters for decades. What a belting idea, Dave! And don't forget the punchline. We've got to compete against top chefs at their own game, in their own restaurants. *And we are not even chefs.* Do we need our bumps feeling or what?'

Si wasn't serious, of course, but put like that the series was pretty bloody daunting.

'Let's just give it a go,' I said, which was a phrase Si and I had used many times over the years, and had become a bit of a mantra to us.

We knew the biking alone would be tough, but we had no intention of cutting corners and were committed to doing the whole tour authentically, on two wheels. I'm glad we did. It turned out to be an absolutely belting series. We met wonderful food producers and did some whacky things, like making proper Cornish pasties at the Eden Project and Cheshire cheese soup in the jaguar house at Chester Zoo, and we even had tea at the Dorchester with the Duchess of Cornwall, who was supporting British Food Fortnight and was simply wonderful.

To our surprise Si and I actually won seventeen out of the thirty cook-offs with the top chefs too. The chefs were incredibly gracious and generous, and we learned a great deal from them. For example, in one of the early weeks the Dorset-based chef Alex Aitken taught us how to make the most fabulous fondant potatoes, which we cheekily cooked a few weeks later in another chef's kitchen . . . and we won!

We had a couple of disasters along the way, which was inevitable. At the start it really was a question of the two of us getting in the kitchen, throwing out ideas and testing them out before we hit the road.

'Eee this is just like Huntly in the old days,' Si said when we embarked on our research for the series, and in terms of how we interacted with each other in the kitchen he was right.

'Have you seen the . . . ?' he'd start.

'Lemon zester?'

'Aye. Thanks, mucker.'

We'd move around each other effortlessly and almost telepathically, and even though this was work, we were always looking for the next laugh and trying to make it as fun an experience as possible.

As always, everything we cooked was made with great care and love, because we both agree that if you don't do that then it simply doesn't work. One crucial thing had changed, though. In the old days we cooked dishes based on the ingredients we had to hand, like the time we made pizzas with scampi on top for Si's boys. Now we could ask a home economist to source practically any ingredients we wanted, which was a huge luxury, as was being able to cook in fabulously well-equipped kitchens instead of on rigged-up barbecues and makeshift street kitchens in remote parts of the globe.

This raised the bar in terms of what was expected of us, but it didn't change the fundamental way in which we operated, and as we devised our recipes we always focused on the joy of the cookery rather than the potential deep embarrassment we might suffer on national television if our dishes flopped.

In Essex we made a stuffed turkey ballotine that was an absolute stinker and just grew like Topsy until it resembled a Polaris missile, and in Kent we decided to deep-fry seaweed, but it blew up all over the kitchen of Michelin-starred chef David Pritchard.

'Sorry about that, David, and, er, we're having trouble with this sauce too. Can you give us a bit of advice?'

We were trying to make Dover sole and beer sabayon sauce, garnished with the deep-fried bladder wrack, but the sauce had gone horribly wrong and needed rescuing. David graciously obliged, but unfortunately that segment never made the final cut of the programme and the judges, who had no idea we'd received help, went on to choose Si and me as the winners. We felt quite guilty, though as usual we couldn't help seeing the funny side too.

'First we wrecked David's kitchen and then he had to suffer the humiliation of losing to us pair of clowns on telly!' Si said. 'And he is such a lovely, helpful guy. Sometimes life is so unfair . . .' He then of course exploded in a fit of giggles.

By May 2009 we were reaching the end of the food tour and were in Suffolk, cooking pork and apples, when Si's mobile rang. I could tell immediately it was bad news.

'It was our Gin,' he said, ashen-faced. 'She said Mam's gonna go.'

Stella had been in hospital but Si had not expected this news at all. I knew she'd had several health problems as she got older, but

I was shocked too. As I knew from my own experience, you just never think it's going to happen to your mam, and I felt desperately sad for Si.

He hightailed it back up north on the bike just as I'd done for my mam all those years earlier, and then he spent a fortnight at his mam's bedside. Stella's health issues and her age had finally taken their toll, and she was very frail and slipping away. I volunteered to make an episode for the tour on my own so Si could forget all about work, but nevertheless he felt guilty leaving me in the lurch and was in turmoil, not wanting to let anybody down.

Stella passed away on the morning of 15 May, which was a Friday, and Si rode up to Scotland that afternoon, to film something to do with Aberdeen Angus steaks. He was in absolute bits and in retrospect this was totally the wrong thing to do, but Si felt under pressure to please everybody, and he was not himself at all. I wish I'd put my foot down and insisted he took time off, but we both agree that hindsight is a wonderful thing. Si did what he thought was right at the time, and he did his best, and that is just how life is sometimes. To this day he says he feels he hasn't grieved properly for his mam, and he thinks this is the reason why.

Something else very sad happened that summer. John Stroud died from brain cancer in August, aged just fifty-four. He was a brilliant man, and we could not begin to imagine the loss his family suffered. Si and I owed him our careers, and we felt very fortunate and grateful for the lives we had.

The Hairy Bikers' Food Tour of Britain cookbook did extremely well, selling more than a hundred thousand copies. Doing the series and the book had not just been a huge commercial success, but we had learned a hell of a lot from it too, improving our cooking skills no end. We'd effectively been trained by thirty of the top chefs in the country for months on end, picking up tips and skills we have used ever since, like how to make a demi-glace by twice-reducing the stock, or the trick of cooking your vegetables 'just so' then plunging them in ice-cold water before drying them, so they are ready to warm through in a sauté pan with butter when you need them. For two blokes like us it was an absolutely priceless result to have been welcomed into so many incredible kitchens, and to have such skilled chefs share their experience with us. We couldn't believe our luck really.

After *Food Tour* we soon got another programme lined up, called *Mums Know Best*. This was an idea that came from Gill Tierney at BBC Birmingham, who had been our executive producer on *The Hairy Bakers*. Gill liked big event telly, and the idea was to start each show with a 'recipe fair' in the style of an old-fashioned summer fete, where mums would proudly share their favourite recipes. Then me and Si would travel to the homes of some of the mothers behind the recipes, to learn about the origins and family history attached to each dish.

This was music to our ears. Si and I have always loved meeting new people, and we could see that this would be great fun to make, and was something we could both really identify with. I was still as passionate about my mam's favourite old recipes for Yorkshire puddings and cheese-and-potato pie as I always had been, despite travelling around the world and sampling delicacies like, er, goat's penis. Si was the same; Stella's recipes for flat rib broth or sherry trifle still floated his boat just as much as trying a zebra burger, barbecued in the Namibian desert.

As anticipated *Mums Know Best* proved to be a cracking show to make; we had a great crew, most of whom who we still love to work with now, and of course we met some amazing mums along the way, who bowled us over with their warmth, good humour and passionate love of food and family cooking.

The vast majority of visits were very successful. Muriel Bell from Worcestershire was terrific and made the most fantastic chicken in brandy and double cream, plus mouth-watering seventies-style desserts like lemon soufflé.

'This is absolutely delicious, Muriel,' we enthused, because it really was.

'Oh, I am glad you like it, have some more.'

'Ooh, thank you. This is wonderful! Where did you learn to cook like this?'

It turned out one of Muriel's relatives had worked as a cook in the royal household, and the luxurious but incredibly heavy recipes had been passed down into her family.

'That's amazing!'

'Thank you. You must try this one too . . .'

'OK then, Muriel. Blimey, I don't think I'll need feeding for a week after this. I'm right royally stuffed!'

After we sampled Muriel's fabulously calorific food we nearly couldn't walk. I was filmed getting on my Ducati afterwards and a motorcycle magazine commented that I looked like a pot-bellied pig mounting an antelope. It was cruel, but unfortunately rather accurate!

'I've just realised, we don't actually have to polish off every single thing we're offered, do we?' I said to Si.

'I was thinking the same myself,' he replied, loosening his belt. 'I think we need to be a bit more strategic, Dave. And not so greedy.'

Up until this point we'd been terribly well-mannered, trying everything that was offered, but the trouble was that the mums were very polite too, and the more we ate, the more they brought out. We were filming approximately twenty-five times as much footage as would make it to air, which is pretty standard, so there was no way we could stuff our faces in every kitchen we visited; Si and I were already well overweight as it was.

After *Mums Know Best* we had another commission to honour before the end of 2009, making a one-off special called *The Hairy Bikers' Twelve Days of Christmas*. This was a quirky idea of ours that would see us cooking various dishes tenuously linked to the Christmas song.

On the second day of filming, in October 2009, I'd arranged to meet Si at a Newcastle call centre, where we were cooking *poulets de bresse* for four workers – our 'four calling birds'. At 8 a.m. I was riding through morning rush-hour traffic in Gosforth when I saw an accident up ahead.

'Oh no, some poor bastard has come off his new bike,' I thought, seeing the blue flashing lights of an ambulance. I could see a shiny motorbike lying on its side, and as I got closer my heart thumped in my chest. The bike was exactly the same as the one I was on, which was a wonderful 1100cc Ducati Streetfighter. The BBC had got me and Si one each, especially for the Christmas show.

I pulled over, hoping my fears were misplaced, but there was Si being carted into the ambulance. He was clearly shocked but seemed alright in the circumstances.

'I've got a pain in me leg,' he winced as I reached his side, which made me relax a bit. At least he was compos mentis, and the pain didn't appear to be too severe as he was talking normally.

I called Jane and went with Si to the hospital, where the news turned out to be not too bad at all. Thanks to the fact he'd been wearing some really good leathers, Si had got away with a bit of soft-tissue damage to one knee and a bash to the base of his spine. His bike had not been so lucky; it was a write-off.

'What on earth happened, mate?'

'A woman in a Renault Clio pulled out in front of me so I tipped the bike. I'd have T-boned her otherwise.'

After he dropped it, Si's bike had skidded across the road and hit the Clio while he shot off in the other direction, into oncoming traffic.

'It was a bloody miracle nobody hit me, Dave. I was lying there going: "Oh no, man, this is it!" It was quite surreal. Then the woman got out of her car wearing bobbly pink pyjamas and I was saying: "I'm OK, sweetheart." Then someone asked me: "D'you want your lid off?" I said, "I'll take me own lid off, thanks", and when I pulled off me helmet some woman yelled: "Bloody hell! It's a Hairy Biker!" Dude, you couldn't make it up.'

It was a bit like our show, in fact. After Si had a couple of days to recover, we did all kinds of loony things, like cooking a partridge and pear dish in Norwich while in search of the real Alan Partridge, making a goose risotto at the Seven Swans brewery in Gloucestershire for 'seven geese a-laying' and preparing a Christmas ale stew for the 'ten lords a-leaping' cast of *Riverdance* at the Sunderland Empire. All the recipes were devised using a mixture of research, ingenuity and a dash of creative craziness. For example, Si and I happened to bump into the great chef Antonio Carluccio in a car park one day.

'Antonio! Do you mind us asking what you would do with a partridge and some pears? How would you cook it?'

'I would make a festive stuffing for the partridge and I would pickle the pear and serve it with that.'

'What a fabulous idea! Thank you!'

It was a recipe delivered off the top of his head, and that is exactly what we cooked.

When it came to the goose risotto, we decided to have a bit of fun by covering one of us – namely Muggins here – in goose fat and chucking me in the river, to see if it kept me warm the way it does for cross-channel swimmers. It was absolutely freezing, and it didn't keep me warm at all, of course. Worse than that, the fat I was covered in was really hard to wash off, and I stank like a giant roast potato for days.

Si wasn't fit enough to ride a bike for a while after his accident and I had to go to Bristol to get a customised three-wheeler trike for us to share. We wrapped red tinsel around the handlebars and the pair of us looked like Dastardly and Muttley. Si had to sit behind me, and was very grumpy.

'Cheer up,' I said. 'Have you seen how many people love you?'

The story of his crash had hit the news, and the reaction from the public surprised us both. Messages of support were flooding in from all over the country; it was a heartening revelation that so many people who'd seen us on the telly cared, or were even interested.

We had further news to be grateful for around the same time. A BBC memo leaked to the press named us as 'top tier' talent who were worthy of investment. Apparently, we were as highly valued as the likes of Stephen Fry, Jeremy Paxman and Rick Stein, which was a terrific surprise, and very promising for the coming year. We already had the first *Mums Know Best* cookbook coming out in 2010, and we started preparing for the second series of *Mums Know Best* and also began work on a show called the *Hairy Bikers' Cook Off*. It was what I would describe as a 'proper shiny-floor show', filmed at Studio 7 in Television Centre. *Blue Peter* had been filmed in the same studio and I'd obviously started my career at

TV Centre, so to see my name on a door there was thrilling. The idea of the show was to search for Britain's best cooking family, and it involved me and Si giving food tips, having a bit of a chat, welcoming a celebrity guest and judging a cook-off between competing families.

Before we started work the BBC asked us both to have a routine medical, which was the norm for presenters filming fast-paced studio shows of that nature. My weight had crept up a stone every decade since my twenties so I was now pushing eighteen stone, which was way too heavy. I was taking Ramipril tablets for high blood pressure and statins to lower my cholesterol, both prescribed by my GP several years earlier. On top of that, during the *Food Tour* I suffered from painful feet and my legs broke out in sores and eczema. I blamed the bike and all the miles we rode that winter, but when I went for a precautionary check–up afterwards I was diagnosed with high blood sugar and warned that I was borderline Type 2 diabetic; the sort that is caused by lifestyle, not genes. I was put on the drug Metformin and told that one in three people in my position end up on insulin, but despite this I hadn't got a grip of myself in the way I should have done.

'I hope I don't eff this up for us, Kingie,' I said, ruing the fact I was such a hopeless glutton.

'I hope I don't, mate,' Si replied, looking nervous. He wasn't far off twenty stone, but I felt it was different for Si because he'd always been naturally big.

Anyhow, we both trotted in for our check-ups. The doctor seemed pretty ferocious to me, and I was terrified of what her verdict would be. However, by some miracle I scraped through, and the doctor deemed me fit for filming. I emerged shaking my head in disbelief, but when Kingie came out he was ashen and spluttered: 'I've been told to go straight to the doctors. My blood pressure is incredibly high, and it's spiking dangerously.'

Both in shock, we rode immediately to Harley Street on the bikes, and Si was given a repeat prescription for the same brand of blood pressure tablets I was on, only much stronger. The doctor also gave him some vials of Vitamin D when she found out he'd be working long days in a studio, barely seeing daylight for a month.

'Can I have some for me mate too?' Si asked, and the pair of us then rode straight to a chemist on Edgware Road and came out rattling with bags of medication.

It was a shameful state of affairs. I had only passed my check-up because I was already taking a load of pills, so we were both in the same boat really.

'It's not very good this, is it, Kingie?'

'It's not really, mucker, but what can we do?'

'I don't know, but I tell you what, Kingie, I'm glad I wasn't on my own back there.'

'Same, Dave. Can you imagine? At least we're in this together, eh? Come on, let's get ourselves a glass of water and take the pills. At least we're doing something about it . . .'

By his own admission Si had got it down to a fine art when it came to ignoring his weight or making excuses about it, while I had just been burying my head in the sand for years. Subconsciously, I'm sure the pair of us justified our eating habits because of our work and the image we had as men who appreciated good food, and plenty of it. We couldn't be skinny sparrows, picking at our food, could we?

The fact we were snowed under with work now provided us with another handy avoidance tactic; we simply didn't have time to deal with our weight issues.

Cook Off went alright, though we felt the format wasn't the best and it didn't go any further, which was a shame. You can't win them all.

Anyhow, it was good to be in a position where our lives didn't depend on one particular show being given the green light, and for the first time we were actually turning down work if we didn't think it was right for us.

Our star was very much in the ascendant at the BBC and it wasn't long before we began negotiating our best contract yet, to make a string of cookery programmes for BBC2 over two years. One of the shows being discussed was a four-part campaign series called *Meals on Wheels,* to highlight the fact the service was dying on its feet and needed rescuing. This was something that really appealed to us both, on a personal and professional level. I knew how much it would have helped my family if Mam had had hot dinners delivered when I was a kid, and in more recent years Si's mam could also have benefited from the service, but it wasn't available to her.

It was a gentle series, but Si and I got a real buzz out of working on something so worthwhile. When it aired, the BBC portal crashed because so many people got in touch, and the series went on to be nominated for a BAFTA, which was just fabulous.

There were various other programme ideas in the mix too. Si and I were both very keen to do something on the history of British food, because we were genuinely interested in it. We developed the idea of doing a journey of discovery around the country, celebrating British food and learning about traditions and trends through the decades, then cooking some of the dishes in a kitchen studio and having a bit of a chin-wag while we did so. This eventually became our long-running *Best of British* series, which turned out to be very popular. *Bakeation* was also in the offing, which was to be a 5,000-mile road trip across Europe, with me and Si sampling the best baking we could find and meeting up with local artisan bakers and some of our old mates along the way. Si and I were knackered just thinking about all this, but we certainly weren't complaining. To have so much work lined up was lush, and we both felt pleased with ourselves to have reached this position. What we both want, more than anything else, is to look after our families as best we can, and to be able to give the kids a bit of a leg-up in life, the sort we never had. Ultimately, we want to make sure the kids always have a roof over their head and a bit of financial security. Si and I have both worked very hard to achieve that, and we know how hard it is to have no back-up, and to have to do it all by yourself.

Before the two-year contract was signed and before any of those shows were made, however, I had something else a bit special in the diary. On 8 January 2011 Lil and I finally got hitched. We'd been talking about it for a while but just hadn't found the time. Lil's parents were coming over from Romania for the New Year, and so we decided to book the wedding during their stay, and surprise them.

Lil organised everything because I was so busy working, and she did a spectacularly good job, which didn't surprise me at all. From the day she moved over Lil had worked extremely hard, throwing herself into local life.

'I'm not going to tag along behind you, Dave,' she had told me clearly. Lil volunteered for the local rotary club and she found herself a job doing clothing alterations for Debenhams, because she felt guilty not earning money. Sewing is Lil's first love. She'd worked in a clothes factory for thirteen years before moving into tourism, and she eventually left Debenhams and started a thriving business of her own, specialising in making designer dresses.

Lil made her own wedding dress, which was a silk off-the-shoulder number and was absolutely knockout; she looked stunning. I wore a kilt and so did Si and Dr Dave, who were my two best men. The Mayor of Barrow, Rory McClure, is a good mate and he loaned us his mayoral limo for the day and suggested we got married in the drawing room of the town hall. The ceremony choked me. We had a string quartet and Serge read a very moving poem in English and Romanian, while the room was decked out with the most fabulous white roses. Honest to God, I wanted to blub. Afterwards we had a hundred guests for dinner and the home-made *pálinka* hooch came out.

For the evening do Lil had booked out the 99 Club in Barrow, which I was a bit sceptical about as it was no longer the uber club it had been in its heyday, when I was a kid. I needn't have worried. Four hundred guests partied like there was no tomorrow, and we had the night of our lives. Si's son James kicked things off brilliantly with an indie band he was the drummer with at the time; Si had taught him to play when he was a teenager. Lil had also found an incredible Blue Brothers tribute band called The Briefcase Blues Brothers, and they really got things stomping. In the end the dance floor was so rammed it was like being at a full-on rave, with the ground bouncing beneath your feet, and guests packed onto the balcony area above the dance floor.

What I enjoyed most of all was looking around the room and seeing so many people who had shared my life, in so many different ways. They were an eclectic crowd too, reflecting the diverse adventures I'd been lucky enough to experience. For example, the lovely ladies from the local Thai community who have a stall on Barrow market, and had appeared on telly with us, did a wonderful buffet. I was incredibly grateful and impressed, because it was no mean feat feeding four hundred guests as fabulously as they did. Producers we'd worked with and good friends we'd made in the publishing world danced the night away alongside old mates of mine like Graham Twyford and Chunky the lifeboat man.

Of course I had a whole new Romanian family surrounding me too, and I'd gained an amazing stepson and stepdaughter. Si's oldest son Alex met Lauren, who was an assistant to one of the home economists we'd worked with, and they have been together ever since. Even my old art teacher Mr Eaton was there. I'd bumped into him by chance a few years earlier, when I was in Ulverston with Lil. He spotted us through the window of a coffee shop and came rushing out saying: 'David Myers! Well, I never!'

He was as flamboyant as ever and told Lil he'd love to paint her.

'You have the most *amazing* cheekbones,' he said admiringly. 'I can tell you're not from these parts.'

He must have been in his eighties by then but he gave Iza some art lessons after that and seemingly worked his magic once again, because Iza is a talented artist, currently doing an art degree at Manchester University. Mr Eaton passed away not long after the wedding, but it was just wonderful that he had been there. I told him how much he influenced me and I hope he believed me, because I am certain I would have lived a completely different life if it weren't for him.

I'd had my stag do the night before the wedding at the Prince of Wales pub in Foxfield, which you have to get a train to. When the last train's coming through you can hear it hoot from the pub, and the landlord gives everyone plastic glasses so they can finish their pint on the way back. Needless to say, by the time me and my stag party had boarded the train home to Barrow we were in quite a loud and lively state, so much so that the police had been called to meet us at the other end, to check everything was all in order! The Lord Mayor was with us, so when we staggered off the train we shoved him to the front of the group.

'Go on, Rory,' I said. 'No one's going to arrest the mayor!'

I think the police officers were quite stunned to see a merry Hairy Biker in a kilt shoving the Lord Mayor towards them and saying: 'Please forgive us if we've been a bit noisy, officers. I'm getting married in the morning!', and in the event we escaped with a very mild ticking-off.

'Who'd have thought you'd end up being my best man, and after all these years,' I'd said to Si that night. 'Isn't life funny?'

'It is, Dave. I wonder where the pair of us would be if we hadn't worked on the Cooksons, and met like we did?'

'God forbid! I might still be making prosthetic moles and noses!'

'Don't even think about it. God knows what I'd be doing. But I do know this, Dave. I wouldn't have this career without you.'

'I wouldn't have this career without you, Si,' I said, coming over all emotional. 'We're a pair of bloody lucky buggers. Come here!'

We had a hug and one last pint, remembering how we'd chinked our glasses for the very first time some sixteen years earlier, at the Egypt Cottage pub next door to Tyne Tees TV, and thanking our lucky stars that we had.

Lil and I didn't have time for a honeymoon because I had so much work lined up. A few weeks after the wedding our new contract with the BBC was finalised, and to fulfil it Si and I would be away filming for two hundred days a year. Neither of us wanted to spend all that time away from our families but, as usual, we were both of the opinion that we had to seize the opportunity while we could, as we didn't know what was round the next corner.

The deal was announced to the press in February 2011, with the BBC2 controller, Janice Hadlow, saying she couldn't imagine the channel's cookery output without us, and describing us as a 'knowledgeable, fun and warm duo'.

'Blimey! High praise indeed,' we giggled. We were chuffed to bits; it was the best endorsement we could have wished for.

18

Si's

Christmas-Pudding Vodka, Mississippi Pulled Pork and Low-Fat Rice Cakes

'Kingie! Are you there?'

Dave was knocking frantically on the door of my hotel room in Turin, where we were filming for *Bakeation*.

'What is it, Dave? Is everything OK?

'Can I borrow your blood pressure tablets, mate? I've run out!'

'Course. Come on in, but are you sure, Dave? I know we're on the same brand but mine are four times stronger than yours . . .'

Desperate as he was, in the end Dave didn't take the chance and found himself a local doctor who gave him the correct prescription. It was a sobering experience for both of us.

'What the hell is going on?' he reflected later. 'This is insane, Si, me trying to get pills off you! I don't know about you but this has given me a bit of a wake-up call.'

'You're right, dude. It's not cool, at all, but what can we do?'

We'd both been feeling heavy on the bikes, which wasn't pleasant either. We were covering thousands of miles all over Europe and it should have been a pleasure, but we were uncomfortably hot every day. The focus of our work wasn't helping matters in any way. We were on yet another gastronomic road trip, and as *Bakeation* was essentially a celebration of baking we were chomping our way through bread, cakes, pastries and pies every day, all in the name of research, of course.

On the day Dave banged on my hotel room door, we'd made a chocolate cake that was to die for – perhaps quite literally in our case. Another day we filmed in Norway, sinking our teeth into delights like *pierogi*, which are calorie-laden ham and Jarlsberg-filled pastries. I can still recall the delicious melt-in-the-mouth taste, though it has to be said the *pierogi* weren't nearly as memorable as the authentic knitted underpants we both treated ourselves to in Norway. They had a sleeve for your willy, and Dave and I inevitably modelled them and were filmed doing so. For the record, Dave cheated and stuffed socks down his so he looked like an elephant.

'The knitted pants on the *Hairy Bikers* are possibly the most unpleasant and frightening thing I've seen on TV,' one viewer tweeted after that episode was broadcast.

Anyway, I digress. To give the *Bakeation* series an added dimension we met up with old friends and family on our travels. We called in on my sister Ginny, who had moved to Florence, we visited Dave's in-laws in Transylvania and, hilariously, Dave decided to track down his old housemate from his student days in London, the attractive au pair he called 'French Pat'. He found her on Facebook and we arranged to meet her in a street in France, with the cameras rolling. It was a hoot. Dave's jaw completely dropped because she was just as glamorous as he remembered her thirty years earlier.

'I was so 'orrible to you, Dave,' she said, playing along wonderfully and recalling how Dave had behaved like a lovesick puppy around her in their youth. 'If I 'ad known you would 'ave been rich, I would 'ave been nicer to you!' she joked.

The reunion made a great bit of telly and we still laugh about it, but Dave admitted he felt terribly lardy standing beside elegant Pat. I completely understood how he felt. In recent times we'd both looked at publicity pictures of ourselves and thought: 'Oh noooo!' and we'd had a demoralising exchange with the designer Paul Smith, who we met in a hotel during the food tour.

'What have you got for fat blokes?' Dave had asked, hoping to buy some posh designer gear.

'Socks and cologne,' Paul smiled, trying to make light of it. 'You'll be alright in the ties as well.'

We laughed gamely, but deep down we didn't find it funny. We wanted to be able to buy decent clothes and jeans that didn't come from the fat-boy rail. More importantly, we needed to face the fact our weight wasn't just compromising how we looked and what we wore, it had become a serious threat to our health. How to lose the blubber was obviously a big problem in itself, not just because of the effort it would entail, but because of our line of work and image.

'Do you think the BBC would even want us to lose weight?' Dave pondered.

'You've got a point there, mucker. I'm really not sure. We're the big fat Hairy Bikers after all. Maybe it's not feasible . . .'

Half-hearted conversations like these took place for months and months as we polished off eight shows for *Bakeation*, completed the second series of *Mums Know Best*, put together the thirty episodes of *Best of British* and did a one-off special, *The Hairy Bikers'*

Christmas Party. As always, the people we met along the way were amazing and we couldn't help ourselves when it came to sampling dishes made by contributors, or recipes we unearthed on our travels. Dave and I were tucking into all sorts of loveliness on a daily basis; it was rude not to. We're talking substantial food here, too, like Wakefield mum Dee Briggs's 'biggest meat-and-potato pie in the world', delicious Rustic Spanish bread on *Bakeation* and calorific beef and suet pudding on *Best of British*. For the Christmas Party special we really had a blowout, throwing ourselves with abandon into a huge knees-up and feast that included a turkey vindaloo, bacon-and-egg canapés and Christmas-pudding vodka. We talked Wizzard legend Roy Wood into performing a version of 'I Wish It Could Be Christmas Every Day', but thank God it wasn't; me and Dave would have exploded.

On top of all that indulgence, we were compiling two more books called *Perfect Pies* and *The Hairy Bikers' Big Book of Baking*. Clearly, they both needed a lot of hands-on research if we wanted to keep things authentic, like we always had. By the way, we'd come a very long way from our cobbled-together beginnings. Thanks to Sammy-Jo we'd learned that recipes for publication needed to be triple-tested, and we always got stuck in with more than our fair share of taste-testing.

In a roundabout way, it was the Olympic Games that saved us from putting ourselves in an early grave. Don't go getting any daft ideas now; we didn't start training for a medal. It was much simpler than that. When we started to dream up our next batch of programme ideas the 2012 London Olympics were looming and we wanted to do something relevant. The idea for me and Dave to lose weight and get fitter on telly came out of a conversation with one of the television production companies we worked with, Optomen.

At first there was some concern that the BBC wouldn't buy us slimming down, because our branding as two large chaps was very clear, but our bosses at BBC2 didn't hesitate in supporting us; in fact, they thought it was a great idea for a programme. The result was that Dave and I were commissioned to make four shows to coincide with the Olympics that summer, called *Hairy Dieters: How to Love Food and Lose Weight*.

The thrust of the series was simple. We were going to discover how people like us could continue to eat delicious food but still shed kilos, by compromising on calories rather than taste. Naturally, for the show to work Dave and I would have to lose a significant amount of weight, and our progress would need to be shown to the nation. This was a daunting prospect, but also a great motivator. As Dave put it: 'Most people have a fat picture on the fridge to keep them on track; we've got the shame of failing on national television.'

The first step was to get weighed and measured, and then have a fitness and diet assessment at Newcastle University, with the metabolism and diabetes expert Professor Roy Taylor and dietician Professor Ashley Adamson. This was bloody terrifying. On the day, I weighed in at nineteen stone six with a fifty-inch waistline and Dave was seventeen stone twelve with a forty-nine-inch waist. Then it was into a 'Bod Pod' fat-measuring machine, which showed I had forty-two per cent body fat and Dave had thirty-eight per cent. On the scan pictures you could see all the blubber hanging around our hearts and internal organs. It looked like we were wearing aprons of fat under our skin, which was incredibly alarming. That wasn't all. We were then both given the very shocking news that we were, in fact, morbidly obese. It's such a frightening and grisly phrase, but Professor Taylor insists on using it, to help make people like us face the truth.

'No wonder we feel so rubbish,' Dave said, looking like he'd seen a ghost. 'Look at all that fat we're carting around. I'm tired just thinking about it.'

I'd had such a shock I could barely speak.

'Basically, we're like walking duck confit, Dave,' I stuttered eventually. We laughed nervously. This was deadly serious, though, and I was acutely aware that my lifestyle was going to have to radically change.

When the experts looked at our diets they calculated we were eating around 3,500 calories a day each, which is 1,000 calories more than the recommended daily allowance for men. Forty-five per cent of my intake was from fats, and for Dave it was forty per cent. The professors were lovely people who genuinely cared, and they told us straight how it was: Dave and I were shortening our lives with our eating habits, but the good news was that it wasn't too late to change if we followed the simple rule of burning off more calories than we ate each day.

It was early spring when we filmed at the university, and we were told that if we wanted visible results by the time we shot the final episode of *Dieters* in July, we would have to cut down to around 1,200 calories a day and increase our exercise for three months. That way we'd lose about a kilo, or two pounds, each week, which is the sensible and healthy way to do it.

'It's simple really,' Dave said through gritted teeth. 'Eat less, burn off more. Oh, and cut out all those "empty" calories consumed in alcohol.'

'Simple?! I don't bloody think so, mate. How the hell are we going to be that disciplined?'

The deeper we got into this, the more nervous I was feeling. I was taking a huge gamble with my reputation. I thought about my school-days, and the burning embarrassment I felt when the headmaster announced to the packed dining hall: 'Simon King is on a diet.' The fear of failure was terrifying, then and now. Even though I'd lost weight at the slimming club Mam and Ginny took me to, in the long run I failed to keep it off.

'I'm six foot two and I've been big all my life,' I panicked. 'It's my identity and it's just the way I am. I don't honestly know if I can change the habits of a lifetime on telly, in front of millions of people.'

Dave was also feeling anxious about the sacrifices we were going to have to make, though his fear of failure wasn't as intense as mine. He hadn't been fat all his life like I had and he knew there was a thinner person inside, though he did share the worries I had about actually putting in the hard work to get the results we needed. He normally chips in with a positive comment if ever I start to flap, but he looked at me gravely.

'All this, and we're off to Mississippi. And doing *Everyday Gourmet*.'

My jaw dropped. The fact I was morbidly obese was still sinking in. I was in a terrible state, and I hadn't got as far as thinking about the timing at all, but Dave was right.

Before *Dieters* we'd been commissioned to make the series *Mississippi Adventure*, which was going to be an epic 3,000-mile food and music tour of America's Deep South, and as soon as we got back we'd be dining with Michelin-starred chefs to learn how to make gourmet meals on a budget at home, for the series *Everyday Gourmet*.

Doing *Mississippi* had been a dream of ours for many years, and we had decided we'd visit New Orleans for jazz and blues, Lafayette for Cajun music, Memphis for soul and rock and roll and Nashville for country. Along the way we were going to eat the best pulled pork, fried chicken and Mississippi mud pie on the planet . . . at least, that had been the plan.

'It's only a few weeks,' I said to Dave, thinking about the food. 'We'll just have to cut down as best we can, not be gluttons and then we'll start the full-on three months of calorie-counting when we get back.'

We flew over in April. Our director, Simon Kerfoot, was brilliant and had set everything up so we could just arrive in New Orleans, collect a couple of Harley Davidsons and start filming practically straightaway. Dave and I were both absolutely buzzing when we set off on the bikes, and the entire trip really did turn out to be a dream come true, with every day bringing a new highlight.

One of the first things we did was meet a couple who ran a tamali shop in a fire station.

'Our shop got decimated in the floods,' they told us. 'And the firemen who rescued us loved our tamalis so much they said we could open a shop in the fire station, so they could have our tamalis whenever they wanted them.'

The well-fed firemen all smiled in appreciation. 'Why not?' they beamed. 'Everybody wins.'

'Can you imagine something like that happening in the UK?' Dave commented. 'This truly is another world.'

'I know, mucker. How fortunate are we to be here?'

We were not just having a bird's-eye view of another culture, we were invited into it with open arms. That night we went to listen to some fabulous jazz at a club on the famous Frenchman Street. Dave's not as big a fan as I am and he had jokingly likened jazz to a 'musical migraine', but after listening to a wonderful singer he was a little bit in love, and completely sold on jazz.

'I think we've had what you might call a pretty good day out,' he grinned, and we couldn't believe that we'd barely got started.

The treats kept coming. I played drums at Sun Studios, standing where greats like Otis Redding and Isaac Hayes had stood. We sampled pulled pork that had been slow-smoked for fourteen hours at the famous Central BBQ diner in Memphis – without going mad, I hasten to add. We also fished for oysters in New Orleans and attempted to find catfish in the swamps in Lafayette. I say 'attempted' because on the day we turned up on our Harleys with our fishing rods there was a proper tropical rainstorm and the road was a foot deep in water.

'How can we salvage this?' I said as we immediately started racking our brains for ideas. We never panicked when a hitch like this threatened our filming schedule, because experience had taught us that something always came up.

'D'you know, Kingie, this takes me back to that day in Portugal, sitting in that cafe in the pouring rain with Stroudie, when the playboy baker didn't show up.'

'You're right, Dave! Now I wonder if we can get hold of catfish anywhere else around here . . . and I wonder what else they catch in these swamps.'

The upshot was that we got some catfish from a helpful fisherman's freezer to use in our planned cookery item, and we ate frogs. We're not talking delicate little frogs like the French eat either, no. These were massive frogs that were definitely as good a talking-point as catching catfish would have been.

We found there was a generosity of spirit everywhere we went along the Mississippi River. Mam's phrase, 'there's a greater community spirit in people who have nowt', rang in my head many times on this trip. Everybody we met had a story to tell or something to share that enriched our day.

When it came to the food we did reasonably well, cutting down on our usual portions each day and taking it steady if we had a beer. After the shock we'd had it would have been incredibly foolish not to. We simply couldn't make lame excuses any more, and we couldn't justify over-indulging.

We were also more honest than before about how uncomfortable we felt in our leathers. 'Dude, I feel massively hot,' I'd say, nearly every time I got off the bike. 'I feel lethargic too. We haven't made life easy for ourselves, have we?'

'Aye, I'm sweating cobs an' all, Kingie. That's because we're massively fat and a couple of heart attacks waiting to happen.'

'Correction! We *were* heart attacks waiting to happen, but now we're going to do something about it.'

We ended our *Mississippi Adventure* in Nashville, where we met the Sweethearts of the Rodeo country music duo, sisters Janis Oliver and Kristine Arnold, who had recorded a string of hits in the late eighties and early nineties. They're in their fifties now and incredibly glamorous and friendly, and while Sammy-Jo prepped some food one night they sang to her, just for the pure pleasure of it. There were no cameras rolling and it was a magical moment to witness. Afterwards me, Dave and all the crew sat around a camp-fire and ate pulled pork while we chatted and chilled out with Janis and Kristine.

'Honey, you're so sweet I could mop you up with a biscuit!' one of the sisters told me, which pretty much made my night. I bloody love this place!

Back home, we brought the cameras into our houses for the first time when we started filming *Dieters* again, as we knew that having the support of our families was crucial to our success. Jane had been concerned about my size for many years and Alex and James were old enough to have worried about my health too. They were all very proud I was getting a grip on it at long last, and they all said they'd happily eat the same food as me, to support me.

I told Dylan I was looking forward to going sea kayaking with him when I was thinner and wouldn't capsize the boat. That was a great goal to aim for; it should not be too much to ask when you are forty-five years old and the father of a twelve-year-old. I also imagined myself on the beach, not feeling as self-conscious as I had done in the past, but by far the biggest motivator was telling myself that I'd be around longer for my kids.

'How about your lot, Dave?' I asked, once we'd got properly started. 'Are they joining in with the dieting?'

'No. They took the mickey out of me when I was filmed lying on the bed at home, trying to squeeze myself into an old pair of jeans. And I had a row with Lil last night, so she ordered herself a takeaway tandoori curry while I was sat there with me Marmite rice cakes!'

Lil and the kids did encourage him over the months, of course. Lil had shared Jane's worries about what the Hairy Biker life-style was doing to our long-term health, and underneath all the mickey-taking she was very happy Dave was getting himself in better shape. With Lil being a very no-nonsense character, her take was simple.

'Yes, Dave, you're fat and you need to lose weight,' she said. 'Good! Get on with it!'

With the first wage-packet she ever earned in the UK, Lil had bought Dave a lovely shirt that was too tight, and she wanted to see him in it after the diet. Wearing it on TV was one of Dave's incentives in moments of weakness. Like me, though, his main motivation was to not drop dead prematurely.

Dieticians helped educate us about calories, so we could work out our daily allowances and start creating low-calorie recipes with the help of a nutritionist. We were pretty clueless at the start. I mean, when we were on the road Dave and I would think nothing of buying an all-day-breakfast sandwich each and sharing a box of forty cocktail sausages.

'How many calories do you think are in each sausage?' the dietician asked us.

We both looked blank and said hopefully: 'Ten? Fifteen?'

'No, there are twenty-five calories in each sausage.'

'Oh! So if we had twenty each that would be . . .'

'Five hundred calories. Plus another five hundred for the all-day-breakfast sandwich.'

'Bloody hell, Kingie!' Dave said. 'That's a thousand calories just having lunch on the go!'

'No way, man! I cannot believe it.'

We had to believe it, though, because it was the truth and we had a top dietician spelling it out for us.

The calorific lunches had to stop, obviously, as did many of our other habits. We swapped fried breakfasts for lean ham, beans and rye bread with no butter, cut out milk in coffee, sprayed oil in the pan instead of lashing in a large glug, and we started experimenting with low-fat replacements in all our favourite recipes. It didn't take us long to suss out that half-fat crème fraiche or coconut milk were as tasty as the full-fat versions, for example, and it came as a pleasant surprise when we really started to enjoy leaner copies of our favourite dishes.

This was absolutely crucial; Dave and I would not have lasted five minutes if we'd been told to drink diet shakes or faff around with plates of leaves. If we were going to give up an all-day-breakfast sandwich or a takeaway curry we needed a replacement that still filled us up and tasted great, and so we started to devise lovely alternatives like prawn, mango and avocado wraps, tofu and vegetable stir-fry and low-calorie Indian chicken with vegetables.

We knew the people watching at home would be like-minded, because our audience is made up of people just like us, and for that reason we also felt we could be very honest about our goals, and how we felt.

'We're not this shape for nowt!' we said on camera. 'We're two blokes who love food and this is a huge challenge. We know we're never going to be skinny-minnies, but that doesn't mean we can't get healthier and trim down.'

I live in my head and I knew that once I'd cracked it psychologically I could do it, so when I started making statements like that for telly, it really helped. Dave's more practical. It was a job he'd committed to, and therefore he did not want to fail and would give it his best shot.

We both got push-bikes and exercised when we could. I did circuit training and boxing, and Dave did a couple of personal training sessions a week with the ex-rugby player Martin Ostler, who lives in Barrow. It was bloody hard, but we both felt better once we got going. I found it was a great stress-reliever when I gave the boxing pads a good pounding, and Dave said he felt more mellow, and generally nicer to be with after he'd had a training session with Martin.

We didn't touch a drop of alcohol for a month. This was murder for me when we had a big family party for Jane's birthday and Ginny came over; to me, socialising is intrinsically linked to having a few drinks. Dave found it much easier, largely because he enjoyed not having hangovers, which he'd always suffered dreadfully from. It was worth the sacrifice. One month in, the weight started dropping off. We each lost well over a stone, but we had a bit of a hurdle ahead of us.

We now had to start filming *Everyday Gourmet*, which would mean meeting some of the country's best chefs who were going to show us how to cook top-notch dishes on a budget at home. We knew from experience that these guys are generally extremely hospitable and that we would no doubt be invited to sit at their tables and appreciate their fine cuisine. Some of them had been known to feed the whole crew; providing amazing food was their raison d'être and we did not want to offend them, or ruin our diets.

'How are we going to deal with this?' I said to Dave. 'We need a plan, mate, or all our hard work will go to pot.'

'Right. Remember what happened on *Mums Know Best*, when we had that amazing revelation that we didn't have to eat a huge portion of every single thing that was put in front of us?'

'I do.'

'That's it. We have to do the same. Only it won't be Muriel's soufflé but a Michelin-starred feast we'll be dealing with. Remember, have a taste, be polite, but don't feel obliged to lick the plate clean. Or ask for seconds.'

'Right-ho. Simple. Easy-peasy. We'll nail it.'

The fantastic chef Nigel Haworth invited us to stay at Northcote Manor and very kindly made us steamed halibut, as he knew we were watching our weight. When the sommelier came over Dave and I were suitably restrained and ordered one glass of wine each, a red for me and a white for Dave, but then a little devil popped up on my shoulder.

'Sod it,' I thought, before I told the waiter to leave the rest of the bottles on the table.

The next morning we were both full of remorse and guilt, but that spurred us on for the next month. At Tom Kerridge's Michelin-starred restaurant in Marlow he cooked a curried cauliflower soup with a curry oil and a pakora, and belly pork that was very hard to resist. We picked meagrely at the delicious food even though we wanted to devour several platefuls, and afterwards we both had some low-fat rice cakes round the back, away from the cameras. When we lost a few more pounds that week we felt very proud, which encouraged us too. After that we got into the habit of taking plenty of snacks wherever we went, to keep us going when we couldn't cook for ourselves.

At home and when we had days off it was much easier, because we'd been working incredibly hard on devising all kinds of low-calorie recipes that were satisfying and tasted great. This helped us no end, because in moments of weakness we could focus on the vegetable stew or curry we had waiting for us, or were look-ing forward to cooking. This was the key to our success, and it was great to know that not only would the recipes help me and Dave lose weight, but ultimately other dieters too.

One of the hardest days of all was when we filmed with Olivier Limousin, the head chef at L'Atelier de Joël Robuchon in Covent Garden, which is a two Michelin-star restaurant. Olivier gener-ously invited us and the crew to stay for lunch when we'd finished shooting for the day. We accepted, of course, but then Dave and I just had to nibble on these amazing langoustines like a pair of little mice. Every bite on camera was our lunch and half of our dinner; it was bleedin' torture.

Sammy-Jo was working with us on this show, and she said we were very bad-tempered some days, which we undoubtedly were. We spent six weeks like that, rubbing our own noses in it as we doggedly stuck to the calorie count during the day, desperately looking forward to tucking into one of our own recipes whenever we could.

Away from work, we were feeling loads better. When I first started exercising I'd felt a pain in between my shoulder blades, like a knife stabbing me in the back. The more the pain subsided the more I knew I was making progress, and in the second and third months I could honestly feel the weight dropping off my body. Dave's barometer was clothes. As well as the shirt Lil had bought him he had all sorts of other stuff he'd never got into that still had the labels on.

'Honestly, it's like dressing a wok,' he used to say, but that was slowly changing and he promised he'd buy himself a Paul Smith suit as his final reward. Lil's attitude helped him too. She was practical and unemotional about the dieting, cracking the whip if he had a moment of weakness.

Thank God, our efforts were not in vain. When we went back to Newcastle University three months after starting our calorie-controlled diets we were visibly thinner, but we still had to go through that nerve-racking moment of truth when you step on the scales.

I found the day incredibly emotional.

'I feel like I've been on this journey all my life,' I found myself saying to Dave. 'I feel exactly like a little boy again, going to the slimming club, and gearing myself up to step on the scales in front of all the ladies. Even when I was sure I'd lost a bit of weight it was terrifying, like waiting for exam results and never quite knowing if you'd passed or failed. I feel exactly the same today. It's taken me right back, and I'm still scared of not doing well enough.'

Dave was less emotional but still nervous, and in typical style he tried to lighten the tension with a joke. 'Look, Kingie, it'll be fine. We're no longer casting shadows like a pair of Walnut Whips, are we? It's going to be good news, no way it can be anything else.'

To our utter delight, when the moment of truth came we found we had each lost an incredibly impressive three stone. Not only that, our body fat percentages were substantially reduced; mine from forty-two to thirty-two per cent and Dave's from thirty-eight to twenty-five. Best of all, we were told we could come off the various drugs we were taking for high blood pressure, cholesterol and all that nonsense.

'Fooking hell, Dave, we've done it!' I said afterwards. 'I cannot bloody believe it.' The relief was palpable and I was exhaling loudly and rubbing my beard, as I do when I'm feeling emotional and trying to take things in.

Being more logical than me, Dave had had more faith that we'd succeed, but even so the sense of achievement was overwhelming for both of us. We were triumphant, and felt incredibly proud. This had been the toughest challenge we'd ever faced and we'd smashed it. Doing it together had been crucial; I know I wouldn't have managed it without Dave and he felt the same way. We'd shared so much together over the years, and to know your best mate was going through exactly the same process, and that you didn't want to let each other down, had really helped keep the pair of us on track.

We both got a Paul Smith suit to celebrate, Dave proudly wore the shirt Lil had bought him the next time we filmed, and I went sea kayaking with Dylan. I still capsized a few times, but at least I didn't sink like a rock as I would have done before. All my boys are into rugby and for a long time I coached a local team, but it had been years since I got stuck into a bit of practice with the lads. I could do that now too, and Dyl was made up. He'd also got himself a bit leaner over the months by eating the same meals as me, as had everyone in the family, so it was a win-win.

The show was a great ratings hit, with 2.5 million people tuning in to BBC2 each week. Throughout the series viewers were asking for more and more recipes, and almost as a public service exercise we agreed to bring out an accompanying book full of our tips and favourite low-calorie dishes. Letters and messages we'd received from viewers had really moved us. People were saying they'd struggled for years to lose weight but had finally got results after seeing me and Dave do so well.

'If you two fatties can do it, anyone can,' was the gist of how the majority of viewers had reacted.

The book had to be compiled quickly as we hadn't planned to do it, but with the help of a crack team we managed to get a paperback, *The Hairy Dieters,* on the shelves on 2 August.

Creating the book, and in fact the whole *Dieters* experience, undoubtedly made us better cooks.

'There's no calories in flavour' became our mantra, and we found ourselves improving the taste and freshness of all kinds of recipes we'd made before by experimenting with spices more than ever. We re-examined some old-fashioned basics too, like working on the art of making the best reduced stock we possibly could to flavour our dishes.

The diet expert Justine Pattison helped us massively with the recipe-writing, because it was absolutely crucial that the numbers added up and the balance of vegetables, carbs and protein was correct. She was brilliant at ensuring we achieved our aims, whatever we threw at her.

'Justine, we want to make low-calorie pastry. We know that's like searching for the holy grail, but can you help?'

'I'll try something using a pizza dough mix. It won't be the best pastry ever, but it could work.'

It was a bit like 'beer mat' pastry, as we called it, but it was pastry nonetheless, and we and our fellow dieters were delighted with it.

Dave and I didn't expect the *Dieters* book to sell in huge numbers;

we simply hoped it would be useful to people who wanted to lose weight like us.

However, just over a fortnight after it was published we got the most hilarious phone call from Nicola Ibison, who was in charge of our management at James Grant.

'Congratulations!' she said. 'You've knocked *Fifty Shades of Grey* off the top of the Amazon bestseller list!'

We laughed our heads off, and Dave and I had great fun putting together a press release. 'We've always known our food is sexy, but this is mad,' we said. 'Sex may be important but the way to a nation's heart is still through its stomach. We're delighted and thrilled that people have taken the programme in the spirit in which it was intended. You can still have a pint and enjoy your food.'

Our editor, Amanda Harris, pitched in with: 'It's official – two hairy Englishmen are hotter than Christian Grey.' She added: 'Si and Dave understand how the average household shops and cooks. They also understand, from personal experience, that it's really hard to lose weight if your appetite is not sated. They've lost three stone each so the proof is in the low-cal pudding. And we all have to eat, of course. Sex is optional.'

We'd sold 150,000 copies already and our publishers couldn't print *The Hairy Dieters* fast enough. The sense of personal pride and victory we felt was one thing, but to know that thousands of people were potentially going to lengthen their lives because of us was mind-blowing, and incredibly gratifying.

'Listen to this,' Dave said one day. 'You're gonna love this story. One of our readers has been in touch to say she started giving her husband Hairy Dieter meals without telling him.'

'And did he lose a lot of weight?'

'He did – two and a half stone. But because he didn't know

he was on the diet he went to the doctors, thinking something was wrong with him as he'd lost so much weight for no apparent reason. It was only after that that his wife had to confess what she'd been up to!'

'No way, man! I love it! That's music to my ears.'

We've since heard many more success stories, with one person losing an incredible thirteen stone and loads of members of the online diet club we'd also created reporting that their weight loss had improved their life and made them happier, which mirrored our experience.

'I'd have done this years ago if I'd have known I could still eat so well,' Dave said. 'It's funny, isn't it? I just never realised what a hindrance all the weight was before, which sounds ridiculous, but it's true. I feel like a different person, Kingie.'

I agreed with every word. The weight loss was liberating and life-changing, and for me it was proof that I wasn't destined to be a fat person, which is what I'd believed for so many years.

'I never thought I could do it,' I said. 'To know that I can actually control my weight is mind-blowing. I'm absolutely made up.'

Dave and I felt brilliant in ourselves, and we remained on a massive high long after we'd finished working on *Dieters*. We were on cloud nine professionally too. *Mississippi Adventure* was broadcast in the midst of all the dieting madness and that also received great reviews, so 2012 was shaping up to be an incredibly successful year.

By now we had started talking about making a series on Asia in 2013, plus another *Meals on Wheels*. They were both great projects to look forward to, but before that we were doing our second live tour, *Hairy Bikers: Larger Than Live*. Yes, we couldn't resist going back for more! Dave and I had thoroughly enjoyed the first tour and had always vowed to do another. This time BBC Worldwide were on board as our promoters, and we were confident it would be bigger and better than the last.

The tour was starting at the end of September 2012 and running through to April 2013, with a break for Christmas and New Year when all the pantos would take over the theatres. We knew from experience that when you're facing live audiences night after night you need to be feeling on top of your game, so the timing was perfect; we were really up for it.

A couple of weeks before we went on the road we won a *TV Choice* award in the Best Food Show category, beating stars like Jamie Oliver and our old mucker James Martin. It was the first award we'd won of that nature, and as the votes are cast by viewers it was really special and meant a great deal.

'Can you believe it?' Dave giggled at the awards ceremony. 'People really do like us, Kingie!'

The thrill of the occasion seemed to have gone to his head, because when Dave got chatting to a TV producer later in the evening I couldn't believe what I was hearing.

'Would you do *Strictly Come Dancing*?' Dave was asked, very seriously.

I nearly spat my drink out laughing, and when Dave replied, 'Oooh yes, I'd love to,' I nearly split my posh trousers.

'What about you, Simon?' the producer asked.

'Me? You're asking *me*? No, mate, I'd rather have a red-hot poker shoved up me arse, if I'm perfectly honest.'

When it came to working out what to put in the next live stage shows I'm sure our recent triumphs fuelled our enthusiasm and creativity, giving us the confidence to be even more daft and outrageous than before.

We decided to open the show with a short film, which was a

spoof of us backstage, supposedly being our true selves, scoffing kebabs, wearing dirty T-shirts and saying we hated each other and didn't even like cooking. I was sticking Haribos up my nose and blowing them out, and then an alarm clock rang and we shouted: 'Oh no! We've got a show!' The next minute we were in a chaotic flap getting ready. I was having my back waxed, and Dave was putting on red spangly high heels and running up Islington High Street half-dressed, still wearing his dirty old T-shirt, plus a pair of lederhosen.

The second short film we made was inspired by our recent encounter at the *TV Choice* Awards, and showed us pretending to audition for *Strictly*. I was dressed up like some bleeding tango god and Dave was twirling around in a pair of size sixteen gold lamé pants from Primark, plus stockings and his red stiletto heels. We actually managed to get the *Strictly* dancers Kristina Rihanoff and Robin Windsor to appear in the film, and we had an absolute hoot shooting it with them. I danced with Kristina, who was just fabulous, and Dave got the short straw and had to dance with Robin. I don't know how we decided that, but there you go, you can't win 'em all, Dave!

Dave was dancing cheek to cheek with muscle-bound Robin.

'I've never been this close to a man before!' I heard him say slightly nervously.

'Oooh, neither have I!' Robin grinned in a camped-up voice, which cracked us all up.

We played Newcastle City Hall in the November, and though I rarely got worried before a show I was very nervous as we prepared.

'Bloody hell, Dave, I've seen Jimi Hendrix and Peter Gabriel play here!'

'I know, Si, it's a bit special for you this one, isn't it?'

'Aye, and you know there's nothing like a Geordie homecoming. I think we could be in for a great night.'

This turned out to be a huge understatement. The two thousand-strong audience went wild, and as I stood on the stage and listened to the applause at the end I was filled with an unbelievable amount of pride. I would never in a million years have thought that I would be in receipt of such love and appreciation in this venue, in my home city.

'Mam would have loved this,' I thought, and to this day I remember it as one of the best nights of my life.

Though we had a gruelling schedule, eventually putting on more than eighty shows in seventy-odd theatres and travelling ten thousand miles around the UK, Dave and I got ourselves into what we both thought was a very manageable routine. We'd have a hearty but healthy breakfast in whichever hotel we stayed at, potter around in the morning and then head to the next venue for late afternoon. We always shared a dressing room and so I'd make us a cup of tea while Dave did the ironing, then we'd have a bite to eat, do the sound check and be ready for action from 7 p.m.

'Right – let's rock!' I'd say every night before we went on stage, and we'd play some AC/DC dead loud and jump up and down together, to get ourselves going.

Afterwards, we'd have a pint back at our hotel because you really can't just go straight to bed after coming off stage, as you're too pumped up. It was too late for us to eat as we'd finish at about 10 p.m., and so it wasn't a bad set-up in terms of keeping our weight stable. We'd come off the calorie-controlled diet by now but we'd learned a hell of a lot on *Dieters* and were both eating much more wisely than we had before. On a personal level we obviously didn't want to undo our hard work, and we also had our reputations to think about.

In December *Hairy Dieters* won Food and Drink Book of the Year at the National Book Awards, and we naturally wanted to be a good advert for it.

Work-wise, Dave and I were still flying high, but the downside of our success was that not only were we away from home all the time, but we were living in each other's pockets. We couldn't remember the last time we'd just hung out as mates like we used to, because we simply hadn't had the time.

We'd become like a pair of comfy old slippers together off stage, rather than the exuberant chaps we prefer to be, but there was no way around that with the schedule we faced; our down-time had to be rest-time, or we wouldn't have been able to manage.

I think the set-up worked better for Dave than me. He missed Lil and the kids like mad of course, but he likes order and routine and he's incredibly pragmatic. The tour was a big deal to us. Most of the shows were sell-outs and we'd added extra dates to meet the demand for tickets. Dave knuckled down as he always does in such circumstances, but I started to buckle near the end, though I didn't realise it at the time.

The first sign I had that all was not well was when I went to the loo and noticed blood in the pan, which freaked me out.

'Not again!' I thought. 'Why do I always have a medical drama? This is just ridiculous.'

After the initial shock I calmed myself down, figuring there had to be a reasonable explanation, and that it was probably just some kind of digestive problem. I really didn't want to burden Dave yet again with another health problem and so I kept it to myself and said nothing. However, then I started having abdominal cramps and pains and feeling generally a bit unwell, at which point I did mention it to Dave.

'It's probably nothing, but I do feel a bit ropey,' I said, playing it down.

'You should go and get checked out, Kingie.'

'I will, mate, I will. But I'll soldier on for now. It might get better on its own.'

'Look, Si, your health's more important than the shows.'

'Honest, Dave, I'm not that bad. I'll make an appointment after the tour if it hasn't gone away, I promise.'

'You do that, Kingie. I'll be checking up on you.'

I went on stage that night, and the next night, and the night after that, though if I'm honest I was feeling gradually worse and I knew I should have got myself to a doctor.

'It's probably just caused by stress,' I told myself. 'What do I expect, going on stage every night and being on the road? I'm sure it'll calm down when I'm back in a normal routine.'

I have to admit the stress I was under was not just down to work, because sadly Jane and I had been having marriage problems for a while. Fundamentally, because of my continued absences, it was incredibly difficult to keep things on an even keel and to stay together. In recent times our lives had taken different paths and we were struggling to make things work, so I suppose it was no wonder at all that I was feeling considerably below par.

I finally took myself to the doctors when the tour was over, and I was sent to hospital for exploratory tests, which involved having a camera shoved up my arse.

'Do you want to have a look?' the doctor asked me, swivelling a screen in front of me.

'Well, I can't help it now you've moved the telly round, can I?'

There was clearly something dodgy going on, because the doctor pointed out a noticeable bulge in the wall of my colon.

'Is it bad news?'

'We can't say at this stage what it is,' the doctor said calmly. 'We'll have to do a biopsy, and we'll know in two weeks' time. It could just be inflammation, which can be caused by many things.'

I spent the next fortnight taking painkillers and antibiotics and worrying about the results. In the meantime plans were afoot for Dave and me to make not just the *Hairy Bikers' Asian Adventure* and *Meals on Wheels: Back on the Road*, but also the *Hairy Bikers' Restoration Road Trip*, in which we'd be helping to mend all kinds of weird and wonderful machines from the industrial age. That was a bit of a departure for us, but as Dave said: 'We're both men of ambition, so why not?'

We also had a new curry book out and there would be a cookbook to accompany Asia too, plus a second *Hairy Dieters* book called *Eat for Life*, as people were still going crazy for more recipes. Thinking about all this work made my brain ache. Dave and I had barely had a break for two years now, and I knew this was taking a toll on me.

'I want some time off after Asia,' I said to Dave, after I finally got the biopsy results.

The diagnosis wasn't particularly serious, but I was adamant I still wanted a break.

'Is everything alright, Si?' Dave said, looking alarmed. 'What did the doctor say?'

'Oh, I hope I haven't worried you, mucker. It's only diverticulitis.'

'Diverticu-what?'

'Di-ver-tic-u-li-tis, Dave.'

The pair of us collapsed in giggles once I'd explained what it was, though it was no laughing matter really. The funny word meant the bulges in the lining of my colon had become nastily inflamed and I effectively had a serrated bowel. It sounded nasty, but the doctor assured me it was nothing that couldn't be put right with medication, and by continuing with healthy eating and good, clean living.

Once this had sunk in, Dave was a tad perplexed about me wanting time off, and looking back I can understand why. We were at the top of our game and having a ball. Back in the day I'd have been eager to crack on and capitalise on our success, but here I was wanting to step away. I told Dave I wanted three months off in addition to the usual breaks we took for summer and Christmas holidays.

'Are you absolutely sure about this, Kingie? I'm gonna miss you, mate!'

He looked a little bit hurt, actually.

'I am sure, Dave, and I'll miss you too. It's not about you, though, you know that, don't you?'

'Course, Kingie!'

'To be honest, Dave, how great will it be just to see each other when it's not all about work? We could go on a lads' weekend or something, couldn't we? I'd absolutely love that. I just need to take my foot off the gas when it comes to work, that's all.'

'All right, Kingie, if that's what you want, and if you're sure it's the right thing, I'll support you, you know I will.'

It was not a conversation I had been looking forward to. When you are half of a double act you have a huge responsibility to the other person, but I felt I had no choice. The diverticulitis felt like a warning. I was pushing myself too far and expecting too much of my body when I was also trying to deal with my personal issues. I was very grateful to Dave for being so understanding, and I counted my lucky stars that I was in the incredibly fortunate position of having my best mate as my other half at work.

I had decided to move out of the family home while Jane and I worked through our marriage problems, and I was very honest with Dave and told him I was feeling emotionally as well as physically frail.

'Put it this way, if I don't take a break I think I'll be suffering from far worse that divertic-u-bloody-litis,' I said.

He laughed and, as only Dave could, he said: 'Kingie, go and get your blistered arsehole sorted out and then get your arse back to work.'

19

Dave's

Prawn-and-Scallop Stir-fry, Beans on Toast and Steak and Chips

'I'm not going to bed now, mucker!' Si hissed. 'It's way too early. Shall we nip out for a pint?'

We were at a Buddhist monastery in Kyoto on our *Asian Adventure*, where Si and I had believed we were simply doing a recce. When we arrived, however, two novice monks showed us to a room with a couple of bamboo mats on the floor, and at about 7 p.m. we were swiftly bid goodnight by the monks and our crew.

'I suppose we could nip out over the wall, Kingie,' I replied, looking out the window.

Si was in complete agreement, and the pair of us skedaddled like a couple of truanting schoolboys.

'Quick, before the monks come back,' Si whispered. 'Leg it, Dave!'

Once over the wall we found a really nice restaurant where we had some sushi and lots of Japanese beer before sneaking back to our room. The plan for the next day was that we were to rise at 5 a.m. and make sesame tofu, so we tried to get our heads down.

'I can't sleep!' Si said. 'This mat is ridiculously uncomfortable. I'm gonna have to find something to put me head on.'

We'd ridden hundreds of miles across Japan on a couple of big Honda CVR 1300 road bikes and were aching all over, and it was also freezing cold. Si went rummaging around and came back with a cushion for his head, and the two of us eventually nodded off until 2 a.m., when we were awakened by the sound of a chanting vigil that was going on in the monastery.

'This is bloody madness!' Si complained.

I had to agree. 'I'm dehydrated,' I moaned. 'I wish we had some water.'

It felt like we'd only just nodded off when the film crew came in at 5 a.m., with the cameras on. 'Oh nooo!' we both wailed, though of course we got our act together and threw ourselves enthusiastically into the tofu-making.

Asia had been on our wish list of places to cover for as long as we could remember, and it was an incredible trip, taking in Hong Kong, Thailand, Japan and Korea. One of the major highlights was eating sushi for breakfast at the famous Tsukiji fish market in Tokyo, because sushi is our all-time favourite food. Visiting the market had been on our bucket list for as long as we could remember, and we even got the chance to go round the back of one of the counters and help make some sushi, which was a complete thrill.

Our whole *Asian Adventure* was so amazing, in fact, that some incredibly spectacular footage never made it to air, because there was just so much of interest to see and do. For instance, one day we joined in with some fancy-dress dragon-boat racing in Hong Kong harbour.

'Look over there,' Si said, eyes on stalks.

'Oh yes, it's a supermodel dressed as Superman, beating a drum,' I said, deliberately deadpan.

'That's not the sort of thing you see every Sunday afternoon, now is it, Dave?'

It was gloriously sunny and what with the fantastic colours of the boat and the backdrop of glistening skyscrapers, it was a breathtaking spectacle that bombarded your senses, yet not a single frame made the final cut, as we simply had so much material jockeying for space.

The day we filmed at a Sumo school was a definite shoe-in, though, and it was simply unforgettable. Our director wanted to capture the moment when we first met the sumo wrestlers on film, so all Si and I had before the initial introduction was a bunch of notes given to us by the researchers.

'Bloody hell, Kingie,' I said. 'It says here that they train for four to five hours in the morning, then have a ten thousand calorie lunch, then sleep, so the food sticks.'

'Sounds like the complete antithesis of what we learned on *Dieters*, Dave. The experts at Newcastle uni could have something to say about that . . .'

'That's not all, Si. Listen, they then wake up and consume another ten thousand calories, including a load of beer, and then they sleep again, in a kind of big fat-boys' dormitory. Wait a minute. Oh, right, I've just read on in the notes.'

'What is it, Dave?'

'Well, the plan is for us to have a go competing with one of them, in the sumo ring. And I've just read the ominous words: "mawashi loincloths to be provided".'

'Awww noooo!' Si groaned, but to be honest, we weren't really surprised, and this was the sort of thing the crew knew we loved and were also going to throw ourselves into, possibly quite literally.

I don't think I've ever laughed so much as when I saw Si naked except for his loincloth, complete with his hair greased back and fixed in a little neat Japanese ponytail.

'Look at your little lychees!' I'd said as his nether regions were bound and wrapped. 'I hope they'll be alright in there. Take care of them!'

Si laughed back at me. 'Could have done with one of these nappy things when I had that strangulated testicle and one of me lychees was more like a mango . . .'

What with our matching Che Guevara tattoos on display, we were a sight for sore eyes. When the moment came for us to come face to face with a sumo we both genuinely blanched, which of course was what the director had anticipated, and it did look funny on telly. Si's eyes widened like saucers as he took in the enormity of the thirty-five stone sumo wrestler standing before us. I've never seen him look so alarmed and reticent, in fact, and for the first time in our lives we were actually the skinniest and smallest kids on the block. It was all quite surreal, and now we had to take turns trying to push this gigantic man out of the roped sumo circle.

'I think it might be your go first, Kingie!' I said, and Si reluctantly shuffled forward, then braced himself for the challenge. His shoulders went forward and he planted his feet firmly on the ground before trying to shove the sumo away, but it was a completely lost cause.

'It's like pushing a brick wall!' he said, puffing and panting and admitting defeat.

Hilariously, the sumo then told him, 'You have to try to push me,' because I think he thought Si hadn't understood the rules.

'I did, man, but I cannot, I just cannot!'

When it was my turn I was equally feeble, and I felt ridiculously small and weak as I locked eyes with the serious-faced sumo. After four hours of training he was understandably quite sweaty, and all I can remember thinking is: 'This is like doing battle with a gigantic, smelly walrus!' Inevitably I wimped out too after failing to budge him an inch, but I'm glad I had the chance to try. It was a priceless experience and the photos we came away with are classic images that never fail to make us chuckle each time we see them.

We also still laugh at the memory of us making a prawn-and-scallop stir-fry at a street-stall in Hong Kong.

'Hey, Dave, why don't we sing the theme tune to the cartoon show *Hong Kong Phooey* while we cook?' Si said, out of the blue.

We sang the song and really went for it, complete with karate-chopping dance moves, which we thought were hysterical. I'm not sure the confused locals who looked on quite got our sense of humour, but never mind, eh? It made us laugh even more when we attracted strange looks, and the stir-fry still got cooked, so what was not to like?

Throughout the trip it was great to see Si having a really good time after how he'd been feeling at the end of our stage tour. Before we went to Asia we had made the most of the *Hairy Bikers' Restoration Road Trip* and *Meals on Wheels: Back on the Road*. I found both programmes extremely interesting and good fun, but looking back there were days when I could see Si was not quite himself. He didn't complain, but I can tell when Si goes into his 'hail fellow well met' routine, even though he doesn't quite feel that way. He's a professional to his boots, and he got stuck in with gusto whether we were reforging the wheel of a steam train or revisiting volunteers making meals for the elderly, which I really admired him for.

Si was genuinely on good form in Asia, though, and I was very pleased to see it. I'd obviously been concerned about his marriage breakdown, and I was keeping a close eye on him. Si was living alone in a cottage near the family home while he and Jane sorted things out, and I knew he wasn't going to find this easy. He was under a tremendous amount of pressure, and I made it clear I wanted to be there for him and support him as much as possible.

After Asia, Si was going to take the time off we'd talked about, and the two of us now needed to work out exactly how long he'd be out of the game, and what I was going to do with myself in the meantime. We always tried to have most of August and December off so I knew that, realistically, if Si wanted an extra few months off on top of that, then we wouldn't be back at work together until early 2014. We'd been talking to the BBC about doing a series on the Baltic in the spring of 2014, which would be good timing, but I didn't want to sit around doing nothing until then.

So, when Si said he wanted time off, I decided to have a go at *Strictly*, and I asked my agent to put in a call and see if they were serious about having me on. To my delight they were, and within a matter of weeks I was being sworn to secrecy and making plans to start work on the show at the end of the summer. I was made up, and Lil was all for it too, as I knew she would be.

'It'll be an excuse to flaunt your flamboyant side, Dave,' Lil teased. 'Good for you.'

When it came to putting my money where my mouth was, I was incredibly nervous. The first step was to get measured for costumes and meet my fellow 'celebs'. I hit it off immediately with Deborah Meaden; somehow we felt we'd known each other for years, and I was relieved to see a friendly face in Susanna Reid, whom I'd met before on breakfast telly. Clocking the rugby player Ben Cohen blew me away, though. When he played for England I'd jumped up and down on the sofa with Si and his three boys, watching the team win the Rugby World Cup in 2003. I was starstruck, and also quite spooked by the idea of competing against an athlete of his stature, although I felt better when he confided that he was absolutely terrified!

Being matched with a dance partner is another nail-biting experience. You all get chucked in a room together with a load of producers with clipboards and then it's like speed-dating got absurd, as mere mortals like me mingle with all these stunning dancers. Luckily world mambo champion Karen Hauer and I clicked, as unlikely as that may sound, and we both hoped we'd be paired up, which of course we were. I discovered that she's not only a spectacularly good dancer, but Karen genuinely loves food and cooking, so we seemed to be a match made in heaven, sort of. Karen's fiancé, the dancer Kevin Clifton from Grimsby, told me later: 'Karen was hoping she'd get you, even though you've got six left feet.'

'Well, I hope she's got feet of steel, that's all I can say!' I replied.

I had bought a Dutch barge that I moored on the Thames near Reading so I could stay there during *Strictly* rather than in hotels, and Karen would come over and dance on the deck with me, under the stars. It was ace. When she taught me the cha-cha-cha for my first dance to 'Moves Like Jagger', she made me chant 'beans on toast' to get the rhythm, and even though I was so big and clumsy next to her she treated me with great respect and never made me feel rubbish. I did thirty hours a week in the gym for three weeks at the start which made me lose inches, if not weight, and Karen and I would also rehearse together at the Royal College of Dance, where we'd prop four cushions up against the wall and pretend they were the judges.

'This is surreal,' I said more than once. 'I'm a hairy northerner and I'm dancing where Darcey Bussell has danced. I think I need to pinch myself to see if this is really happening!'

'It's really happening, Dave,' Karen would say. 'You had better start believing it!'

On the Saturday night you get two rehearsals with the band and then a dress rehearsal. When I stepped out on the famous *Strictly* set for my very first band rehearsal I was feeling absolutely petrified, not least because this is the first time your fellow contestants get to see you dance.

'Come on, Myers,' I was saying to myself. 'You can do it!'

I'd had so much support from Lil and the family, and from Karen and everybody on the show, and I didn't want to disappoint anybody or let myself down. When the music started my heart was beating like a drum and my legs felt like a couple of wobbly blancmanges. I'd never felt so nervous on a stage before, and I really missed Si. I thought back to the first time we'd been on a stage together, when we cooked Vietnamese crispy beef and lemongrass noodles at the Good Food Show in Birmingham, and I wished he was by my side, to pick up the reins if I needed him to, as we always did for each other.

Hearing the big sound of the live band striking up snapped me back to the present, immediately bringing home the enormity of what I'd got myself into.

'God help me! I'm going to dance on live telly! I'm going to dance to "Moves Like Jagger" on live telly!'

I looked at Karen and thought, 'Right, beans on toast', and then I just gave it my all, trying my absolute best with each and every move Karen had painstakingly taught me. It seemed to be all over in a flash and I stood there panting. Then I spotted Deborah Meaden, who was clapping and smiling, and I dared to hope I'd been alright.

'What do you think, Deborah?' I asked hopefully once I'd got my breath back.

'Dave, if you can do that tonight the whole nation will be in love with you!'

'Really? Blimey, I can't tell you what a relief it is to have got that over with. Thanks, Deborah!'

Still, when it came to the real thing later that evening I was shaking like a leaf when I took to the floor, and I really had to concentrate and give myself a good talking to as the music started and I had to perform all over again. I gave it my absolute all and the audience roared wildly, which I took as a good sign, but afterwards the judges said they felt the same way as I did: terrified! I was just pleased to have got through it without falling over or having a heart attack, to tell the truth.

'What have I done?' I said to Lil the next morning. We'd had a knees-up in the bar with everybody after the show and now I was lying hungover and as stiff as a board on the barge, looking at the *Strictly* Facebook page. Crazily, my routine had attracted 10,000 likes.

'I don't know, darling, but you've done it.'

Lil came to the show to support me every week, bringing either Serge or Iza with her. They all loved it. Abbey Clancey gave Serge a cuddle so he had a great picture for Facebook, and Iza taught Abbey, who went on to win, how to twerk. As the weeks went on I got more and more into the competition and I desperately didn't want to get voted off. To my amazement and delight the public really supported me, and then Sir Bruce told me I was his favourite contestant of the series. What an honour! I was tickled pink.

I had a bit of a setback in rehearsals in week three, mind you, when Karen and I did the pasodoble to Meatloaf's 'I'd Do Anything for Love', and I fell flat on my face in the dance studio.

'I am the bull and you are the matador,' Karen said, refusing to let my spirits drop. 'The bull is about to tear you apart. You need to have a strong face, Dave. You need to look like a matador who is not going to be torn apart.'

I did my level best, but on the night I suspect I looked more like a walrus who'd been kicked in the bollocks.

There are two St Tropez tanning tents backstage at *Strictly*, and every week I embraced the fake tan with relish. I'd have a double dip for Latin and a single dip for ballroom and usually ended up looking like a Greek fisherman, but I absolutely loved it. Halloween week was a bit different. I had to jive to the 'Monster Mash' while dressed as Beetlejuice. It had seemed like a good idea at the time but in hindsight I looked more like an angry panda, or Alice Cooper after a car crash. To add to my woes, for the first time in many years I also lost a bit of hair, which shows the sort of pressure I was under. I'd not had alopecia since the cyst was removed, and in my mind there is still a big question mark over whether I'd actually had the condition for all those years, or if my hair loss was solely due to the cyst. Whatever the truth, I certainly had it now; clumps of hair came out in my hand, and this time I was in no doubt it was the stress that did it. It was an exhilarating kind of stress, though, and I wasn't complaining; the experience was just priceless.

'How's it going, mucker?' Si would ask when we spoke on the phone. 'I've been sitting at home pressing re-dial when the voting starts.'

'Thanks, mate, I appreciate it. I'm doing alright. How are you?'

'Not bad at all, Dave. It's odd spending so much time apart though, isn't it? I don't think we've ever gone this long without seeing each other.'

'I know. I miss you, mate!'

'Aw! I miss you too. Now look after yourself and don't go breaking any bones or anything daft like that.'

'Did you really just say that, Si? With your track record you're probably more likely to break your leg walking out your front door than I am doing the tango!'

'Alright, mate, no need to be like that! Any more lip and I won't be hitting re-dial come this Saturday . . .'

We really did miss each other a lot, but it was good for Si to have a proper rest and for my part it was refreshing to break out and do something completely different, and *Strictly* was certainly that.

Karen and I went on to survive for seven weeks, which was a great achievement, and something I am very proud of.

Me and Si met up again in December, to do a turn at the Good Food Show in Birmingham, and it was fantastic to see him, and to be cooking together again.

'You doing alright, Kingie?'

'Aye, Dave. I tell you what, I've missed this though.'

He was enthusiastically chopping onions and garlic and squeezing limes like I'd seen him do hundreds of times before, and it felt like our few months spent apart had never happened. If someone had told me *Strictly* had been a crazy dream I might have believed them, because it just felt like I'd blinked and then Si and I were here together, never having missed a beat.

'Can you pass me that, er, doo-dah . . .' he said, and without looking up from my breadcrumbs I passed him the grater he wanted for his Parmesan.

'Thanks, mate!'

'You're welcome. Don't eat that, Si.'

'What?'

'Don't eat the chorizo. We need all that.'

'I wasn't gonna, Dave. Well, only a little taste, check it's alright, like.'

After the Good Food Show, Si spent Christmas with his family and had a holiday and I went to Romania with Lil and the kids, which was a lush way to round off 2013. Si was then going to have another couple of months off before our next diary commitment, which was a book tour we had coming up in March 2014, for our *Asian Adventure* cookbook. After that we would be cracking on with the Baltic series we had scheduled for later in the year. The plan was to ride from Moscow to Copenhagen, taking in wonderful places like Lithuania, Poland, Finland, Latvia and Estonia. It would be more than twelve months since our Asia trip once we hit the road again, and I was already raring to go. The Baltic series was one I'd wanted to do for a long time, and being back on the bikes with Si would be brill.

Having said all that, I had lots to occupy me in the New Year. *Strictly* opened a lot of doors for me, and in January 2014 I travelled to Cambodia with Oxfam to make three films to help spread awareness about clean water. I didn't hesitate when they asked me if I wanted to get involved; why would I not? I spent a week roughing it, travelling around in a minibus and thinking: 'And me and Si thought we'd had it rough on the road sometimes . . . we didn't know we were born.'

I came home with a real passion for Oxfam's work.

I'd also agreed to be a contestant on the last ever *Who Wants to Be a Millionaire?* with *Countdown*'s Rachel Riley as my partner, as I couldn't resist the chance to win a wedge for charity. Unfortunately, on the night, we mucked up our last question, which was worth £50,000. We ended up with a mere £1,000 instead, which was horribly frustrating.

I did *Room 101* too, which was a fun opportunity for me to tell the nation why I hated wigs. I enjoyed the buzz of doing something slightly out of the ordinary on different shows like that, but when March came around I was itching to get back to normality with Si. For his part, Si was feeling miles better, and to kick things off before our book tour we happily accepted an invitation to a burlesque-themed charity do at the Savoy Theatre in London, along with some friends and colleagues, including my *Strictly* partner, Karen, and her fiancé Kevin.

Me and Si hadn't had a big night out together in ages and we both threw ourselves into the proceedings with wild abandon. It was a wonderful night. I took to the dance floor wearing lederhosen to do a burlesque-style 'Moves Like Jagger' routine with Karen, who wore very little. Then Kevin came on to show everyone how it should be done. We also had cocktails made by the world champion cocktail maker, Eric Lorincz, whom Si and I had filmed with in the past. The drinks were fabulous, and may well have accounted for the fact me and Si were both exceedingly merry as the evening wore on. It felt like old times, and it was great to see Si really letting his hair down. He complained he had a terrible headache the next day, mind you, but to be fair I think quite a few of us did, given the amount we'd all had to drink.

Si and I hit the road on our week-long *Asian Adventure* book tour straight after that, once again clicking back into work mode together like we'd never been apart. On a typical day we signed about six hundred books and posed for a similar number of photographs, having lots of laughs as we did so. Working with Si was so easy and familiar compared to the crazy mix of jobs I'd done in recent months. He was in his element, joshing with the blokes and flirting with the ladies as per usual, and you would never have known he'd been through a tough time. However, after about three days Si told me he still hadn't got rid of his headache.

'This is nuts,' he said. 'I just can't shake it off at all.'

I didn't think too much of it. Even though book tours are good fun, it is a bit like attending two parties lasting four hours each per day, and you do tend to feel a bit run over by the evening. I had quite a bad head myself at the end of each day, and it wasn't exactly unusual for Si to have a malady on the road, was it?

We ended the book tour in Newcastle, on a Thursday night, and Si invited me to stay at his cottage. It had been a long time since I'd stayed over at his and I readily accepted; it would be a great way to round off the week. We went out for steak and chips and a couple of pints at the Broade Chare pub at Quayside, which is run by Si's mate Terry Laybourne. It was lush but we were both knackered and Si suggested we knock it on the head early-doors and get a good night's kip. I readily agreed, as we were getting up at 8 a.m. the next day to go to Fish Quay at North Shields.

'D'you know what, mate, I've still got a proper headache,' Si said when we were stood in his kitchen the next morning.

'Are you sure you want to bother with Fish Quay then, Si?'

It was a daft question really, because Fish Quay is one of Si's favourite places in the world. The fish is superb and the folk are just lovely, and always make a big fuss of the two of us. I was planning to fill up the boot of my car with fish and seafood and drive back to Barrow, but I didn't want Si to feel obliged to go if he was feeling rough.

'I'll manage,' he said, predictably. 'You know me, I'll never pass up an opportunity to go there. This is nuts, though. I just cannot get rid of this headache, man.'

I was feeling as fresh as a daisy, and I wondered if Si was just taking longer than me to recover from the book tour as he was only just getting back into work mode. Anyhow, we had the usual wonderful time at the Quay, treating ourselves to a bacon sandwich and a cup of tea as we chatted to the fishmongers, and picking out loads of lovely fresh plaice, halibut, prawns and scallops. I loaded my car up, enthusing about how much Lil would love all this healthy fish, and Si seemed to have perked up because he was planning what to cook that weekend, and what to put in his freezer.

'Tell you what, Dave, I'm really looking forward to pottering around the cottage, doing a bit of cooking and having a bloody good rest,' he said.

'I'm not surprised, Kingie. You've worked hard. Go and put your feet up, mate.'

20

Si's

Hospital Pork Pie, Farm Shop Picnic and Well-Earned Pint

I went to bed at 8 p.m. on the Friday night, feeling absolutely dreadful. I was alone in the cottage and all I could think about was my banging head. It had got worse and worse all day, ever since I waved Dave off at Fish Quay that morning. I'd maxed out on paracetamol to no avail and now I didn't know what to do but try to get myself to kip. I couldn't blame a hangover any longer; it was a good week since the Savoy bash, so that had to be long gone. It was odd, though, because there was no other logical explanation as to why my head should be hurting so much. It was bloody killing me and I was feeling generally unwell now too; the sensation was unlike anything I'd experienced before. It was actually getting a bit scary, and so I went to bed early because I had no idea what else to do to try to block out the pain.

I tried telling myself this was probably a result of the hectic time I'd just had, and that things would no doubt start to settle down now I had the chance to rest and be alone. I lay awake for an hour or so, wishing myself asleep. All kinds of thoughts went through my head. I reasoned that I had probably been under more strain than I realised, giving it my all on the book tour. So many people had come to meet us, have a cookbook signed and take a souvenir selfie. I'd made a huge effort day after day, because I would never do anything less, and Dave and I never want to short-change anyone. I love meeting people and I genuinely enjoy the craic, but now I was thinking the tour must have really taken its toll on me, because I'd not been working for a while, and it was maybe a shock to the system.

I woke up at 10 a.m. on the Saturday morning after sleeping for more than twelve hours but I still felt absolutely terrible. I made a cup of tea and took a few more painkillers but my head was banging away, worse than ever. I wandered around the cottage for a bit, lighting the fire, trying to relax and eventually putting the rugby on the telly at about half past one in the afternoon, as it was an early kick-off. I sat there for a bit just staring at the screen and not really focusing properly. The pain in my head was insane by now; it had started to feel like someone was driving a rusty nail into my skull.

'Damn it,' I thought. 'I'll just go back to bed.'

Suddenly, when I looked back at the telly, stuff started sliding off the screen, and that's when I knew I was in serious trouble. It reminded me of Dave's description of what happened to him before his brain surgery, when he was making up the actress Pam Grier and the make-up appeared to slide off her face. Now it was happening to me, and I began thinking all kinds of dark thoughts. I managed to call a taxi and asked them to pick me up straight away and take me to the Royal Victoria Infirmary in Newcastle. Then I called the hospital, told them I was coming in and said: 'I'm not feeling very well at all. I'm sorry to ask this but can you please not put me in a room with a load of people who will put camera phones in my face?'

I have never done anything like that before, but I knew I would not have been able to cope with that sort of thing as I was now feeling very sick, and my eyes were closing because I felt incredibly light-sensitive. My headache was literally blinding, and my neck was sore and stiff. I could barely string two words together with the taxi driver because all my energy and concentration was going into coping with the excruciating pain.

Thankfully, as soon as I arrived at the RVI I got whisked through inpatients and put in a quiet assessment room round the corner from A & E. A lovely lady doctor then asked me some questions and took my blood pressure. By now I couldn't sit still and I could barely open my eyes at all, because the light was killing me. Then all hell broke loose.

I was laid flat immediately, rushed to the intensive care unit for more tests and rigged up to some tubes and wires, but nobody could tell me exactly what was wrong because the doctors weren't yet sure themselves. I understood it was serious, though, because I knew I was in ITU.

'Who do you want to inform?' a nurse asked.

'What do you mean? I don't want to inform anyone.'

Her question made me panic on more than one level. I was starting to slip a bit further by now, and in my pounding head I wondered if they thought I was going to die. My dad had died after I'd seen him in intensive care, at this very hospital.

Is that why I needed to contact my next of kin? Then my brain went into a horrible scramble as I realised I didn't know who I ought to call. It should be family, I thought, but Alex and James were away on a trip to Bruges and I wouldn't want to worry them, or Jane.

The person I really wanted to call was Dave. He would know exactly what to say and do and he'd also cheer me up, but I knew he'd get straight in his car and drive to the hospital, and I didn't think that was fair. He'd only just driven home, and was probably cooking some lovely fresh fish for Lil and having a well-earned break.

'I don't want to inform anyone,' I repeated.

'Yes, but you really do need to let somebody know what is happening. Who should that be?'

'Nobody.'

'I don't think that's a good idea. You need to let someone know you are here.'

'I don't want to. I'm not. I don't even know what is wrong with me yet.'

I knew this wasn't a responsible way to behave, but I wasn't changing my mind.

I spent the Saturday night alone, being stabilised and monitored in ITU, and having scans. I was also drugged up on painkillers. They must have taken the edge off my anxiety, because I managed to stay surprisingly calm. I was in good hands and I was going to get the treatment I needed, that's what I was focusing on. It was a relief to be in hospital instead of alone at the cottage. I was exhausted, though, and all I wanted to do was fall into a deep sleep.

I had more tests and then a lumbar puncture, to take fluid from the base of my spine, which was unbelievably agonising. The next day the hospital was even more adamant I should call someone.

Reluctantly, I phoned Jane, and asked her to bring me some pyjamas.

'What?' she said, completely taken aback. I think she was as shocked about what was happening to me as she was about the fact I had called her in my hour of need. It says a lot about Jane that she drove straight to the hospital with an overnight bag for me, and she also called Dave.

'I'll come straight over,' he said without hesitation.

I got more news that day, and it wasn't good at all. I had a brain aneurysm, which meant one of the blood vessels in my brain had bulged out like a balloon. Worse still, it had ruptured, causing a brain haemorrhage, or a 'bleed on the brain'. Left untreated this could cause a massive stroke at any moment, so I basically needed an operation to save my life. I got the gist of most of this and I was properly scared now, and started having terrible thoughts about being left brain damaged if things went wrong. I didn't know it at the time, thank God, but about three out of five people who have the type of haemorrhage I had die within two weeks, and half of those who survive are left with severe brain damage and disability.

I can remember being prepped for surgery. Alex and James came in and were both brilliant, and then Dave brought Dylan in. I was drugged up on painkillers but apparently I was still trying to have a craic with the lads, which was a bit confusing for poor Dyl. Dave told me afterwards I was brimming with bonhomie and coming out with what he calls my 'Kingie speak', being all 'hail fellow well met', as he says. Dave said it was just terrible to see me like that, because my eyes were telling a very different tale. He could see the fear I had inside, and he held my hand before I went to theatre.

I've got no idea how long I was on the operating table for, or when I started to fully comprehend what had happened, but I pieced it together over the next few days as I recovered from the surgery. I learned that the doctors knew I'd had a haemorrhage once they did the lumbar puncture, because there was blood in my spinal fluid. The scans and tests they did helped them to build

328

a 3D image of my brain and work out exactly where the aneurysm had occurred. They pumped dye into my system and found out it was near what is known as a branch, where two veins joined into each other, and so they blocked it up with a piece of titanium that looked like a tiny bit of Brillo pad, forcing the blood to reroute down a healthy vein. I was told the process was called an 'occlusion' and my surgery was done through the femoral artery in the right-hand side of my groin, which is pretty mind-blowing when you think of it.

I really couldn't register all this for a while. I'd had brain surgery through the top of my leg, for God's sake. It was just ridiculous, and bizarrely enough, the aneurysm was on the front, left-hand side of my head, exactly where Dave had his cyst operated on.

Dave came in again as soon as I was allowed visitors. He'd stayed over with Jane and the boys, and he told me Alex and James had been wonderful, looking out for Dyl and trying to reassure him that his dad would be alright. I felt very proud of all of my boys; they are lovely, cracking lads. Jane had been incredible too.

'How are you feeling, Si?' Dave asked. He looked like he hadn't slept much, and I could tell he was trying to act all normal, when really he wanted to wail, 'Thank God you're alive!' He's admitted this to me since.

'Actually, I'm hungry mate,' I said. 'Can I have a pork pie?'

Dave started laughing. 'That's just classic! Only you could order a pork pie from your hospital bed. Hang on, Kingie, I'd best check with the nurse.'

'Cheers, mate,' I said. 'I'm just proper hungry, and you know what it's like when you fancy a pork pie?'

'I do, mate. You're talking to the right fella. Leave it with me.'

Dave was visibly relieved to see me behaving in my usual manner, planning what I was going to eat next. The nurse said it was fine and Dave scooted off to the shop downstairs and got me a pie and all sorts of other goodies. I sat there tucking in, still with a central line in place, and Dave said he was very pleased to see me 'stuffing my face like a good 'un'.

I know now that Dave had been absolutely scared to death when Jane told him it was an aneurysm, because he knew quite a lot about the condition. He had a friend back in Barrow who'd suffered the same symptoms as me, but she was sent home from hospital after the initial scare and then went on to suffer a massive stroke that had left her quadriplegic. Dave also had the experience of seeing Glen in ITU, of course, and he was under no illusions about how serious it was to be there.

I was in hospital for about four weeks all told, and to give you an idea of how poorly I felt it wasn't until about three weeks after my operation that I started wishing I could be discharged. Up until then I was very grateful to lie in a hospital bed and be looked after. I can't tell you how superb the staff at the RVI were. Everyone, from the cleaners up to the consultants and registrars, was absolutely fantastic, and I'm incredibly lucky to have such a marvellous hospital on my doorstep.

I eventually learned that the official term for what I'd suffered was a 'subarachnoid haemorrhage, caused by an aneurysm'. In a nutshell, the bulging vein in my brain had bled underneath the protective 'arachnoid' layer of my brain. The fast-acting doctors and nurses at the RVI really did save my life, and I will never, ever be able to thank them enough.

'I was so frightened I'd lose you, Si,' Dave told me eventually. 'I can remember having this terrible, terrible thought when I heard the diagnosis. I thought, "What if I lose Kingie? I can't lose my best mate, it simply can't happen".'

Dave was actually in shock when he'd first arrived at the hospital, and in hindsight he did an incredible job of keeping himself together and not losing it in front of me. I know I would have been in bits, but Dave was very strong and stoical, just being there and holding my hand when I really bloody needed him. I'm very touched by his reaction, and also by the way he dropped everything and supported my family. Whatever plans he had at home went straight out the window, and of course he also dealt with the inevitable impact my illness would have on our work, which I knew nothing about at the time.

Dave and I should have been packing our bags for the Baltic while I was in hospital, but he had spoken to the BBC commissioner, Alison Kirkham, and she had readily agreed to postpone the series, understanding that we'd have to just wait and see how long I was out of action for. After my operation she phoned me in person to offer her support, which was very much appreciated not just by me, but also by Dave. We both felt valued, which is something that has always been very important to us, and meant a great deal. The BBC had really come up trumps for us when we needed them to, and it was a tremendous help to have them rooting for me and offering such unconditional and genuine support.

'You certainly get to know who your friends are when something like this happens,' I said to Dave. 'It makes you think, doesn't it?'

'It does that, Kingie. More to the point, it makes you realise what's important in life. Honest to God, when I thought I might lose you, nothing else mattered.'

'Thanks for everything you've done, Dave. I really do appreciate it.'

'I know you'd do the same for me, Si. You're family, one of my loved ones. You know I'll always stand by you through thick and thin, through hell and high water. Come to think of it, I've already done quite a bit of that. Aye, remember that time when the road got flooded in the swamps in Mississippi . . .'

Then we were off, reminiscing about some of the mad-cap adventures we'd had and looking forward to many more.

The Baltic was kept on ice indefinitely and Gill Tierney, who was due to be our producer again, came up with a great idea to fill the gap in the schedule. She suggested the series *A Cook Abroad*, which would follow six cooks on a dream trip, Dave being one of them. He was offered several other jobs to keep him ticking over too, such as *Back in Time for Dinner* and *The Great British Sewing Bee* celebrity special, both for BBC2. It was a great endorsement for him to be offered such a variety of work. Mind you, I thought Dave was maybe taking his have-a-go attitude a bit too far with the sewing bee.

'I'd have understood it if it was make-up or hair, but I didn't think sewing was your bag, mate.'

'It's not,' Dave replied. 'I'm only doing it to make Lil jealous. It's her favourite show on the telly.'

He did *Countdown* for Channel 4 too, and not for the first time someone started chatting to him about being a Geordie.

'Wey aye, man!' Dave replied, because he didn't want to point out the mistake.

It's not unusual for people to mix us up and Dave's given up explaining he's the one from Cumbria – he says people usually react with disappointment!

'So long as one of us is on telly it keeps the Hairy Biker flag flying!' Dave commented cheerfully, and I was very grateful he was out there, not just enjoying himself but doing such a great job, for both of us.

I couldn't return to work until a scan gave me the all-clear, which could take months, but it was right for me to take more time off. During my recuperation in the cottage I noticed I wasn't concentrating as well as I normally did. I'd drift off in the middle of a conversation or when I was watching the telly, and I found it really uncomfortable being on the phone. Dave came to visit and I told him all this, and he said he was in a similar state after his brain surgery, feeling like he 'wasn't quite with it'.

'I had an Irish surgeon who summed it up quite well, telling me: "Dave, the brain's like a computer and I've just had me hands in your hard drive".'

To cheer me up, Dave took me to the Knitsley Farm Shop one day, which turned out to be a real highlight of my recovery, because I wasn't allowed to drive and I'd been stuck indoors a lot, on my own. I didn't really feel like going out at first, but Dave knows I love the farm shop and said he'd drive us up there.

It's a wonderful place, packed with fabulous fresh produce, and Dave and I picked out some great bread and cooked meats and all kinds of delicious bits and pieces from the deli. The weather was decent and so we put it all on the bonnet of Dave's car and had ourselves a bit of a picnic, and before we knew it we were talking about food and enthusing about fresh ingredients, just like we always had. I had a moment when I looked at Dave and was flooded with relief.

'Thank God,' I thought. 'Nothing has changed.'

Several weeks later Dave and I honoured a long-standing commitment to shoot a pilot for a potential new quiz show. It was the first time I'd had to really use my noggin and I felt a bit nervous, but it was so familiar having Dave back at my side that I felt very much at ease once we were in position.

'Oh, you two have your own "side",' somebody in the crew commented, which made us laugh, as the implication was that we were a bit precious to insist that I was always on the left of shot and Dave on the right. In actual fact, this was something that had evolved naturally. Right from the early days, whenever we lit a fire it seemed to be left of camera, so that's where I gravitated to, as I was the one most likely to be in charge of the flames. Then the crew started saying it was simpler for continuity if we stuck to a particular side on the bikes, and so I chose the left. Dave and I actually do feel a bit off if we're on the wrong side now, it's funny how it just feels comfy somehow, like the right side of a bed.

Anyway, despite feeling very comfortable beside Dave on the set, when filming started on the quiz pilot I struggled to bounce off him the way I normally do. Dave was really kind and said I'd done brilliantly well in the circumstances, but I could feel the sharpness had been taken off my usual banter. The show was never commissioned and the production company was adamant that it had nothing to do with us, saying that the format of the show just wasn't right. Still, I couldn't help feeling bad, like I'd let Dave down.

'You've done nothing wrong,' he insisted. 'It'll come right, you have to give it time, Kingie.'

I knew Dave was right, and after that I went back to spending most of my days at home, going for walks around the cottage with my Dalmatian, Fred, and generally trying to get myself fit and well.

Dave and I received a boost by winning a couple of awards later in the summer. The first was for TV Personality of the Year at the Fortnum & Mason Food & Drink Awards, which we were dead chuffed with, as it's another one that is voted for by the public. I made the effort to travel to London for the ceremony, and I'm so glad I did. The event was attended by a lot of posh people at Fortnum & Mason's flagship store in Piccadilly, and to see some of the toffs blanching at the sight of two hairy northern oiks like me and Dave kissing our golden F & M trophies was worth every ounce of effort. The next award, also voted for by the public, was the prestigious Celebrity Cookbook gong at the *Good Housekeeping* Food Awards, which we won for *The Hairy Dieters: Eat for Life*. The timing was great, because our third *Hairy Dieters* book, *Good Eating*, was coming out in the autumn. Dave had worked incredibly hard on the book, creating and writing up the recipes and liaising with the dietician, as well as taking on all the planning meetings and promotion work we would normally have done together. I felt guilty about that, but again Dave was having none of it.

'This is the good thing about being a double act, Kingie,' he said. 'I'm here to take up the reins. I'll say it again – I know you'd do the same for me.'

'I would, mate, but let's hope it doesn't come to that, hey? I think we've had our fair share of medical dramas!'

It wasn't lost on me that I had my smiling chops on the cover of the new *Dieters* book. In the photograph I was looking slimmer and healthier than I had done in years, but in the months since the photograph was taken I'd put on about a stone in weight because I'd been so poorly and immobile. I really wanted to lose it, and in the September I made a pledge through our online dieting club to follow a six-week diet-and-fitness regime to help get me back into shape. I was acutely aware that critics might have pointed out that my previous weight loss hadn't exactly appeared to do my health any good, but the truth is I might not be here today if I'd had the aneurysm when I was three stone heavier and my blood pressure was through the roof. That's a very sobering thought, and the biggest incentive I could possibly have to get my weight back under control.

As I focused on getting myself fit and well, Dave was cracking on with all sorts of other jobs. He went on *All Star Family Fortunes* with Lil, Serge and Iza, taking along a great old mate of ours, Quirky, aka the fabulous chef Steve Quirke, to complete the Myers team. They won £10,000 for charity, which he was cock-a-hoop about. Dave also did an episode of *Holiday of My Lifetime with Len Goodman*, which saw him returning to the Isle of Man with *Strictly's* head judge and reminiscing about the holiday he had there as a young boy. I was made up he was doing all this stuff, and I was very proud of him too. He'd done so many things he might have never done otherwise, and the best example of all is that he made his panto debut, playing Baron Hardup in *Cinderella* at The Hexagon in Reading. He bloody loved it. Lil went with him and worked as a tailor backstage and they stayed on their houseboat, which was moored in the marina close by at Caversham. That's just so typical of Dave, making the most of a situation and squeezing everything he can out of it. I really admire his attitude, and it's never changed in all the years I've known him.

Dave had chosen to cover Egypt for *A Cook Abroad*, the show that was replacing our Baltic series in the schedule. Before he left I visited him in Barrow to do a little bit of filming to be included in his episode, and this turned out to be quite emotional for both of us.

'This is just weird,' I said, feeling quite choked at the thought of Dave jetting off to do a cookery show without me. 'It's not the way it's meant to be.'

'I know, Kingie, I'm gonna miss you, but you'll be with me on the next one. Don't go getting all emotional on me now. Tell you what, I'll bring you back a souvenir to cheer you up. What would you like?'

'Oooh, now there's a thought. Let me see, how about a camel, and perhaps a nice drum?'

Dave gave an evil laugh, which I recalled later, when he presented me with a gift on his return that was certainly not what I'd asked for – it was an ugly stone ornament with a giant phallus.

'Where's me drum? Or me camel?'

'This is much better,' Dave quipped. 'You can hang your bagels on it!'

Dave was practising a recipe for his show and he made some terrible falafels that disintegrated in the pan.

'It looks like Bombay mix!' he jokingly lamented while I watched from my seat at his breakfast bar and also disintegrated, into a fit of giggles. It was a bittersweet moment because we were back doing what we did best, mucking around in the kitchen, but we had to accept that I was sitting on my arse while Dave was going it alone this time. It was aggravating, but there was nothing I could do to change it. I was still waiting for another scan and hopefully the all-clear from the hospital, and I just had to be patient.

'You just keep yerself safe, mucker,' I told Dave.

'Aye. And you just take it easy and get yourself fully better, Kingie. Chill out and relax while you can.'

Stress had undoubtedly played a part in my illness. I'd been working very hard and had been for an incredibly long time. Dave was right; I did need to keep taking it easy, and the rest helped. At my next hospital appointment my consultant was very pleased with my progress and said my latest scan showed that my brain was repairing itself nicely. Dave and I wouldn't be able to do the Baltic until I was a bit further down the line and able to be insured for such an intensive trip abroad, but I could now start making plans to return to work, which I was very happy about.

After he was back from Egypt, Dave suggested we could nip off on the lads' weekend we'd talked about.

'D'you know what, I'd love that, mate. How long is it since we last did that? I can't even remember.'

'Exactly, Kingie. Let's do it, it'll be a laugh.'

We flew to Amsterdam and had a fabulous time, walking all over the city, having beers in various bars, doing a bit of shopping and taking siestas.

One day we both bought some psychedelic underpants because, as Dave said: 'These look brill for when we're on the bike. Look how snug the undercarriage is, Kingie: ideal for keeping the crown jewels from rattling!'

We laughed our heads off and both agreed that the trip had been a hoot and a tonic, and just like old times.

The first series we started working on after my illness was called *The Pubs That Built Britain*. When we were first approached to do it, Dave had been uncertain.

'What d'you think, Kingie?' he'd said cautiously as he read the details in an email, which basically told us we'd be visiting some of the oldest hostelries in the land to sample their beer and learn about their history. He looked very concerned as he read aloud that filming would begin towards the end of 2014 and run into Spring 2015, and then he started wittering on about various other diary commitments we had. We'd decided to write this memoir by then, as well as our new *Meat Feasts* cookbook, and filming for

338

the Baltic series was pencilled in for May 2015, which was well after my next hospital appointment, when I would have hopefully been given the final all-clear.

'Could we fit in *Pubs*?' he said. 'What d'you think, Si? Do you fancy it? Is it even feasible . . . ?'

I looked at Dave and his knitted brow, rubbed my beard contemplatively and very nearly started to join in with his worrying. Then I suddenly came to my senses and thought: 'What the hell are we thinking of? Have we totally lost the plot?'

I burst out laughing.

'What's not to like, Dave? Honest to God, can you imagine if we'd been offered something like this ten years ago? We'd have been snatching their bleeding hands off!'

The frown immediately disappeared from Dave's forehead and he creased up laughing as well. 'You're absolutely right, Si, what on earth was I werriting about?'

The conversation was a bit of an eye-opener. To be frank, in the aftermath of my surgery, the shock of what had happened made me question whether I even wanted to carry on being in the public eye. I was analysing my life, because I wanted to do my best to protect myself from another medical problem.

I'd cheered up dramatically since then of course, and I'd put a lot of things in perspective. Fundamentally, I was very grateful to still be here, in the game I loved.

Working on a new series was exactly what I needed, and it was yet another fantastic chance for me and Dave to do what we set out to achieve all those years earlier. We'd had blood, sweat and tears along the way, we'd diced with death and burned God only knows how much rubber in the process, but we were still in the saddle, and with opportunities that most people can only dream of, being offered to us on a silver platter, or at least a bar tray.

'You know what, Dave? Wouldn't life be great if we could just ride bikes, cook food and talk bollocks?'

'Aye, and go on an epic pub crawl for a job?! We must be two of the luckiest men on the planet. Let's have a pint to celebrate, I think we've earned it.'

Epilogue

'I've cooked chicken at lower temperatures than this, Kingie!'

I was heading bollock-naked into a seventy-degree Finnish sauna with three large men, and being taught how to whip myself with birch twigs.

'When you sweat, you do it like so, Dave,' one of my bare-arsed companions said before beating the living daylights out of his mate.

I'd expected the 'twigs' to be like little fronds, but they were the size of half a palm tree, and I was petrified.

'Argh!' I shrieked as my hot, naked flesh was whipped. 'What happens when you've had enough?'

'We go to the lake!'

I'd been intimidated before going into the sauna, and now I had to leg it outside and chuck myself in a freezing cold lake, and all in front of the crew filming our Baltic series. I know the crew really well, but even so it was daunting for a man of my age to be running around in the buff!

'Dave, mate,' Si said after we'd done four takes. 'You've been absolutely fantastic. Thanks for taking one for the team!'

'You know what, I was absolutely dreading it but it was brill in the end. I actually feel quite euphoric. Who'd have thought Finland would turn out to be so wonderful?'

Little did Si know, but he was about to take one for the team too, when we rocked up at a wife-carrying competition a few days later. We'd been expecting this to be a very light-hearted affair, but we found out the Finns take it really seriously. It's treated like an Olympic sport in fact, and there are big prizes at stake and serious athletes involved.

The rules are strict. There are three types of lifts and the lady you carry – who actually doesn't have to be your wife – must be over forty-five kilos.

'Can you demonstrate the lifts on my friend here?' I asked. 'He's very strong.'

Before Si had time to think about this, one of the competitors jumped on his back and clung to him like a limpet, and Si obligingly did a little practice run down the street.

'That's the traditional piggy back,' we were told.

Next up was the fireman's lift, and Si deftly lifted the lady onto his shoulders and again did a demonstration run.

'Finally, we have the Estonian-style lift!'

'What's that?' Si asked nervously.

'For the Estonian method, the wife wraps her legs around your neck, like a front-facing rucksack.'

'Oh!' Si said as his 'wife' mounted him crotch first, pushing her nethers into his face and beard.

Si gamely rose to the occasion, of course, and instead of just running down the road he jokingly disappeared round the corner shouting: 'I'm not coming back!'

It was very funny indeed, and it was just fabulous to witness. All these years on, here we were, still doing what we set out to do so long ago, and still having bloody great fun.

The Baltic series turned out to be one of our best ever, if not the very best one we've made so far. Everything about it was epic. The last few weeks, when we did St Petersburg, Finland and Sweden, were particularly special. In St Petersburg we went backstage at the ballet, interviewed a Russian oligarch and had a vodka-sampling session. We also got to ride a Cossack Ural Mars MK 3 with a sidecar, the same as the very first bike I ever bought in my youth. It was an old knacker and we set off down the main street, Nevsky Prospect, which is a very busy six-lane highway, with me on the bike and Si in the sidecar. I found it hilarious . . . until we broke down, that was.

'Have you pulled the clutch in?' Si shouted. He was very worried because buses and cars where whizzing past us and we were causing a dangerous obstruction.

'Course I have! Bloody hell, I'll have to get out and kick-start it.'

I eventually got the bike going again, but unfortunately it shot off sideways across Nevsky Prospect.

'We're gonna die!' Si shouted. 'Bloody hell, Dave, this is it! The end!'

It wasn't the end, fortunately. Several days later, after getting to Finland, we found ourselves sitting outside the cabin we were staying at near the Baltic Sea. The villagers were all out painting the house next door, and Si and I were cooking and sharing our food with them. We did blazing salmon with pepper and lemon juice on a wood fire and made the most mouth-watering rye bread; it all tasted divine.

'Life doesn't get much better than this, Kingie,' I said, looking around. Our bikes were there, standing in this wonderful landscape, and it was just paradise.

'I know, mate. It's lush. We made this happen, didn't we? That's just mind-blowing.'

Si was right. We'd followed our mantra – just give it a go – and this was what we got in return.

We did some great riding throughout the trip, and after one long day of filming we were shattered and Si and I went back to our cabin to change and take a breather for half an hour, before going out to eat with the crew. We started taking off our leathers and boots, like you do, and when we were stripped down to our T-shirts Si flopped on his double bed. I was so tired that I just crashed down beside him instead of going to my own room. The place was full of flies and was a bit rough, but as we lay there looking up at the ceiling we started counting our lucky stars once again, talking about what a terrific trip we'd had and marvelling at the vastness of Finland with its 187,000 lakes and 40,000 islands.

'You know what's great, Kingie? Even after all this time it's still scarily exciting to be on the road. D'you know what I mean?'

'I do, mate. This trip's been off the scale. We're two incredibly fortunate men.'

The Finns like to say that they are comfortable with their own silence, and after that we lay there quietly for a few minutes. I was thinking how cool it was that we could be here like this, so content together, all these years down the line. Lots of people who work as closely as me and Si can't even stand to share a car, yet here we were, lying side by side in our T-shirts and underpants, and all after an intensive few weeks' filming.

'Hang on a minute, Dave, have you got your psychedelic pants on?' Si suddenly blurted out, breaking the silence. 'So have I, dude!'

I looked down and it was true. The pair of us were wearing the psychedelic knickers we'd bought together in Amsterdam, the ones that stopped your crown jewels from rattling on the bike.

At that point we both threw our heads back on the pillows and started laughing uncontrollably, completely cracking up and with tears streaming down our faces.

'Oh God, I just can't stop laughing!' Si said, gasping for air.

'Nor can I!' I spluttered.

Then we just carried on laughing our heads off for a very long time.

We finished the Baltic series having a wonderful time in Sweden, where Si and I were presented with the results of a DNA test we'd taken, in an attempt to find out who we really are, and where we came from.

Because of our looks, Si has always believed he was descended from the Vikings, while I imagined my ancestors might be Jewish, but the tests proved us both wrong.

It turned out I was the Viking, as my ancestors hailed from Norway and had worked their way down to Cumbria via the Orkneys. Much to his disappointment, Si had no Viking blood at all – his ancestors were part Swiss and part German, with a bit of North Italian thrown in.

'From now on I want to be known as Ragnar!' I teased, and then I started making noises like a cuckoo clock, just to wind Si up.

He took it in good spirit, and afterwards we both agreed it was all a bit irrelevant anyhow.

'I've learned more about meself writing this book,' Si said.

'Same,' I replied. 'It's funny, isn't it?'

'Well I bloody hope so, mucker!'

We had no idea that writing our memoir would take us on such an eye-opening journey, and we hope you've enjoyed the ride as much as we have.

Index

Index

Index

Index

Index

Index

Index

Index

Acknowledgements

It is hard to know where to start with 100 years of history between us – it's a huge task to thank all of those who have had an impact on our lives individually and collectively. However it's important to us that we try. We have been loved by our families, close friends and the countless people who have been with us on our world travels – and it is this love that enables us to write this book. We thank you from the bottom of our hearts.

In the making of this book we would like to thank our wonderful team at Orion Publishing Group. Firstly huge thanks to Rachel Murphy – an amazing writer who was instrumental in bringing this book together – she has truly helped to tell our story. Thanks to our publisher Amanda Harris, Abi Hartshorne, Jillian Young, Lucy Haenlein, Hannah Cox, Clare Sivell, Alice Morley and publicist Mark McGinlay, the Peckham massive, and all who have worked so hard to make this a wonderful book. The team at Orion are more than publishers of our books – all have become good friends.

We would like to thank our amazing team at James Grant Management whose work has literally helped change our lives. Love to Nicola Ibison, who was and always will be a source of inspiration and counsel. Thanks to Natalie Zietcer and Sarah Hart, for making our madcap lives work. Thanks also to Rowan Lawton and Eugenie Furniss in the literary division. Thanks to Holly, Neil, Darren and Paul – more than managers, good friends.

Thanks to our families and friends who have put up with our wayward lifestyle over the years. Without all your love, help and guidance, we would never have been able to function. Thanks to all in the mad, glorious food world – chefs and producers alike who have shown us such generosity with their knowledge, time and produce. Not least Sammy-Jo Squires.

We have had some amazing breaks in the business and huge thanks goes to the late John Stroud and the very present Vikram Jayanti, who first took the Hairy Bikers to the BBC. Thanks to Roly Keating for giving us our break. Thanks also to our lovely Anya Noakes at PR Matters alongside Kat Blair, who have been guiding us since the very beginning.

Thanks to the BBC for allowing us to grow and to try new challenging projects. Thanks to channel controllers Roly Keating, Janice Hadlow and Kim Shillinglaw. A big hug to Alison Kirkham who has been our commissioner for many years now – thanks for sticking with us. Thanks to Marcus Mortimer for working with us when John became ill, thanks to all at BBC Birmingham, and all the directors, producers and crew both in house at the BBC and independents. We know we've tested your patience in the pursuit of making entertaining, informative and above all fun programmes – we salute you!

Lastly, BIG thanks to everyone who has watched our shows, bought our books or have just given us a cheery wave in the street. We thank you for your affection for us and the shows we make! Without you we have nothing.